Renewable Energy Management in Emerging Economies

Renewable energy has never been more important than it is today, as climate change becomes arguably the world's most essential problem to be solved. Solving this problem is proving difficult and complex – none more so than for emerging economies that are undergoing rapid economic development with increasing use of fossil fuels. There are many challenges for these countries that are making efforts to promote renewable energy use, with limited resources. Good government policies and corporate strategies are essential to support these efforts as a part of the global climate change crisis.

This important book addresses the very latest developments in renewable energy management plus the key challenges and risks. Potential new policies and strategies for the further growth of renewable energies in emerging economies, together with high-level business case examples of renewable management in emerging economies, are addressed.

This book is essential reading for policy makers, government employees, business executives, professionals, researchers and academics looking to improve global renewable energy policies, investments and management.

Henry K. H. Wang is an international adviser, author and speaker with extensive high-level business experience. He is President of Gate International and a former director of both Shell China and SABIC in Riyadh. He is a Fellow of the Royal Society of Arts FRSA and a Fellow of Institute of Chemical Engineering plus has been invited to join the London University SOAS Advisory Board and the Imperial College Grantham Climate Change Stakeholder Committee. He has published four books as well as over 100 papers and speeches globally. He has been invited to speak at international conferences, leading universities and business schools. He is also undertaking charity work on youth leadership and sustainable developments around the world.

T0371836

Routledge Frontiers of Business Management

For more information about this series, please visit www.routledge.com/Routledge-Frontiers-of-Business-Management/book-series/RFBM

Renewable Energy Management in Emerging Economies

Strategies for Growth

Henry K. H. Wang

Routledge
Taylor & Francis Group

LONDON AND NEW YORK

First published 2020 by Routledge

2 Park Square, Milton Park, Abingdon, Oxon OX14 4RN
605 Third Avenue, New York, NY 10017

Routledge is an imprint of the Taylor & Francis Group, an informa business

First issued in paperback 2022

Publisher's Note

The publisher has gone to great lengths to ensure the quality of this reprint but
points out that some imperfections in the original copies may be apparent.

British Library Cataloguing-in-Publication Data
A catalogue record for this book is available from the British Library

Library of Congress Cataloging-in-Publication Data
A catalog record has been requested for this book

ISBN: 978-1-138-48090-2 (hbk)
ISBN: 978-1-03-233701-2 (pbk)
DOI: 10.4324/9781351061582

Typeset in Galliard
by codeMantra

Contents

Author's note

This book is based on the author's research, literature surveys, high-level business experiences and learnings accumulated over some 40 years of successful international business globally. He has worked as senior executive and international adviser, author and speaker plus as director and board member of leading companies. He has also been invited to advise various international organisations, leading companies plus universities and business schools.

The views expressed in this book are results of research insights, personal learnings and high-level business experiences of the author. This book represented a contribution by the author, as part of his global corporate social responsibilities together with his strong interest to support improvements to climate change and sustainability plus the development of future thought leaders globally. We hope that this book will help policy makers, executives and professional practitioners as well as academics, researchers and students in their studies and research works.

Preface

This new book aims to provide a holistic overview of the institutional, organisational and management issues that underpin successful renewable energy management and growth in the key emerging economies globally.

Renewable energy growth and management are attracting high interests globally, especially in emerging economies. Industrialisation and rising fossil fuel consumptions globally have resulted in rising emissions and pollution globally. These have led to rising global warming and worsening environmental pollution globally, especially for emerging economies. There are currently significant international pressure and drives to reduce emissions and to improve environment. Many emerging economies are promoting clean renewable energy usages and reducing fossil fuel consumptions so as to reduce emissions and pollution. Looking ahead, renewable energy growths are expected to continue as countries push ahead with their Paris Agreement commitments and environmental improvements. Good government policies and corporate strategies will be essential to support future renewable growths and successful clean energy investments. There are also many serious challenges to future renewable energy growths in emerging economies, particularly in innovation, smart city, green finance and governance plus digital and cybersecurity management.

This book will address the latest developments in renewable energy management plus the key challenges and risks. Potential new policies and strategies to promote further growth of renewable energies in emerging economies, together with high-level business case examples, will be addressed in the book.

This book will also compliment the four T&F books already published by the author globally. These included *Successful Business Dealings and Management with China Oil, Gas and Chemical Giants* published in 2014, *Energy Markets in Emerging Economies: Strategies for Growth* published in 2017, *Business Negotiations in China* published in 2018 and *Climate Change and Clean Energy Management* published in 2019.

Acknowledgements

I like to thank the valuable inputs, support and encouragements received from many senior executives, thought leaders and key stakeholders in international companies, leading universities and top business schools globally during research and writing of this new book.

My sincere thanks to Routledge, Taylor and Francis who commissioned and published this book. I like to thank all the editorial and production staff who have contributed to the successful editing, copywriting, typesetting, proofreading, design, publication and marketing of this book.

I would also like to thank various leading universities and top business schools globally for inviting me to speak and work with them on climate change and sustainability. The keen interests from the university staff and students plus the professional practitioners have motivated me to write this book so as to share my experience and research works with professionals, academics and students globally.

I sincerely like to thank my family for all their great support, love, understandings and encouragements which are much appreciated and treasured everyday. Their strong support and encouragements have been critical in helping me to complete this book, especially with large amounts of personal time and efforts required for the extensive research, writing and editing. I also like to thank my mother, sisters and their families plus our close friends globally for their valuable advice and support.

I like to dedicate this book to my two children whom I love dearly. I really appreciate all their love and support, especially after the passing of my dear late wife, whom I am missing dearly.

Abbreviations

ACIA ASEAN	Comprehensive Investment Agreement
ADB	Asian Development Bank
AIIB	Asia Infrastructure Investment Bank
AMAC	Asset Management Association of China
ASEAN	Association of South East Asia Nations
ASW	ASEAN Single Window
B2C	business-to-consumer
BCM	billion cubic meters
BDS	big data system
BECCU	bioenergy carbon capture utilisation
BP	British Petroleum
BPD	barrels per day
BRI	Belt and Road Initiative China
CAGR	cumulative annual growth rates
CASS	Chinese Academy of Social Science
CBRC	China Banking Regulatory Commission
CCAA	China Certification & Accreditation Agency (CNCA)
CCC	Committee on Climate Change UK
CCER	Chinese Certified Emission Reductions or CCERs
CCPC	Chinese Communist Party Congress
cCR	Carbon Climate Registry
CCR	continuous catalytic reformers
CCS	carbon capture storage
CCSU	carbon capture storage utilisation
CCU	carbon capture utilisation
CDM	clean development mechanism
CEO	chief executive officer
CETS	Carbon Emission Trading Scheme
CF	cubic feet
CFO	chief finance officer
CIETAC	China International Economic & Trade Arbitration Commission
CIF	Co-Investment Fund

CJV	contractual joint venture
CNCA	Chinese Certification and Accreditation Agency
CNODC	China National Oil and Gas Exploration and Development Corporation
CNOOC	China National Offshore Oil Corp
CNPC	China National Petroleum Corp
CM	cubic meters
CMI	Confederation of Management Institute UK
CMPY	cubic meters per year
CNPC	China National Petroleum Corporation
CO_2	carbon dioxide
CPCIF	China Petroleum and Chemical Industry Federation
CPEIA	China Petroleum & Petroleum Equipment Industry Association
CSO	combined sewer overflows
CSP	concentrated solar power
CSR	Corporate Social Responsibility
CSRC	China Securities Regulatory Commission
CTO	chief technology officer
DICP	Dalian Institute of Chemical Physics
DNL	Dalian National Laboratory for Clean Energy
DoS	denial-of-service (DoS) attack
E&P	Exploration & Production
ECFA	Economic Cooperation Framework Agreement
EDF	Environmental Defence Fund
EGS	enhanced geothermal systems
EIA	environment impact assessment
EIA	Energy Information Administration of USA
EJV	equity joint venture
EOR	enhanced oil recovery
EPA	Environmental Protection Agency
EPB	Environmental Protection Bureau
EPC	engineering, procurement and construction
ESG	environment, social, governance reporting
ETS	Emission Trading Scheme
EV	electric vehicles
FAME	fatty acid methyl ester
FDI	foreign direct investment
FIT	feed-in tariff
FORESEA	Funding for Ocean Renewable Energy through Strategic European Action Project
FTA	Free Trade Agreement
FTZ	Free Trade Zones
FYP	Five Year Plans of China

GDP	gross domestic product
GFI	Green Finance Initiative UK
GHG	greenhouse gases
GM	general manager
GM	genetically modified
GTL	gas to liquid
GVC	green venture capital
GW	giga watts
GWP	GHG Global Warming Potential
HKEX	Hong Kong Stock Exchange
HR	human resources
IBP	integrated business planning
ICBC	Commercial and Industrial Bank of China
ICE	internal combustion engines
IEA	International Energy Agency
IEFS	Integrated Food Energy Systems
IFC	International Finance Corporation
IMF	International Monetary Fund
INDC	Intended Nationally Determined Contributions
INRM	integrated natural resource management
IOC	international oil company
IOT	Internet of Things
IPM	integrated pest management
ISO	International Organization for Standardization
JV	joint ventures
KPI	key performance indicators
KBPD	thousand or kilo barrels per day
KTPA	thousand or kilo metric tons per annum
LCOE	levelised cost of electricity
LNG	liquefied natural gas
LPG	liquefied petroleum gas
LTO	light tight oil
M&A	merger and acquisition
MENA	Middle East and North Africa
MEP	Ministry of Environmental Protection of China
MBPD	million metric barrels per day
MLR	Ministry of Land and Resources of China
MTPA	million metric tons per annum
MNC	multi-national company
MOFCOM	Ministry of Commerce of China
MOU	memorandum of understanding
MSW	municipal solid wastes
MTG	methanol to gasoline
MTO	methanol to olefin

MTO+OCP	methanol to olefin + olefin cracking process
NAFMII	National Association of Financial Market Institutional Investors China
NDC	Nationally Determined Contributions
NDRC	National Development Reform Commission of China
NELP	New Exploration Licensing Policy of India
NGL	natural gas liquids
NOC	national oil company
NPC	National People's Congress of China
NPM	non-pesticidal management
NSIDC	National Snow & Ice Data Centre
NSSF	National Social Security Fund China
NTB	non-tariff barriers
OE	oil equivalent
OECD	Organisation of Economic Cooperation & Development
OPEC	Organisation Petroleum Exporting Countries
PAR	project application report
PBOC	People's Bank of China
PHEV	partial hybrid electric vehicle
PDO	petroleum development oman
PE	poly-ethylene
PMI	purchasing managers index
PNG	Papua New Guinea
PP	poly-propylene
PPA	power purchase agreements
PRC	People's Republic of China
Q&A	questions and answers
QP	Qatar Petroleum
REC	renewable energy certificates
REDD	reducing emissions from deforestation and forest degradation
RFS	renewable fuel standard
SAFE	State Administration for Foreign Exchange
SAIC	State Administration for Industry and Commerce
SABIC	Saudi Arabia Basic Industries Co.
SASAC	State Assets Supervision and Administration Commission
SAT	State Administration for Taxation
SAT	soil aquifer treatment
SCEPC	State Council Environmental Protection Committee
SECEP	Sinochem Energy Conservation & Environmental Protection Co. Ltd
SECURE	Social Economic and Cultural Upliftment in Rural Communities India
SEEC	Saudi Arabia Energy Efficiency Centre
SDG	Sustainable Development Goals UN

SFJV	sino-foreign joint venture
SG&A	selling, general and administrative costs
SIA	social impact assessment
SIPC	Sinopec International Petroleum Exploration & Production Corp.
SME	small medium enterprise
SMTO	sinopec methanol to olefin process
SNG	synthetic natural gas
SOE	state-owned enterprise
SPA	sale and purchase agreements
SPC	Singapore Petroleum Company
SPR	strategic petroleum reserves
SRI	systems of rice intensification
SSE	Shanghai Stock Exchange
SST	sea surface temperature
TCF	trillion cubic feet
TCFD	Task Force on Climate Finance Disclosure
TCM	trillion cubic metres
TES	thermal energy system
TPA	tonnes per annum
TPD	tonnes per day
TPP	Trans-Pacific Partnerships by USA
UN	United Nations
UNCHE	United Nations Conference on the Human Environment
UNGC	United Nation Global Compact
UN PRI	UN Principles for Responsible Investment
USEPA	United States Environmental Protection Agency
VBM	value-based management
VC	venture capital
VR	virtual reality
VW	Volkswagen Group
WEO	world energy outlooks
WOFE	wholly owned foreign enterprise
WTO	World Trade Organization
WWF	World Wide Life Fund
yoy	year on year growth
ZEV	zero-emission vehicles
%	percent

1 Clean renewable energy growth management

冰冻三尺,非一日之寒
Bīng dòng sān chǐ, fēi yī rì zhī hán
It takes more than one cold day for a river to freeze to three feet deep.
Rome was not built in one day.

Executive summary

Clean renewable energies have been increasingly applied globally in recent years. Many countries globally have enacted new energy policies so as to promote clean renewable energy growths whilst reducing their fossil fuel consumptions. Global renewable energy investments have already grown by over USD1 trillion over the last decade across the world. These have helped to create over ten million new jobs in the clean renewable energy and low-carbon economy sectors in various emerging economies and developed countries. Looking ahead, clean renewable energy growths are expected to continue to rise with investments of over USD200 billion per year for the foreseeable future. The clean renewable energy growth in various key countries will be discussed in more detail in this chapter with international examples.

Overviews of global fossil energy and clean renewable energy transformation

Globally, many developed countries and emerging economies have been implementing new policies and regulations to control climate changes and reduce GHG emissions. These should help to reduce environmental pollution and help them with their compliance with their Paris Agreement commitments. Many countries have enacted new clean energy policies which would significantly change their overall energy mix by boosting clean renewable energy usages whilst reducing fossil fuel consumptions.

Clean renewable energy investments globally have increased, by over USD1 trillion over the last decade, in both emerging economies and developed countries across the world. These global clean renewable energy growths and transformations have already helped to create over ten million new jobs in the clean renewable energy and low-carbon economy sectors in various key countries. Looking ahead, it is expected that clean renewable energy growths should continue with annual investments of over USD200 billion for the foreseeable future (IRENA, Investments in Renewables Analysis, 2018).

The significant shifts in fossil fuel consumptions and clean energy growths across the world have been progressing differently in various countries. The global energy demands have been growing slowly with low demand growth rates of about 0.9% over the period of the last five years from 2011 to 2016. In 2017, the global energy demands actually increased by over 2%. When the global energy growth patterns are analysed in detail, it showed that more than 40% of the energy growths in recent years have been driven by China and India. These two countries have been the fastest growing major emerging economies in the world in recent years.

Detailed analysis showed that the large majority, about 72%, of the increased energy consumptions in recent years have been met by fossil fuel growths and consumptions, which are very concerning. Only a quarter of the new energy growths were met by clean renewable energy sources. The remainder of the global energy rise was met by nuclear energy (IEA, Energy & CO_2 Report, 2017).

The rise in global energy demands in 2017 has also resulted in energy-related CO_2 emissions increasing higher by near to 1.5% in 2017. Global CO_2 emissions reached a historic high of 32.5 giga-tons (Gt) in 2017. The resumption of CO_2 emission growths was very worrying as this has reversed the trends of the last three years of global CO_2 emissions remaining stable.

Analysis of the global increases in CO_2 emissions has shown that there have been different emission trends amongst the key countries. Most major economies have seen rises in their CO_2 emissions. Some key economies had actually experienced some declines in their CO_2 emissions. The key countries with declines in CO_2 emission included the United States, the United Kingdom, Mexico and Japan. These countries have been able to achieve their emission declines with their new energy policies and clean renewable energy transformations. A good example is that the USA has reported its biggest CO_2 emission declines in recent years, mainly, due to its higher clean energy and renewable deployments. These US renewable growths have occurred despite the current US Administration expressing doubts about climate change and introducing some energy policies promoting fossil fuel applications and consumptions (REN, Renewables Global Status Report, 2018).

The total global fossil crude oil consumptions have also risen by over 1.5% with the higher energy demands in 2017. This was equivalent to a rise in oil demand of some 1.5 million barrels per day. These higher oil demand rate rises were more than twice the annual average increases seen over the last decade. Analysis showed that the rising oil demands have been driven mainly by the transport and chemical sectors globally. The rising share of sport utility vehicles (SUVs) and light trucks in many major economies globally has been driving up oil fuel consumptions, especially in the form of gasoline and diesel. In addition, the increased demands from the petrochemical and chemical sectors for fossil oil and gas feedstocks have contributed to the rising global fossil fuel growths.

Demands of global natural gas have grown faster than those of crude oil, with growth rates of around 3% per annum. These higher gas growth rates have been driven by many countries viewing natural gas as a clean transitional fossil fuel, as part of their fossil to renewable energy transformation. There have also been abundant gas supplies from various gas-producing countries with relatively stable and low gas pricings. China alone has accounted for almost 30% of the global gas consumption growths in recent years. In the past decade, about half of the global gas demand growths have come from the power and electricity sectors. However, recent gas demand growths have changed and these have been driven largely by the rises in energy demands from the industrial and building sectors.

Analysis has also shown that the global coal demands and consumptions have risen again, by about 1% in 2017. This concerning rise has reversed the declining coal consumption trends seen over the last two years. The new coal growths were mainly due to rising coal demands from some emerging economies in Asia. These rising coal demands have resulted from increases in their coal-fired electricity generation capacity and new coal-fired power stations being built in some of the emerging economies.

Experts have reported that clean renewable energies have enjoyed some of the highest growth rates of most energy sources in recent years. Renewable and clean energies have been meeting a quarter of the new global energy demand growths in recent years. China and the United States (USA) have led the renewable and clean energy transformations. Together they have contributed around 50% of the increases in new renewable-based electricity generation capacities globally. The European Union (EU), India and Japan have also contributed significantly to the renewable transformation globally. Wind power has accounted for over 35% of the growths in renewable electricity power outputs.

The global electricity demands have increased by over 3%, which has been significantly higher than the increases in global energy demands for the equivalent periods. China and India have together accounted for about 70% of these new electricity demand growths. It is concerning to see that these new rises in electricity demands have been met by traditional fossil fuels, including gas and coal, in addition to clean renewable and nuclear energies globally. Outputs from nuclear plants globally are seen to have risen by 26 terawatt hours (TWh) in 2017, when a significant number of new nuclear capacities have completed their first full year of operation.

It is also worrying to see that the improvements in global energy efficiency have slowed down dramatically in recent years, after the good improvements achieved over previous years. Analysis showed that these global energy efficiency slowdowns have been caused largely by weaker improvements from new energy efficiency policy coverage, as well as lower energy prices, which resulted in higher and less efficient consumptions. Global energy intensity improved by only 1.7% in 2017, which is lower than the average of 2.3% over the last three years.

Looking ahead, global energy consumptions are expected to rise by over 40% from now to 2030–2035. The majority of the new incremental energy growths, estimated to be over 90%, are expected to be coming from the emerging economies. The energy growths in China and India are expected to account for more than half of the total incremental energy increases globally, with their continued high economic growths. Looking ahead to 2035, energy experts have forecasted that the energy consumptions in the non-OECD emerging economies will likely rise by over 65%, compared to their 2012 levels (IEA, World Energy Outlooks, 2018).

Energy experts have also forecasted that after more than a century of constant energy growths, the global energy demand growths are likely to peak or plateau around 2030–2035. This forecast of a global energy plateau or peak is important but it will be dependent on many factors. The key strategic drivers will include fossil to clean energy transition, shifts to lower consumption industries, heavy industry getting more efficient, improved energy efficiencies, implementation of energy-efficient technologies, etc. A good example is that China's total energy consumption for steel production by 2035 could be halved by applying more efficient blast and arc furnaces (McKinsey, Global Energy Perspective, 2019).

Looking ahead, energy experts globally have generally forecasted that the rise of renewable resources should continue for the foreseeable future. Wind power and solar power have so far only constituted a small slice of the global energy mix despite growths. However, it is encouraging to note that they have accounted for more than half of new installed energy capacities globally in recent years.

It is important to note that energy experts have also been predicting that new solar or wind technologies will be becoming more cost competitive, with various innovations and cost reduction measures, against fossil fuel technologies, by the 2020–2025 period. These improvements in cost competitiveness should support new wind and solar generation capacities increasing significantly, by a factor of 10–60 times depending on locations, from year 2015 to 2050. Looking ahead to 2035, clean renewable energies are expected to make up more than 50% of the total power generation capacities globally.

Looking ahead, energy experts have also predicted that traditional fossil fuel growths are likely to decline further but it is unlikely to vanish by the end of 2100. The growths in crude oil and coal demands are expected to slow down further globally. Experts have predicted that crude oil demands are likely to be peaking in the early 2030s. However, experts are predicting that natural gas demands are likely to continue growing until 2035. This is driven by continued rising gas demands in China and other emerging economies. After 2035, experts have predicted that the natural gas growths globally are likely to plateau or peak. This is largely because of the increasing competition from clean renewable energies. These major mega-trend shifts in future fossil fuel consumptions are likely to lead to peaking in global carbon emissions in 2020s–2030s. These should then lead to a likely global decline in carbon emissions, which could potentially start in the mid-2020s. Some climate experts have predicted that there could be an eventual fall in carbon emissions of roughly 20% by 2050 globally. These carbon declines will be heavily dependent on different key policy measures in various emerging economies and developed countries (McKinsey, Global Energy Perspective, 2019).

It is interesting to compare the future energy growths of the developed countries with those of the emerging economies globally. Experts have generally predicted that the energy demands of the advanced developed economies of North America and Europe are expected to grow only very slowly in the short and medium terms. Looking ahead to beyond 2030, the energy demands of the advanced developed countries could even fall if their new energy efficiency policies and improvement plans would work out as planned (Wang, Energy Markets in Emerging Economies, 2016).

Looking ahead to 2035, crude oil is generally expected to have the slowest growth rates amongst the major fossil fuels. The majority of the new net oil demand growths are expected to come from the emerging economies outside the OECD. The combined oil demand growths from China, India and the Middle East will likely account for most of the new net oil demand growths globally. The key emerging economies in Asia are also expected to show the largest growths in liquid oil fuel consumption globally, with China accounting for a majority of the total increases. The non-OECD emerging economies' share of the world liquid fuel consumptions is also expected to grow substantially over time. This is mainly due to their higher economic growth rates and their higher transport sector growths.

Natural gas is generally expected to be the fastest growing fuel amongst all the fossil fuels. Non-OECD emerging economies are expected to generate over 75% of the new gas demand growths globally in the next decade. LNG exports from the gas producers to the key gas-consuming emerging economies are expected to grow, more than twice as fast as the average global gas consumption growths.

Coal is expected, after crude oil, to be the slowest growing fossil fuel globally. Most of the net growths, estimated to be above 85%, in the global coal demands till 2035 are expected to come from China, India and other emerging economies. Some countries, such as Vietnam, Indonesia, etc., have also been planning to install more new coal power plants.

Looking ahead, nuclear energy outputs are also expected to continue to rise up to 2035. China, India and Russia are expected to account for over 95% of the growths of nuclear power globally. In the developed economies, especially the USA and the EU, nuclear power outputs are expected to decline with planned plant closures. Some EU countries have been developing their new nuclear power strategy and have plans to build some new nuclear power stations to supplement their electricity generations. A good nuclear example is the new nuclear power stations in the UK that have been provisionally agreed during the last visit of the Chinese President to the UK in November 2015. There are still many major hurdles and considerable uncertainties on these planned new nuclear projects in the UK to overcome before they would become reality.

Looking ahead, experts have predicted that the clean renewable energy growths globally will continue with annual investments of over USD200 billion for the foreseeable future. Major renewable investment growths will be mostly in the solar and wind renewable energy sectors. Hydroelectric power is also expected to grow moderately up to 2035. Nearly half of the new net hydroelectric power growths are expected to come from China, India and Brazil. There will also be future growths in the biofuel and geothermal renewable sectors in various emerging economies and developed countries globally (REN, Global Status Report, 2018).

Global clean renewable energy growths and investments

Global investments in clean renewable power and clean fuels have been growing strongly in recent year. These have exceeded USD200 billion per year for the past seven years. A good example is that in 2016 the total new investment in renewable power and fuels was over USD260 billion. It is also worth noting that for the fifth consecutive year, the total investments in new renewable power generation capacities globally have been roughly doubled that in fossil fuel power generating capacities internationally. Global investments in clean renewable energies have continued to be focusing primarily on the solar and wind renewable power sectors. Asset financing of utility projects, such as wind farms and solar parks, has dominated global clean renewable investments in recent years. There have also been significant cost reductions in both solar and wind renewable areas in recent years. These have been achieved with new technology innovations and cost reduction measures. Looking ahead, renewable energies are likely to become more cost competitive against fossil fuels in the near future (IRENA, Investments in Renewables Analysis, 2018).

The global renewable power generation sector has continued to attract far more clean investments than for fossil power or nuclear power generating plants. A good example is that in 2016 it has been calculated that nearly USD250 billion of clean investments has been committed to construct new renewable power generation plants globally. These renewable investments have been about twice of the committed investments of USD134 billion for new fossil and nuclear power plants. These included some USD114 billion of investment in new fossil fuel-fired generating capacities and USD30 billion in new nuclear power capacities. Overall, renewable power generation has been accounting for over 60% of the total new power generating capacity investments globally in recent years (Wang, IOD Climate Finance Green Investment Paper, 2018).

Globally, renewable energy investments in the developing and emerging economies have overtaken those in developed countries for the first time in 2015. In 2016, clean investments in developed countries retook their lead over the developing countries. These have mainly resulted from the new renewable drives and clean energy policies introduced by the governments in various emerging economies and developed countries. The clean investment trends in the renewable energy sector have been varying widely by regions globally. China has been leading the global renewable energy investments with about 32% of the global investments. Europe was second with 25% of the global investments, the United States was third with 19% and Asia-Oceania was fourth with 11%. The Americas, Latin America plus the Middle East and Africa regions have each accounted for about 3% of the global renewable investments.

The top ten countries globally with the highest clean energy investments included three emerging countries and seven developed countries. The top five countries included China, the United States, the United Kingdom, Japan and Germany. The next five countries included India, Brazil, Australia, Belgium and France.

However, there have also been significant increases in clean energy investments recently in some specific countries across the world. A good country example is Singapore which has increased its renewable investments by over ten-fold to USD700 million. Vietnam has also increased its renewable investments by over 140% to USD700 million whilst also continuing with some new coal-fired power station investments. Indonesia has also increased its renewable investments by over 80% to USD500 million. Mongolia has increased its renewable investments to USD200 million in 2016 from having no renewable energy investment in 2015. Thailand has increased its renewable investments by 4% to USD1.4 billion. These investments have led Thailand to become Asia's emerging economy with the third highest renewable investments, after China and India (UNEP, Renewable Investment Global Trends Report, 2019).

In recent years, renewable power generation has been achieving its largest annual capacity increases. These have been driven by the new clean energy policies in most countries and their drive to reduce GHG emissions. A good example is that over 160 gigawatts (GW) of new renewable energy capacity was added in 2016 which resulted in total global renewable power capacity being raised by almost 9% compared to 2015 (REN, Global Status Report, 2018).

Solar PV has seen record new capacity additions in emerging economies and developed countries globally in recent years. It has accounted for more new capacity additions than other renewable and fossil power generating technologies. Solar PV has represented about 47% of newly installed clean renewable energy power capacities. Wind and hydropower have accounted for most of the remaining new power capacity additions. Wind power has contributed about 34% and hydropower has contributed about 15%.

Experts have estimated that globally more new clean renewable energy power capacities have been added annually, than all fossil fuel capacities combined in recent years. A good energy example is that in 2016 renewable power generation accounted for over 60% of net additions to global power generating capacity globally. Experts have also reported that renewable power generation has been supplying about a quarter, near to 25%, of global electricity demands. Hydropower has been providing the majority of the renewable power with over 16% of global electricity demands. The other renewables, including solar, wind, geothermal, biopower, etc., have been supplying the remaining 9% of global renewable power consumptions.

The top countries with installed clean renewable electric power generation capacity continued to be China, the USA, Brazil, Germany and Canada. China has continued to be the global leader with more than one quarter of the world's clean renewable power installed capacities.

The ongoing growth and geographical expansion of renewable energy have also been driven by the continued innovation and cost reductions in renewable technologies. Significant cost reductions have been achieved in both solar PV and wind power with new technological innovations and manufacturing cost-cutting initiatives. Solar PV and onshore wind power have already become cost competitive against new fossil fuel and nuclear power generation options in an increasing number of locations globally. These have been due in part to the declines in component prices and improvements in generation efficiency. The competitive bid prices for new offshore wind power stations have also improved significantly in Europe in recent years. These have contributed to making wind power more attractive.

Cost reductions in clean renewable energy are particularly important for developing countries and emerging economies. These have made new clean renewable energy installations more attractive. In particular, new renewable electrical supply systems have become attractive for remote locations, such as islands or isolated rural communities, where electricity prices have been high and access to grid connections is difficult.

Many developing countries have to bring online an increasing number of new power generating capacities in order to meet the rapidly rising electricity demands from their growing population. They have increasingly turned to clean renewable technologies which might be grid-connected or off-grid. They have also been introducing new supporting policies such as competitive tendering or feed-in tariffs (FITs) so as to support their new clean renewable energy growths. A good example is the supply of new clean renewable energy with distributed power systems which have become particularly attractive for supplying clean electricity to remote rural communities in developing economies worldwide (UNEP, District Energy in Cities, 2018).

Cost reductions in clean renewable energy and storage

The ongoing innovations and developments in clean renewable energy technologies have led to significant cost reductions in various clean renewable energy technologies. Large cost reductions have been achieved particularly for solar PV and wind power. Solar PV and onshore wind power have both become cost competitive with new fossil fuel and nuclear power generation in an increasing number of locations globally. These have been due in part to declines in component prices and improvements in generation efficiency. The competitive bid prices for offshore wind power schemes have also dropped significantly in Europe recently which have made them more attractive.

IRENA has reported, in their recent renewable cost analysis report, that the cost of generating power from onshore wind has fallen by over 20% since 2010 whilst the cost of solar photovoltaic (PV) electricity has fallen by over 70% in the same time period. With further price falls expected for these and other clean renewable energy options, IRENA has forecasted that key renewable energy technologies should be competitive on price basis with fossil fuels by the 2020–2025 period.

Globally, onshore wind power schemes have reduced in costs to around $0.04–0.06 per kilowatt hour (kWh) which should be cost competitive against fossil fuel generation. The cost of solar PV has been reduced down to $0.10 per kWh. In comparison, the cost of electricity generation based on traditional fossil fuel power generation routes has typically been within a range of $0.05–$0.17 per kWh, which would be higher than the latest clean renewable energy power generation costs. IRENA has forecasted that offshore wind and concentrating solar power should further reduce in cost to a range of $0.06–$0.10 per kWh by 2020–2025. These would make all the key renewable technologies cost competitive against traditional fossil fuel power generation options in the near future (IRENA, Investments in Renewables Analysis, 2018).

Latest analysis by Bloomberg New Energy Finance (BNEF) has also shown that the benchmark levelised cost of electricity (LCOE) for offshore wind has fallen by over 20%. LCOE helps to measure the all-in expense of producing a MWh of electricity from a new project. It also takes into account various costs of development, construction and equipment, financing, feedstock, operation and maintenance. Onshore wind power and photovoltaic solar have also become cheaper. These have resulted in their respective benchmark LCOE reaching $50 and $57 per megawatt-hour for recent projects. A good example is that for renewable projects starting construction in early 2019 the LCOEs have been reduced by 10–18% compared to equivalent cost figures of a year ago. The improvements in cost competitiveness of these low-carbon renewable options have been achieved due to a combination of technology innovation, economies of scale, stiff price competition and manufacturing improvements. The LCOE per megawatt-hour for onshore wind, solar PV and offshore wind has fallen by 49%, 84% and 56% respectively since 2010. Although the LCOE of solar PV has fallen 18% in the last year, the great majority of these cost declines have happened in the third quarter of 2018. These major cost reductions have occurred then mainly because a significant shift in Chinese policy has resulted in a huge global over-supply of renewable modules which then resulted in sharp price reductions.

The renewable innovation and cost reductions have enabled solar PV and onshore wind to become the cheapest sources of new "bulk renewable generation" in most emerging economies and developed countries. Offshore wind has often been seen as a relatively expensive generation option compared to onshore wind or solar PV. However, recent auction programmes for new offshore wind capacity have produced sharp reductions in capital costs, in particular for offshore wind facilities with larger advanced wind turbines. These have helped to reduce the global generation benchmark for offshore wind technology to below

$100 per MWh. This is a significant reduction, over two times lower than the offshore wind costs of more than $220 per MWh five years ago. These lower off-shore wind tender prices in Europe have resulted in several high-profile projects reaching financial close in recent months. The cost declines in recent months for offshore wind generation have been the sharpest that have been seen for any renewable energy technology globally.

Energy storage systems have also shown significant cost reductions in recent years. One of the most striking cost reductions has occurred in lithium-ion batteries in the first half of 2019. Latest analysis by BloombergNEF (BNEF) has shown that the benchmark levelised cost of electricity or LCOE for lithium-ion batteries has fallen by 35%, to near to USD185 per megawatt-hour, since the first half of 2018. This meant that lithium-ion battery storage costs have dropped sharply by over 75% since 2012. These significant cost reductions have helped to open up new exciting opportunities for many clean renewable energy storage developments. Battery power storage integrated with solar or wind projects is starting to compete strongly in many markets against fossil fuel generation options. In many cases, clean renewables do not require any government subsidies to be cost competitive against coal-fire and gas-fired generation for the provision of dispatchable power. These new integrated clean renewable generation units with advanced energy storage options will be able to deliver clean power reliably whenever the grid needs it, as opposed to only when the wind is blowing, or the sun is shining. Electricity demands are normally subject to pronounced peaks and lows inter-day. Meeting the peak power demands has previously been dominated by fossil fuel technologies such as coal power generation, open-cycle gas turbines, gas reciprocating engines, etc. These traditional fossil fuel generation routes will now face strong competition from new clean renewable power generation units which have been integrated with advanced power storage systems, together with digital distributed power management systems. The new integrated renewable power storage system could supply one to four hours of peak energy storage with latest developments (BNEF, Battery Power's Latest Plunge in Costs, 2019).

The new clean renewable systems integrated with battery storage systems and distributed power management systems are particularly important and attractive for developing and emerging economies. These should make clean renewable energy installations much more attractive particularly for electric supply systems for remote locations, such as islands or isolated rural communities, where electricity prices have been high and it is expensive to install new connections to national grids systems. Many developing countries have increasingly turned to clean renewable technologies which might be on-grid or off-grid. They have also been introducing supporting policies such as tendering or feed-in tariffs (FITs) to back their new clean renewable energy growths. A good example is the increasing use of new clean renewable energy electricity generation systems integrated with distributed power management and advanced battery storage systems. These are becoming especially attractive for supplying electricity to remote rural communities and villages in developing economies worldwide.

These new renewable developments can also help to supply clean electricity to over one billion people worldwide, who currently do not have access to electricity globally.

Clean renewable energy market trading innovations

The clean renewable energy markets in many countries are changing and transforming fast to accommodate and integrate the growing shares of variable renewable energy supplies. The markets have to become more flexible including managing new shorter trading times. In addition, they have to better integrate customer demand responses on both the supply and demand sides. New market participants have often included small- and medium-sized enterprises rather than the traditional large utility companies. The number of decentralised, independent clean renewable energy producers has been rising globally in both developed countries and emerging economies. They have been playing increasingly important roles in providing variable renewable energy and distributed power management.

Some existing major electric utility companies have been developing new strategies and business models which would accommodate the new market drives for variable decentralised renewable energy supplies. This will be in addition to their traditional centralised big fossil fuels or nuclear power generation models. Good business examples of leading utility companies undertaking these important market transformations included RWE and E.ON in both Europe and the UK.

There have also been many new interesting commercial innovations in renewable energy retailing including new B2B and B2C innovations. A good example is that in response to the conceptual shift away from centralised electricity generation utility companies have shown increased interest in virtual power plant developments. These will increasingly involve new advanced networks of decentralised renewable energy generation integrated with distributed power supply management systems and advanced battery storage systems. These systems could also be connected to and remotely controlled by advanced digital process software and operational data systems (REN, Global Status Report, 2018).

There have also been interesting new developments and innovations in clean energy trading and contracting. A good example is a new digital peer-to-peer trading model in which a direct contract could be made between the energy generator and the energy user. Good examples of these included a new trading platform in New York City, USA plus new peer-to-peer trading platforms in Europe, including Germany, the Netherlands, the UK, etc.

In addition, new innovative models of pooling residential storage systems have emerged. These new pooling systems have often been paired and integrated with distributed clean energy management systems for variable clean renewable energy supply and management. These new systems will allow producers and customers to play increasingly active roles in balancing power supply and demands. A good example is that Switzerland had approved new pooling residential storage system services for its grid. Similar models have also been implemented in Vermont in the United States and tested in Germany.

An important new clean energy innovation is in hybrid renewable energy integration projects. These projects would often combine two or more renewable power technologies. Hybrid projects involving both wind power and solar PV have been becoming popular. These are in large parts due to natural synergies of the two clean renewable energy resources in that wind speeds would often accelerate when solar irradiation declines. New hybrid clean energy projects have been built in many emerging economies and developed countries. Good examples included Australia, China, India, Morocco and the USA (Mckinsey, The future of electricity rate designs, 2019).

Regional clean renewable electricity power developments

The global clean energy and renewable power sectors have been growing fast. Many domestic energy markets in different countries have become significant electricity power markets with further growth potentials. Globally, there are noteworthy clean energy and renewable energy developments in most key regional markets of the world. The major developments in key countries and markets are summarised below.

China has been leading the world in installing new renewable energy capacities particularly in solar PV, wind and hydropower. China has allocated USD360 billion of investments in its 13th Five-Year Plan for new clean renewable energy investments. A lot of new investments will be in new solar PV which should raise the country's total renewable capacity by 45%. There will also be significant new planned investments in other renewables including wind, hydro, bioenergy and geothermal which should help to meet China's ambitious national renewable energy targets. These should also help to reduce China's greenhouse gas emissions and meeting its Paris Agreement commitments.

Other countries in Asia have also been investing in clean energy and renewable energy. Most of the renewable power generations in Asia have been from hydropower. However, hydropower shares have been decreasing recently relative to other renewable power technologies, especially solar PV and wind power. A good example is that in India new wind power and solar PV capacities have both increased substantially. Biopower generation in India has also been growing fast especially in the remote rural communities. Indonesia and Turkey have both been investing in new geothermal power installations.

Oceania countries have been promoting clean renewable energy applications. Australia has been leading the Asia-Pacific region in clean renewable electricity installed capacity. The majority of renewable power generation in Australia has been from hydropower with close to 60% share. This is followed by wind power with over 30% share. In recent years, solar PV capacity has been growing quickly in Australia which has abundant solar resources.

In Europe, clean energy and renewable energy have been continuing their ongoing growth trends. New clean renewable power plants have accounted for a large majority, over 85%, of all new power installations that are being built in the EU recently. Most of the new renewable power installations have been dominated by wind power and solar PV.

The new EU clean energy and renewable legislative proposals, the "Clean Energy for All Europeans Package," have been causing some concerns for the renewable sector in the EU. There have been serious concerns from many stakeholders, including manufacturers, project developers, investors and financing institutions. Their concerns have been largely about the new proposals to remove priority access and dispatch for renewable energy. Other serious concerns included the removal from the new 2030 EU targets, the renewable energy and energy efficiency targets plus binding national targets. There are also concerns about the planned mandatory replacement of FITs by competitive tendering for new renewable projects in the EU (EU, Clean Energy for all Europeans, 2018).

In the USA, there have been strong growths in clean energy and renewables, despite the Administration introducing some new federal policies on promoting fossil fuels and coal applications. Clean renewable energies have increased their share in the total US electricity generation market to 15% from 13%. Clean electricity generation by wind energy and solar PV has increased substantially. A good example is that more new solar PV capacities were installed in the United States in 2016 than any other renewable and fossil power sources. The USA has also started operation of its first offshore wind farm in 2016. However, bioenergy power generation has declined in recent years.

In Canada, hydropower has continued to be the dominant source of clean renewable power generation on a national basis. For new clean power plants, new wind generation plants have been the largest source of new clean power generation being installed for the past 11 years.

Various Latin American countries have been promoting clean renewable power. Some countries have achieved high shares of electricity generation with variable renewable energy. Two good examples include Honduras which managed to supply near to 10% of its electricity with solar PV and Uruguay which has used wind power to supply over 20% of its electricity consumption recently. In addition, a number of Caribbean islands, including Aruba, Curacao, Bonaire and St Eustatius, have managed to achieve clean renewable energy shares of over 10% in their total power mix.

In Brazil, there have been some concerns about the cancellation of the renewable power auctions. These cancellations have been induced in part by declining electricity demands and the recent economic downturns. Their cancellations have caused uncertainties in the growing clean renewable technology markets in Brazil. Many clean power producers, manufacturers and stakeholders would be affected. Substantial clean hydropower capacities have also been commissioned in Brazil but there are growing public concerns on potential environmental impacts.

Many Africa countries have been promoting clean renewable energy applications. Egypt, followed by Morocco, has been leading the MENA region in installing new renewable power capacities. Both countries have significant hydropower capacities installed. South Africa and Ethiopia have been leading sub-Saharan Africa in their total installed renewable power capacities. Their clean renewable power generation capacities have reached 5% of their total electricity generating capacity in recent years.

South Africa and several countries in northern Africa, including Algeria, Egypt and particularly Morocco, have also become important markets for concentrated solar power (CSP). They have also become the new centres of industrial activity for solar PV modules and wind turbine components in Africa. These new clean renewable energy-manufacturing capacities have helped to create new jobs and employments to support the new low-carbon economy developments in Africa. Several Africa countries, including Ghana, Senegal and Uganda, have commissioned new solar PV plants recently. Kenya was one of the few countries worldwide to bring additional geothermal capacities online. Several new large hydropower projects have also been under development in various African countries but some have caused environmental concerns.

Middle East countries have started to actively promote clean renewable energy applications. Current renewable capacities of solar PV, wind power and CSP in the Middle East region are comparatively small. A number of Middle East countries have been building and considering new wind power and solar PV projects. They have also been developing new domestic renewable manufacturing capacities which have helped to create new jobs and employments in the region. Renewable projects exceeding 200 megawatts (MW) are being planned in Jordan, Oman, Saudi Arabia, the State of Palestine and the United Arab Emirates (UAE). Middle East governments and power suppliers have both been favouring the competitive tendering model for new clean renewable power installations. Jordan, Saudi Arabia and Abu Dhabi and Dubai (UAE) have all held solar PV tenders for their planned new solar renewable projects in recent years (REN, Global Status Report, 2018).

Clean renewable energy power grid and off-grid developments

Substantial new investments have and still have to be made in many emerging economies and developed countries globally to upgrade their national power electricity grids so that these can better accommodate the variable clean renewable energy supplies. Good country examples included the modification and expansion of the national electricity grids in leading emerging economies and developing countries, including India, China and Jordan, so as to enable them to better transmit the rising variable renewable power supplies generated in these countries. These major new investments in grid improvements together with reforms in their national power markets have been essential to better utilise their newly installed clean renewable energy supplies.

The developments of new technological innovations for off-grid clean renewable energy power supplies will be very important for more than one billion people worldwide, who currently do not have easy access to electricity supplies. Most of these people are living in remote rural communities in the emerging economies in sub-Saharan Africa and Asia. New clean renewable power generation systems integrated with power storage and new advanced digital distributed power off-grid energy management systems appear to be attractive. These new advanced systems could help to offer new cost-competitive power supply options for these people, especially those living in rural areas far away from the national grids in their countries. Many countries have been considering these new cost-effective options to provide electricity access for their remote villages and rural communities. A good example is that the number of off-grid solar PV power generation systems integrated with power storage and decentralised power distribution systems has been increasing rapidly in many rural communities in developing economies in Asia and Africa. Multilateral and bilateral financing institutions globally have also been providing ethnical impact investment funds to enable accelerated deployment of these renewable energy projects (Wang, FT Asia Climate Finance Summit, 2018).

Globally in both emerging economies and developed countries, there have been expanded applications of new decentralised electricity mini-grids, together with clean renewable power supplies. These have been driven in part by the strong desire to improve the reliability of power supply in the face of rising numbers of extreme weather events, which have been occurring more frequently due to climate change. These included hurricanes, typhoons, flooding, etc., which have often caused more frequent power cuts. So many leading companies, especially those in the IT, digital and data service sectors, have decided to make major new investments in their own secured renewable power generation and storage systems. A good business example is that the leading IT and data companies in the United States and other developed countries have been investing heavily in their own electricity mini-grids together with stand-alone power generation and storage capacities. These have also resulted in a rising number of interconnections of these new local mini-grids with regional or national electricity grids in many developed countries. In a rising number of developing countries, renewable power mini-grid systems have also been applied. These are also helping to meet the important UN goal of providing electricity access for all, especially for remote villages and rural communities (UNFCCC, Distributed renewable power generation and integration, 2015).

Looking ahead, there are also some ambitious plans to consider interconnecting existing national electricity grids across different countries so as to build up some "super-grids" across key regions. These plans are still in very early stages of consideration. There are also many technical, commercial, controls and political hurdles to overcome. Good regional examples included the potential new future super-grids being discussed for Europe, Africa, Asia and America. Many of these potential new super-grids should help to advance the integration of renewable energy supplies across countries and continents. These should then help to promote clean renewable energy growth and applications plus improved international power security across different countries globally.

Clean renewable heating and cooling energy growths management

Globally, the energy uses for heating and cooling have been rising in both emerging economies and developed countries. Various heating applications have included water and space heating, cooking, industrial processes, etc. The global energy demands for cooling have been lower, but these have been increasing rapidly in many countries, particularly with the rising temperature caused by global warming in many temperate countries.

Clean renewable electricity has also been used increasingly for heating and cooling applications in many emerging economies and developed countries globally. Various clean renewable energy sources have been used increasingly to meet directly various heating and cooling demands globally. Different forms of clean renewable energies used have included both solar and geothermal. Increasingly, biopower is also being use and could be generated from various solid biomass, liquid biomass and bio-gas sources.

In line with their Paris Agreement commitments, a number of countries, including emerging economies and developed countries, plus some leading regional organisations in the world, have included in their NDCs, which have been delivered to the UNFCCC at COP22, some specifically mentioned new goals to expand the use of renewable heating applications in their countries and regions.

A good example is the European Commission's proposal for a new Renewable Energy Directive to 2030, which was released in November 2016. This included a recommendation to increase the share of renewables in heating and cooling by 1% annually. The EU has left the specific implementation strategies open for its individual member states so they can choose which renewable energy sources to apply. For the first time in EU policy discussions, their strategies have specifically highlighted the importance of renewable energy for district heating and cooling. There are still many barriers and hurdles on the deployment of clean renewable energy in these markets. Some of the key constraints include limited awareness of available renewable technologies, distributed nature of consumptions, fragmentation of markets, comparatively low fossil fuel prices, ongoing fossil fuel subsidies and a comparative lack of policy supports. In developing countries, the lack of installation know-hows has remained an important additional barrier, particularly for industrial-scale heating systems. Looking ahead, there will still be a lot of additional work required globally to push for more clean renewable energy applications in the heating and cooling sectors (EU, New Renewable Energy Directive to 2030, 2016).

The share of clean renewable energy in the total energy consumption of the heating sector has grown to about 25% for the whole sector. More than two-thirds of the clean energies have been generated by traditional biomass heating. These have been used predominantly in the developing world, including many emerging economies in Asia and Africa. Industrial users have been consuming more than 50% of the heat generated by modern clean renewable energy technologies. The second highest heating consumptions have been from the commercial and residential district heating systems, which have consumed another 5% of the heat generated. A significant amount of clean renewable heat energy has been increasingly consumed by residential households in developed countries and emerging economies. Good heating examples included the use of modern biomass stoves in domestic kitchens plus the application of solar thermal heat systems in modern energy-efficient homes in the developed countries and emerging economies.

The use of solar process heating has continued to increase in the food and beverage industries as well as in the mining industry. These industries have substantial demands for low-temperature heat sources and solar process heating applications have been meeting these requirements. Solar process heating has been expanding into other industrial sectors as well. A good example is that Oman has been constructing a 1 GW solar thermal plant to generate steam for advanced oil recovery. More details will be given in Chapter 2.

Biomass has traditionally been the primary renewable energy source being used for district heating globally. However increasingly, solar thermal heating has been incorporated into new district heating systems. Several large solar district heating projects have been implemented or are being constructed in some leading European countries. A good example is that Denmark has built and commissioned the world's largest solar district thermal heating plant with a capacity of 110 megawatts-thermal (MWth). Denmark's success has inspired solar thermal project developments elsewhere in Europe, especially in Germany and Poland. Solar district heating has also been attracting attention in China with its rising urbanisation and city growths.

Advanced district heating systems are also being considered and installed in some developed countries. Good examples include Denmark, Finland and Sweden. These new advanced fourth-generation district heating systems have begun to move beyond the conceptualisation stage and have been moving towards design and eventual implementation. These new district heating systems will involve advanced integrations with clean renewable energy supplies, smart electric grids, large-scale heat pumps, natural gas and thermal grids, long-term infrastructure planning processes and energy-efficient buildings. The combination of all these advanced features should help to improve their overall system energy efficiency and promote the use of clean renewable energy in district heating. An interesting development is the new residential district heating systems integrated with urban waste incineration systems being installed in London. A good example is the new district heating system that has been installed by EON for district heating and supplying hot water, with renewable thermal heating energy generated by recycled waste incineration in London, to the New Capital Quay residential developments in Greenwich in southeast London (Guardian, London Energy District Heating Systems, 2017).

Looking ahead, there are also growing interest on expanding the use of district heating to provide flexibility to urban electricity power systems. These could involve innovative means to convert clean renewable electricity into heat.

A good example is the new seasonal heat storage systems which involve both inter-seasonal and short-term storage. These systems have been used in conjunction with both electric grids and mini-grids. These new seasonal heat storage systems would use excess electricity capacity to generate power via new power-to-heat process. These systems have been applied on a fairly limited scale so far. More of these renewable heat power systems could likely be applied in future especially in developed countries. Good examples included the seasonal storage system integrated with heat generated by clean renewable energy-based district heating systems which have been applied in a number of European countries.

The use of clean geothermal energy for commercial and residential heating systems has been gradually increasing globally, as several European countries have expanded their use of geothermal district heating plants in recent years. There are currently more than 260 geothermal residential heating systems across Europe. Details of these will be discussed more in Chapter 5.

Clean renewable electricity heating has accounted for only an estimated 1.5% of the total renewable heat consumptions in buildings and industries to date. Looking ahead, the electrification of both residential and industrial heating has been receiving increased attentions in recent years. In many countries, there has been growing interest in the potential to store electricity generated by small-scale renewable energy systems, especially solar PV, in batteries or energy storage systems. The stored electricity can then be used for self-consumption, or to use to produce hot water when required. In addition, the use of heat pumps has continued to rise, particularly in new energy-efficient family houses or buildings with low heat loads.

The number of hybrid clean renewable energy systems for heating has also continued to rise. These systems would combine the application of multiple clean renewable energy technologies to ensure a secured supply of heat. In many hybrid renewable systems, solar thermal heat has often been coupled with different renewable or fossil fuel technologies. A good example is that in Germany solar thermal systems have been combined with natural gas burners to provide secured heating. In China, solar thermal heating is likely to be combined with electric heating systems.

These hybrid energy systems can also apply various combinations of renewable energy technologies, such as solar thermal coupled with biomass boilers or advanced power storage systems. A good example is that in the United Kingdom a new demonstrative hybrid district heating project, which has combined solar thermal, heat pump and energy storage systems, has begun trial operations to supply heat and hot water to new energy-efficient homes.

Space cooling has accounted for only about 2% of total energy consumption globally to date. Most of the cooling demands have been met by means of electrical coolers and air conditioners. Global warming has led to rising demands for space cooling especially in developed countries in the temperate regions of the world. Many temperate countries in Europe and America have recently experienced record-high summer temperatures induced by climate change and global warming. A good example is that Paris has experienced abnormally high summer temperatures, of above 40°C in summer of 2019. These abnormally high summer temperatures have led to dramatic increases in peak electricity requirements and cooling demands in many European countries. These have also helped to spur interest in solar cooling, particularly in sun-rich countries. Some field tests and demonstrative projects of new cooling systems integrated with solar PV panels and heat pumps are being developed to meet these new market demands.

Regional clean renewable heating and cooling developments

There are major differences across various geographic regions in their demands for heating and cooling as well as in the use of renewable energy to provide these services. These are dependent on important key local drivers, which include access to clean renewable energy, biomass availability, heating and cooling requirements, policy supports, etc. Improving the integration of clean renewable energy systems with district heating and cooling systems could help to improve the energy efficiencies plus promote clean energy applications in both residential and industrial heating and cooling systems. In addition, recent analysis has shown that across China, India and the rest of developing Asia, around 50% of the local population have been relying on traditional biomass for cooking, especially those in remote rural communities. There are encouraging new developments on integrating heating and cooling with clean renewable energy sources which we shall discuss more below with regional examples (UNEP, District energy in cities, 2018).

China has become the world's largest consumer of clean renewable energy and heat energy. District heating systems have grown significantly in China. In the past, these have been powered by coal-fired power stations. In the last decade, many coal-fired thermal stations in China have been replaced by gas-fired power stations, as part of China's drive to reduce air pollution. Clean renewable heating has only been supplying around 2% of district heating demands in China. This was due in part to the slow uptake of renewable energy applications in new residential construction projects as part of their basic designs. Looking ahead, there are plans to integrate municipal recycled waste incineration systems together with district heating systems in China. These should offer new opportunities for incorporating clean renewable heat energy supply with district heating systems across China. These developments would be in line with the new integrated district heating and waste incineration systems that have been installed in other developed countries, such as Greenwich, London in the UK, which have been discussed earlier in this chapter (Yale, China Waste to Energy Incineration, 2017).

In India, around 10% of the national heat demand has been met with clean renewable energy to date. These energies have mostly been in the form of bioenergy such as bagasse, rice husks, straw and cotton stalks. A number of solar thermal systems for process heating have been installed in India. These have been supported by the international programmes of the United Nations Environment Programme (UNEP) and UNIDO. There are potentially new interesting developments in India on integrating heating and cooling with clean renewable energy sources. These have been discussed in an interesting UNEP workshop on new district energy developments in India recently (UNEP, District Energy in India Workshop, 2019).

In Europe, various EU states have continued to produce more heat from renewable energy than other regions globally. Most of these clean renewable heat energies, estimated to be over 60%, have been consumed in various residential or commercial building heating systems. Experts have estimated that some 20% of the EU region's total heating and cooling consumption has been met by renewable sources to date. These have primarily been from solid biomass but the uses of solar and wind renewable energies have also been growing. Interestingly, the use of recycled solid biomass in EU domestic heating has been rising with the environmental drives in various EU countries in recent years. These have included advanced biomass kitchen stoves in houses, burning of recycle paper logs in domestic fireplaces plus increased wood log or pellet burning. At the same time, the rising biomass consumptions have generated some negative environmental side effects and concerns. These included increased greenhouse gas emissions plus rising particulate atmospheric releases from chimneys, across the EU region.

Germany is currently Europe's largest consumer of clean renewable heat energy. Germany's total generation of renewable heat has increased by 6% annually on average. The share of renewables in its heating and cooling sectors has been stable. Most of these have been generated from biomass sources. Sweden has the highest shares of renewables in its heating and cooling mix in Europe. Biomass has accounted for 60% of the heat provided to district heating systems in Sweden. Denmark has generated a majority of its renewable heat supplies to its district heating systems from biomass and recycled waste incineration. Interestingly, Demark has also been making significant strides in developing new hybrid renewable systems which have included new integrated solar thermal heating together with biomass and waste incineration. These have been supplying green thermal heat energy for its district heating systems.

North America has been the world's second largest producer of renewable heat. Clean renewable heat energy has been used to meet around 10% of the region's heat demands. The US markets for wood biomass and pellet boilers have grown in past years but these have been levelling off recently. Strong interest has continued in using wood chips for district heating or small commercial boilers. Some electric utilities and companies involved in the fossil fuel delivery industry, including oil, LPG and propane suppliers, have begun to diversify their portfolios by launching new programmes to lease air source heat pumps for both heating and cooling purposes. In Canada, clean renewables have been providing around 22% of their industrial heat demands. A good example is the recycling of biomass residues from the pulp and paper industry in Canada for green thermal heat generations and supplies.

Across Latin America, renewable heat energies have been supplying some 35% of the heat demand in the region. About one quarter of renewable heat energies has been met with traditional biomass, particularly in Latin America's emerging economies and countries. Good country examples included Bolivia, Colombia, El Salvador, Guatemala, Honduras, Nicaragua, Paraguay, Peru, etc. A few countries in the region have been relying heavily on renewable sources for industrial heating. They have largely been using solid biomass fuels such as bagasse and charcoal. Good country examples included Paraguay, Uruguay, Costa Rica and Brazil. The use of solar thermal heating in industry has also growing rapidly in Mexico, where over 95 new solar thermal process heat plants had been installed in recent years.

In Africa, some 2.7 billion of its population have been using traditional solid biomass for cooking every day, especially in remote rural villages. This would be equivalent to over 69% of Africa continent's total population. Access to modern clean renewable heat supplies has been increasing in many African countries. South Africa and Tunisia have been leading the Africa continent in newly installed solar thermal heating capacities and applications. In South Africa, the deployment of solar thermal systems for water heating has been driven by the need to reduce peak electricity demands in their supply-constrained electricity power markets, especially to the slums and remote areas. In Tunisia, the deployment of new solar thermal heat capacity has been driven by their desire to reduce fossil fuel imports and to improve energy security. Egypt has also installed its first demonstrative solar thermal cooling plant in 2016.

In the Middle East, there is rising interest in solar thermal energy for both domestic water heating and commercial and industrial heating applications. There are large projects under consideration and development in Kuwait, Qatar, Oman, Saudi Arabia and the UAE. In the UAE, the 2012 Dubai solar thermal obligations have continued to have positive effects on the solar thermal market developments. In Jordan, about 15% of all households have been equipped with solar water heating systems. Looking ahead, there are likely to be rising use of clean renewable energy for green heating and cooling applications in the emerging economies and developing countries of the Middle East.

Renewable transformation case study: China fossil to renewable transitions

The economic growths of China have created one of the biggest and fastest growing energy markets globally. The energy markets in China have been undergoing significant transformation recently. These have been driven by the new energy and environmental policies enacted by the PRC government to reduce environmental pollution as part of their Paris Agreement commitments. These have resulted in the slowing down of crude oil and oil product consumptions, especially gasoline and diesel, in China. Looking ahead, fossil fuels and oil product consumptions will likely reduce further more in the foreseeable future. However, China's natural gas and clean renewable energies have been growing significantly and these should continue growing for the foreseeable future. More details and background reasons for these significant energy transformation megatrends in China will be discussed in the following sections with business examples (Wang, House of Lords WEG Paper, 2018).

China's clean renewable energy market transformation and outlooks

China has been leading the global renewable energy investments with over 30% of investments. Europe was second with 25% investments, the United States was third with 19% and Asia-Oceania was fourth with 11%. The Latin American, Middle East and African regions have each accounted for 3% of global renewable investments (REN, Global Status Report, 2018).

On renewable and clean energy investments, the National Energy Agency (NEA) of China has announced that China is planning to invest 2.5 trillion yuan or over U$ 360 billion into China's renewable sector. It also announced that China, world's largest energy market, will undergo significant energy transformations. It has been planned that China will shift away from coal power generation towards cleaner fossil fuel and renewable power generation. It has also forecasted that these higher renewable and clean energy investments in China should help to create more than 13 million new jobs to support the low-carbon economy developments in China. The NEA has forecasted that the total installed renewable power generation capacity in China, compromising of wind, hydro, solar and nuclear power together, should be contributing to about half of the new electricity generation capacities in China by 2020–2030 (China NDRC, 13th Five Year Plan, 2016).

The National Development and Reform Commission (NDRC) of China has said that solar power will be receiving some one trillion yuan or over USD140 billion of new investment. China is planning to increase its solar power capacity by five times. This is estimated to be equivalent to about 1,000 major new solar power plants across China. In addition, new investments of some 700 billion yuan or USD100 billion are planned to go into new wind farms across China. Another new investments of 500 billion yuan or over USD70 billion are planned to go into new hydropower stations across China. New investments by China into new tidal and geothermal power generations are also planned in future.

In addition, the planned new China "ecological civilisation" national environmental transformation programme will require green renewable investments of between USD470 billion and USD630 billion in the period from now to 2030. Leading economists have said that China's central government will only be providing some 15% of these new green investments from public funds. The private sector and companies in China will have to generate sufficient new green finance to fund at least 85% of the required future green investments across China. These planned investments should also help to boost more growth of public private partnerships (PPP) across China.

In addition, China is planning to introduce a new China carbon emission trading scheme (CCETS) nationally. It has started to introduce the CCETS for the power sector. It is planning to expand the CCETS to cover other important industrial sectors in future. The introduction of the CCETS is estimated to create new carbon trading and financing values ranging from USD9 to

USD60 billion in future, together with creating many new jobs in the rising green finance sector in China.

These planned new renewable investments and green climate financing in China should create excellent opportunities for international co-operation and advanced knowledge sharing between the leading international banks, finance houses, investment firms plus professional service companies globally with equivalent companies in China.

China's oil market transformations and outlooks

The strong economic growths of China in the last few decades have helped to create one of the biggest crude oil and oil product markets globally. Growths of oil products in China have been fuelled by strong rising demands from the automotive and transport sectors. The oil markets in China are also fiercely competitive with many state-owned enterprises (SOEs) plus national and international oil company players.

The total oil demands in China have been rising by 5.5% per year to 11.77 million barrels per day in 2017. Looking ahead, international oil analysts have forecasted that the apparent oil demands in China are likely to rise by only 500,000 barrels per day. This would be equivalent to a year-on-year growth of 4.2% which is a significantly lower growth rate than the 5.5% growth rate recorded in 2017. One key reason for the lower oil consumption growths is that China's GDP growth is expected to slow down to 6.7–6.5% range in the 2018–2020 period, which is lower than the growth of 6.9% recorded in 2017.

In the transportation sector in China, gasoline and diesel have still been the dominant oil transport fuels. The consumption growths for both gasoline and diesel have been slowing down in recent years. Looking ahead, these will likely reduce further in future which are in line with the new government energy policies to reduce fossil fuel consumptions and promote renewable energy applications.

Looking ahead, China's oil consumptions, including both gasoline and diesel, have all been predicted to fall gradually over the next five to seven years. These oil fuel reductions have mainly resulted from new energy and economic policies from the Chinese government which are focusing more on shifting from quantity to quality, improving energy efficiency, tightening environmental controls plus improving the national environment. All these new strategic policy drivers are expected to contribute to further reducing consumptions of crude oil and oil products in China in the foreseeable future plus promoting renewable growths.

Both gasoline and diesel consumptions in China have been slowing down and are expected to reduce further due to strong downward market pressures in the foreseeable future. These reductions are mainly due to growths in alternative and renewable fuels, expansion of vehicle sharing, increasing ethanol-based gasoline supply, etc. In addition, the expansion of efficient high-speed rail networks across China has also reduced long-distance automotive traffics and lower fossil fuel consumptions.

The growth of new energy vehicles and electric vehicles has also been encouraged in the new policies of Chinese government. These will in turn contribute to further reductions in China's transport oil fuel consumptions and demands. Both gasoline and diesel consumptions are expected to further weaken up to 2020 and beyond.

The PRC government is also expected to further tighten fuel-efficiency standards and vehicle emission standards as part of its drive to improve environment and reduce pollution. These should further dampen and reduce transport oil fuel demands across China. The strong environmental drives in China and the higher oil fuel prices are also expected to enhance the economics of both natural gas and electric vehicles. Looking ahead, new energy vehicles and electric vehicles are expected to continue their growth in the transport sector in China for the foreseeable future.

China's gasoline and diesel demands have been weakened by rising electric vehicle sales plus new government energy and environmental measures. Looking ahead, gasoline demands in China are likely to moderate to 2% by 2020. These reductions will be caused by increased sales of alternative new energy vehicles and electric cars plus fuel-efficiency gains. In addition, the growths of bicycles and urban bike-sharing schemes in various cities in China have reduced short-distance urban driving.

The growths in China's gasoline demands are likely to further constrained in the foreseeable future by the new Chinese biofuel policy mandate for 10% ethanol blends by the end of the decade in the transport sector in China. Gasoline demands will be further reduced and capped by the slower growths in private car sales plus the rise of electric and natural gas-fuelled vehicles in China. Details of China's biofuel and biomass growths will be discussed in Chapter 6.

Diesel has been the largest component of China's major oil products. Slowdowns in its consumption in recent years have severely dented demands for oil products in China. Demands for diesel have been waning amidst moderating economic growths and tighter environmental scrutiny. China's diesel demands had fallen by 3–5% in recent years due to the slowdowns in industrial output growths plus the growth of natural gas-fuelled vehicles and electric vehicles.

Looking ahead, diesel consumptions, like gasoline, are also likely to remain weak as China's economy shifts towards consumption and services led growths plus transform away from heavy industry and manufacturing to service sectors. One of recent new transport policies of the Chinese government is to replace one million heavy-duty diesel trucks, which represented almost 20% of the national truck fleet, with new low-emission trucks which would burn cleaner fuels, such as natural gas and lower-sulphur fuels. These are in line with the new Chinese government policy on tightening environmental controls and reducing air pollution nationally as part of it Paris Agreement commitments.

There are also increasing numbers of electric vehicles as well as heavy-duty trucks powered by liquefied natural gas running on the roads in China. These will further weaken the future demands for gasoline and diesel in China. The production of large LNG trucks broke new records in 2017 in China. There have been over 96,000 gas-fuelled vehicles produced in China recently. This is nearly five times more than 19,600 produced in 2016.

Energy analysts are generally estimating that the demands for natural gas-fuelled trucks in China will likely to continue its rise in the next few years, especially in the logistics, postal services and public transportation sectors. China Environmental Authorities have also reported that several major ports in China, including those in Hebei and Shandong provinces and Tianjin Port, have been replacing their diesel trucks with railways to carry coal and other bulk materials.

The Chinese government has also, via the National Development and Reform Commission (NDRC), raised the retail prices of gasoline and diesel in early August 2018. It has increased the retail prices by 70 yuan ($10.2) per metric ton for these two types of refined oil products. These fossil fuel price rises have further depressed consumer oil fuel consumptions nationally. The Chinese government has asked the leading Chinese national oil companies, including CNPC, China Petrochemical and China National Offshore Oil, to ensure stable supply and pricing of gasoline and diesel nationally. The PRC government and National Development and Reform Commission have also said that they will be closely monitoring the impacts of the current pricing mechanisms and price rises so that they could make appropriate policy and pricing changes in response to global fluctuations and local market reactions, especially the public acceptance to the rising fossil fuel price.

Latest oil fuel research results by leading Chinese oil companies have shown that China's diesel demands have already peaked across the country. In addition, the gasoline demands in China will likely peak in 2025. Looking ahead, China's total oil demands are forecasted to top out by 2030 at around 690 million tons a year, or 13.8 million barrels per day (bpd). Leading Chinese oil and gas energy companies have also advanced the timeline for peak total energy demands for China to 2035, an advance of five years from their previous forecast of 2040.

Leading Chinese oil companies have said they will continue to maintain annual domestic crude oil production of 200 million tons, or about four million barrels per day, up to 2030. Chinese state-owned oil company, CNPC PetroChina, has announced its plans to boost oil exploration and production in China by 1% over the next five years. At the same time, CNPC is planning to boost gas exploration and production by 4–5%, over the next five years. These efforts should help to reduce China's current high foreign oil and gas import requirements.

The declining gasoline and diesel consumptions are serious blows to China's oil refineries, as both gasoline and diesel are important contributors to their fuel sales revenues. Recent new additions to China's refining capacity have also outpaced China's future oil fuel demand growths. Experts have predicted that there are currently more than 50 million tons of surplus fuel refining capacities by 2050 in China. These are likely to lead to some oil refinery closures in China plus some serious job losses in certain oil refining and oil products' sales areas.

China has also become the world's top crude oil importing country. It has sur-passed the USA to become the world's largest importer of crude oil in 2017. It has imported some 8.4 million barrels per day (bpd) compared with 7.9 million bpd for the USA, according to US Energy Information Administration statistics. Some 56% of China's imports had come from OPEC countries, most of which are situated in the Middle East. Amidst warming ties between Moscow and Beijing, Russia's crude oil sales to China have also been rising. Its crude oil im-ports to China reached 1.2 million bpd in 2017. Its crude imports have risen to constitute some 14% of the total oil imports to China. Russia's oil imports have surpassed the Saudi oil imports to China at one million bpd for the same period. This has made Russia to be the top crude importer to China and displaced Saudi Arabia to second place. These significant changes are in line with China's new crude import diversification strategy plus the Belt and Road Initiative (BRI). The diversification of crude imports has contributed to improved energy security in China. The new crude and gas import pipelines and infrastructures are also in line with the China BRI investment plans.

China's gas market growth outlooks

China's strong drives to reduce pollution and improve environment have in-creased gas and LNG demands nationally. Whilst oil and oil product consump-tions in China are forecasted to decline, demands and imports of the natural gas in China are forecasted to continue to increase over the next two decades. These natural gas consumption rises are driven by the PRC government's new energy and environmental policies to promote the use of clean natural gas as part of their drives to improve environment and reduce air pollution. These should also support China meeting its Paris Agreement commitments.

China has now become the fourth largest natural gas-consuming country in the world. Demands for the cleaner burning gas fuel in China have risen strongly by 15–20% in recent years. Leading Chinese energy companies have forecasted that China's natural gas demands are expected to reach 620 billion cubic metres (bcm) by 2035. This will represent a significant growth of 160% from the gas consumption levels for 2017. According to a 2018 report by the International Energy Agency, China is expected to account for more than one-third, about some 37%, of the global increases in natural gas consumptions for the period 2017–2023 (IEA, World Energy Outlooks, 2018).

Domestic gas productions in China are expected to increase in coming years. It is expected to reach 300 bcm by 2035 with gas productions from onshore and off-shore gas wells plus shale gas resources. This will be more than twice the 147 bcm of gas produced in China in 2017. The higher domestic gas productions are still ex-pected to be insufficient to meet the rising domestic gas demands in China. Hence, China will still be reliant on imports of liquefied natural gas (LNG) and piped gas from different gas-producing countries globally. China has risen to be the second largest LNG-importing nation globally. Looking ahead, China is likely to become the largest LNG-importing country by 2030 with its rising LNG imports.

China's oil lubricant market transformation and outlooks

The strong economic growths of China have helped to create one of the biggest and fastest growing base oil and lubricant markets globally. Lubricant growths have been fuelled by strong rising demands from the automotive industry and transport. The growing manufacturing and machinery sectors have also supported significant growths in China's lubricant market. The lubricant market in China is also fiercely competitive with many national and local lubricant manufacturers with their different brands and grades.

Looking ahead, oil and lubricant markets in China are likely to continue expanding at steady rates for the next few years. Growing demands from the automotive industry and transport sectors should continue to offer significant growth opportunities for the market. In addition, the emerging requirements from the renewable sector, especially wind turbines, should add to the overall demands. However, high prices of synthetic and bio-based lubricants are expected to be hurdles for future market growths.

The growing demands for higher quality automotive lubricants will also require new supplies of higher quality base oils and lubricants. These will promote the demands for Group II and Group III base oils plus PAOs. Lubricant suppliers in China are also progressively replacing their Group I lubricants with Group II lubricants. The base oil supply patterns are also expected to continue to undergo wide-ranging changes in China.

On the commercial and marketing fronts, the lubricant industrial sector in China has also entered a new era. A strong brand and its competitiveness have become increasingly important. It is now critical for lubricant companies to have good marketing and branding strategies which will help them to establish distinctive brand positions supported by good channel constructions with strong customer supports in the fiercely competitive Chinese lubricant market. These are key requirements to enable the lubricant companies to remain competitive and have a sustainable future in China's competitive lubricant market.

On the environmental side, China is also planning to phase in some of the most stringent fuel economy requirements over the coming years to cut CO_2 emissions. A good example is that for passenger cars the fuel economy limits are liking to be increased from the 2015 figures of 6.9l/100 km to 5l/100 km in 2020 and then to 4l/100 km in 2025. These new Chinese limits are comparable to the latest requirements in the EU and US markets. These more stringent fuel economy requirements will pose challenging target for OEMs in China. These will also encourage the OEMs to consider the use of higher-quality low-viscosity lubricant grades to improve fuel economy. It is also critical to strike the right balance between engine reliability and fuel economy performances. It would mean that the thinner higher-quality lubricating oils must still be able to deliver excellent wear protection together with lower viscosities in order to succeed in the fiercely competitive Chinese lubricant market in future.

Currently, the consumer lubricant segment appeared to be the best performing oil lubricant market segment in China. Looking ahead, there are also good opportunities for growths in the industrial and commercial lubricant segments. In addition, there should be rising requirements for lubricants and grease from the renewable sector, especially for wind turbines, switchgears, etc. Lubricant companies will need to have good market intelligence of different market segments so as to take advantage of new emerging opportunities. Lubricant companies must also be prepared to adapt to new governmental regulations and societal requirements so as to continue to prosper in the modernising Chinese lubricant market.

2 Solar renewable energy growth management

十年树木,百年树人
shí nián shù mù, bǎi nián shù rén
Ten years for a sapling to grow into a tree and a hundred years to develop enterprises.
Good wine takes time to mature.

Executive summary

New solar renewable energy growths have taken place in many emerging economies. Solar energy has become a key element of the new renewable energy transformation plans of many key emerging economies and developed countries globally. They believe that new solar renewable applications should help them to meet the challenges of lowering fossil fuel consumptions, reducing environmental pollutions plus meeting their Paris Agreement commitments. Technological innovations have helped them to reduce solar energy cost significantly thus making it competitive against fossil fuels. This has promoted solar growths in recent years globally especially in emerging economies. Looking ahead, experts have predicted that solar growths should continue especially with integration with energy storage systems. Details of solar renewable energy growths and future developments will be discussed in more detail in this chapter with international examples.

Overviews of global solar renewable energy growths

The growths in new solar renewable energy applications have taken place globally. These have been driven by the new energy policies and renewable energy transformation plans of many emerging economies and developed countries globally. They believe that these should help them to meet the challenges of reducing fossil fuel consumptions and to control their environmental pollutions plus meet their Paris Agreement commitments. Recent technological innovations and cost reductions have helped to reduce solar generation costs significantly. Experts have reported significant cost reductions in various solar applications in recent years and are predicting more cost reductions in future. These have helped solar energy to become more cost competitive against fossil fuel generation costs. These in turn should promote solar energy applications in both developing economies and developed countries globally (IRENA, Renewable Cost Analysis, 2017).

The world is building more solar power plants because they are getting cheaper and solar applications also do not produce any GHG emission. Since 2009, the total installed costs of solar plants have fallen by as much as 70% around the world. New power purchase agreements (PPA) have recently fallen below $100 per megawatt-hour. These lower solar renewable energy prices have put a solar plant at or below the generation cost of a new natural gas co-generation plant. In addition, new regulatory measures, such as the Investment Tax Credit in the USA, have further supported to improve the economics of solar plants. These have contributed to the growth of solar renewable applications in recent years. A good international business example is that a rising number of leading multinationals have signed new solar renewable power supply deals recently. These deals will help to reduce their GHG emissions and provide them with green credentials. In addition, these will help to lower their energy generation costs and diversify their sources of energy supply plus improve energy security.

Looking ahead, energy experts have forecasted that 2,000–3,000 GW of solar capacity, which is equivalent to almost half of the total electric power capacities in the world today, will likely to become economical by 2025. The innovative integration of solar capacity with new advanced battery storage systems or with gas generation systems could help to overcome the aged old problem of providing reliable power supplies when the sun does not shine. These solar cost reductions and innovations will likely transform the future energy markets in both the emerging economies and developed countries around the world (Mckinsey, Solar Energy, 2016).

Currently, solar power is contributing only some 1–2% of the total worldwide electricity production though it has been growing fast at over 30% per annum (year on year (yoy)). Looking ahead to 2050, solar power is forecasted to provide the world's largest source of clean renewable electricity generation. Globally, solar photovoltaics and concentrated solar power (CSP) have been predicted to contribute about 16% and 11% of the global electricity consumptions respectively. Most new solar power installations will be in China, India and the Middle East plus other emerging economies.

Solar photovoltaic (PV) has been leading the way in renewable power generating capacity in both the emerging economies and developed countries. Solar energy has become a cost-competitive source of new renewable power generation against fossil power in many emerging markets across the world. As a result, solar PV has been the world's leading source of additional renewable power generating capacities in recent year. A good example is that the annual solar PV market has increased by nearly 50% to over 75 GWdc globally.

Globally, China has been leading the world in new solar power renewable installations. It has accounted for 85% of the new solar renewable power additions globally. In addition, the emerging markets have been contributing significantly to global solar growths. Many emerging economies have seen solar PV as a cost-competitive source of clean electricity production. In particular, many developing countries have also found that solar renewable energy integrated with advanced digital distributed power systems have become important clean power supply for their remote rural communities where access to electricity via their national grids has previously been difficult (REN, Renewables Global Status Report, 2018).

Globally, over 17 countries have installed enough solar PV capacity to meet 2% or more of their national electricity demands. Several other countries have installed significant numbers of solar PVs to generate far higher solar power shares in their country's energy mix. Good examples included Honduras in Latin America with nearly 10% solar power supply. In Europe, both Italy and Greece have installed sufficient solar renewables to supply 6–7% of their power demands (Mckinsey, Solar Energy, 2016).

A key reason for the rising solar renewable growths is that solar power generation has achieved unprecedented price reductions, particularly for modules, with new technological innovation and cost reductions. The large downward pressures on prices have challenged many solar manufacturers. At the same time, the declining capital expenditures and improving capacity factors are helping to make solar PV increasingly competitive against traditional power sources. A good business example is that new record low bids of solar generation costs were set in various solar competitive tenders undertaken in 2016.

Falling solar prices and rising demands have lured many new players to enter into the solar industry globally. These included many traditional electric utilities plus some traditional oil and gas companies. These new market entrants and increased competition should lead to further solar cost reductions and wider choice for customers in future. These should be favourable market conditions to promote further growths of the solar renewable energy applications globally.

Concentrated solar power (CSP) has been an important solar renewable energy development. The integration of thermal energy storage into CSP plants is enabling the provision of dispatchable power in many markets, especially in emerging economies and developing countries. A good example is that 110 MW of concentrating solar thermal power (CSP) capacity has come online, bringing global capacity to more than 4.8 GW by the end of 2016. Looking ahead, CSP should remain on a strong future growth trajectory, with over 900 MW of new CSP capacity expected to enter operation in the foreseeable future.

It is interesting to note that many new CSP facilities that have come online have also incorporated new thermal energy storage (TES) facilities. This is a key new technology innovation which should optimise the values that CSP technology can add by providing dispatchable power to grids with variable renewable power supplies. The applications of parabolic trough and tower technologies have continued to dominate the CSP market. There are active ongoing research and developments globally, including Australia, Europe, the USA, etc., on improvements in TES for CSP.

CSP renewable applications have furthered their market push into various developing countries that have high direct normal irradiance (DNI) levels.

These should help to maximise the specific strategic and economic benefits and alignments by CSP technology. CSP has also been receiving increased government policy supports in various emerging economies, especially in developing countries with limited oil and gas reserves. In addition, CSP has contributed to constrained power networks, energy storage, support industrialisation and job creations. These developments should help to maximise CSP values to various countries and its contributions to their national economy.

Solar thermal heating and cooling capacities have also been growing worldwide across different sectors. A good example is that over 35 gigawatts-thermal (GWth) of a new solar thermal capacity was commissioned in 2016 which helped to increase the total global capacity by 5% to over 450 GWth. China is the global leader and has accounted for about 75% of new global additions. It is closely followed by Turkey, Brazil, India and the USA.

The globalisation of solar thermal heating and cooling applications has also continued with accelerated sales picking up in several new emerging economies and developing markets. These included Argentina, the Middle East and parts of Eastern and Central Africa. A good example is that in Denmark the installed area of new solar district heating had almost doubled in 2016 relative to 2015. The successes in Denmark have also helped to promote rising interest in other European countries, especially Germany, which saw new solar heating and cooling project developments.

There have also been significant growths in solar thermal heating and cooling in several non-residential segments. A good example is that the solar air collector systems for drying agricultural products have grown strongly in Germany and Austria. The use of solar thermal technologies in industry has also expanded quickly in Mexico and India. Solar cooling systems have also been used increasingly in sun-rich countries to supply cooling in both commercial and public buildings in conjunction with year-round supply of solar-heated water.

Solar PV regional market growth management

Solar photovoltaic (PV) has continued its growths in both the emerging economies and developed countries. A key reason is that solar PV has become a cost-competitive renewable power supply against fossil fuel generated power in many developed and emerging markets across the world. As a result, this has led to an increasing number of new solar PV renewable capacities being added in recent year. A good renewable example is that the solar PV market had increased by nearly 50% to at least 75 GW in 2016. This was equivalent to the installation of more than 31,000 solar PV panels every hour. This helped to raise the total global solar PV capacity to over 300 GW (REN, Renewable Report, 2018).

Globally, Asia has led the solar PV growth amongst different markets globally. Asia has accounted for about two-thirds of new global solar PV capacity additions. The top five markets were China, the United States, Japan, India and the United Kingdom. They have collectively accounted for about 85% of the new solar PV additions globally. The other countries in the top ten globally for solar

PV additions included Germany, the Republic of Korea, Australia, the Philippines and Chile. For cumulative solar PV capacity, the leading three countries included China, Japan and the USA. Whilst China has continued to dominate both the use and manufacturing of solar PV, emerging markets on all continents have begun to contribute significantly to global growths. A good example is APEC where there have been strong solar PV growths, especially in three APEC emerging economies of Malaysia, Thailand and Indonesia (APEC, Photovoltaic Systems, 2019).

The growing solar PV market expansions have been driven by the improving cost competitiveness of solar PV generation compared to fossil fuel power generation options. These solar PV cost reductions have resulted from new technical innovations and manufacturing cost reductions. In addition, the rising demands for clean electricity and solar PV's potentials for application in both cities and remote rural locations have encouraged more emerging economies and developed countries to install new solar PV capacities as they seek to alleviate pollution and reduce CO_2 emissions.

In Asia, China has been the solar market leader and has increased its total solar PV capacity to over 75 GW which is far more than that of any other country. Xinjiang province in China was the top solar PV market in China with over 3.5 GW of solar PV installed capacity. This is followed by Shandong with over 3 GW capacity and Henan with over 2.5 GW capacity. Large-scale solar PV plants have continued to represent most of the newly added capacities and more than 86% of the cumulative total installed capacities. The PRC government has started to encourage smaller solar PV renewable power plants, integrated with power storage systems and distributed power systems, to supply clean electricity to more remote rural locations in China. The rapid increases in solar PV capacity in China, which has gone up by 11-fold since the end of 2012, have caused some grid congestion problems and grid interconnection delays. To address these renewable curtailment challenges, China has set minimum guaranteed utilisation hours and purchase requirements for solar power plants in some affected areas. It has also continued to build several ultra-high-voltage transmission lines to connect the north-western provinces with the coastal areas. These should enable the export of clean renewable electricity power across China.

Japan is the second largest solar market in Asia. Japan's market was the world's third largest in 2016. This has helped to propel Japan past Germany, to rank second globally for cumulative solar PV installed capacity. Japan solar growths have slowed down recently after earlier growths, which has brought Japan's total solar capacity to over 40 GW. Japan's solar slowdown was caused by declining FIT payments, land shortages and difficulties in securing grid connections. Large-scale projects have driven most of Japan's solar PV expansion in recent years. The large volume of solar PV projects and their outputs have also started to challenge Japan's fragmented electric power grid networks. This has led the Japanese government to revise its regulations. In addition, some Japanese utility companies have refused new interconnections plus curtailed outputs from some existing plants without compensation.

The third largest market in Asia was India, which has ranked fourth globally for additions and seventh for total capacity. The key states in India for solar PV power additions included Tamil Nadu, Rajasthan, Gujarat and Andhra Pradesh. The demands for large-scale solar projects in India have been driven by rapidly falling prices combined with strong policy supports at the state and national levels. India's rooftop solar market has expanded significantly in recent years but has accounted for only about 10% of the country's total solar PV capacity. Financial, regulatory and logistical challenges have hindered growths. India has remained a long way towards meeting its rooftop target of 40 GW by 2022. The most immediate challenges for India's solar sector included grid congestions and curtailments. To help address these challenges, India has been constructing eight "green energy corridors" with new transmission lines to carry power from the solar-rich states to the other regions. This should help to meet the rising electricity demands across India.

In Asia, the Republic of Korea is ranking fourth, after China, Japan and India, on solar PV capacity. The Philippines and Thailand have also been adding new solar PV capacities. Pakistan and Vietnam both have several large solar PV plants under development, but policy uncertainties have been delaying progress.

In the Oceania regions, Australian utilities have been facing major impacts from solar PV. Australia's market has been predominantly residential, although the commercial and large-scale sectors have started to grow recently. About 30% of the dwellings in both Queensland and South Australia have solar PV installations, with high shares also in several other states and territories. Australia's low wholesale electricity prices and high retail prices have encouraged consumers to shift to solar PV, whilst providing them with little incentive to sell their renewable power generation into the grid. Utility companies have also continued to lobby the government to impose further charges on self-consumption by solar PV system owners. These factors have driven a small but rapidly growing market for residential power storage in Australia.

In Europe, many EU states have been adding new solar PV capacities. The EU has become the first region to pass the milestone of 100 GW solar PV in 2016. However, EU demands have fallen recently with the UK accounting for most of the market declines. Europe has become a challenging market for several reasons. The EU region is transitioning from FIT incentives to competitive tenders and feed-in premiums for large-scale systems. In addition, EU electricity demands have been stagnating and the conventional utility companies have been actively lobbying EU governments to maintain their market positions. In Europe, the United Kingdom has remained the region's top market. France has been ranked third in Europe and has been experiencing low solar growths. Germany's annual market remained at about 1.5 GW, which is well below their Renewable Energy Law (EEG) annual target of 2.5 GW. Germany's solar-plus-storage market has been growing rapidly as consumers have shifted from FITs to self-consumption with Germany representing about 80% of Europe's home energy storage market. Germany and Denmark have also opened the world's first cross-border auctions for solar PV, in which companies could bid for installations in either country.

In America, the USA has become a distant second, after China, for new solar PV installations. For the first time, solar PV has become the leading source of new generating capacity in the USA. California has again led the new capacity addition in the USA, followed by Utah and Georgia. The US Renewable Portfolio Standards (RPS) accounted for the largest portion of projects in development in the USA. The increasing cost competitiveness of solar PV against new natural gas co-generation plants has helped to drive solar PV growths in the USA. Large corporate customers have also accounted for a record 10% of large-scale additions. The US non-residential, commercial and industrial markets have also increased significantly. The residential sector has experienced slower expansion, in part, because some major local markets are approaching saturation amongst early adopters. The majority of new residential installations, about 70%, occurred in just five US states. The success of distributed solar PV and falling costs have led some US utilities to establish their own solar programmes and to lobby for revisions or elimination of supportive policies. New net metering, which has driven most US customer-sited solar PV capacities, has continued to be in the centre of regulatory disputes in several US states.

In Latin America, solar PV has been playing important roles in providing energy access and electricity supply to different emerging economies and developing regions. Chile was the region's top installer and ranked tenth globally for newly added solar PV capacities. These expansions were driven by a booming mining industry that has pushed rapid developments in the north. The market was driven largely by the country's first competitive tenders. Distributed systems have accounted for at least one-third of new additions in response to rising electric rates for large consumers combined with falling solar PV prices. Argentina has also been holding solar tenders. In Brazil, solar growths have been stalled by a variety of factors. These included high capital costs associated with their local content rules and the difficulties of obtaining affordable local financing.

In the Middle East, the interests in solar PV renewable power have started to pick up. Countries without domestic fossil fuel resources have begun investing in solar power to diversify their energy supply sources and to improve energy security. Oil- and gas-producing countries have also started to take advantage of their good solar resources, low land and labour costs, plus favourable loan rates to install new solar PV capacity so as to preserve their fossil oil and gas resources for future export sales. Israel has remained the region's leading solar market. Jordan and Kuwait have both brought large solar plants online. Dubai has inaugurated a new 200 MW solar plant. Jordan, Saudi Arabia, and Abu Dhabi and Dubai (UAE) have all held solar tenders recently. Iran has signed several agreements to deploy new solar PV and to build new manufacturing facilities.

In Africa, various countries have also been turning to solar PV to diversify their energy mix plus to meet their rising electricity demands and to provide energy access in remote regions. Solar renewable power with advanced power storage and digital distributed power management systems has become important for providing more easy electricity supplies to remote areas and rural communities. The leading countries for new solar capacity additions included South Africa and Algeria. Several African countries, including Ghana, Senegal and Uganda, have also brought new solar plants online. Tenders for new solar PV projects, both on- and off-grid, have been launched by several countries across Africa, including Algeria, Egypt, Kenya, Morocco, Nigeria and Zambia.

Solar PV innovation and industry developments

Technical innovation and cost reductions, in recent years, have resulted in significant price reductions for solar PV modules, inverters and systems. A good example is that the average solar module prices have fallen by over 30%, to around USD0.4 per watt (W). Downward pressures on prices have challenged many solar manufacturers, whose production costs have not declined as quickly. As a result, many manufacturers have to cut costs aggressively so as to preserve their smaller profit margins. Distributed rooftop solar PV modules have so far remained more expensive than large-scale solar PV. There have also been significant cost reductions and improvements in various elements of the solar PV value chain. These included upstream cost reductions from suppliers of polysilicon, wafers, solar glass, chemicals, back-sheets, etc., as well as downstream actors, such as engineering, procurement downward price trajectories that have made solar PV more cost competitive against other fossil fuel electricity generation prices in many emerging economies and regions globally.

The falling module prices have benefited both solar PV project developers and investors. Lower capital expenditures plus improvements in equipment efficiency and capacity factors have all helped to drive down costs. Subsequently, solar PV is increasingly cost competitive against traditional fossil fuel power generation options. Large-scale solar PVs have recently even out-competed against new fossil fuel projects in some markets, especially in emerging economies and developed regions with low-cost financing. A good example is that in the USA falling PPA prices have made solar PV more attractive than new natural gas co-generation power plants in many locations.

Countries around the world have been increasingly using the competitive tendering system to get the best bids to build their new solar generating capacities. There have been some new record low tenders submitted in some markets recently with bids below USD0.03 per kWh. A good example is that Argentina, Chile, India, Jordan, Saudi Arabia, South Africa and the UAE have all seen very low bids for their solar PV tenders.

The key reason for these low bids was that these tenders have included general expectations that the solar PV generation costs will continue to fall further in future with various new technical innovations and cost-cutting initiatives. In addition, the relatively low weighted average cost of capital and low operating costs in some emerging economies have helped to secure low bids. At the same time, these low bids have also spurred some questions about whether the cheapest projects will be profitable, or will even be built in future. There are also concerns that the low generation prices could threaten plant quality and reliability.

Globally, China has dominated global solar PV shipments and has accounted for about 65% of global solar PV module productions. Asia, including China, has accounted for 90% of global module production. Europe's share has continued to fall to about 5% and the US share has remained at around 2%.

The top ten solar PV module manufacturers globally have accounted for about 50% of shipments during the year. The vast majority of manufacturers have been China-based and some have overseas plants in South-Eastern Asia. The leading solar PV manufacturers globally included Jinko Solar plus Trina Solar and JA Solar in China, as well as Canadian Solar in Canada, Hanwha Q Cells in the Republic of Korea, GCL in China, First Solar in the USA, and Yingli Green and Talesun plus Risen in China.

All the solar PV manufacturers globally have developed corporate strategies to build bigger, more advanced factories to produce solar panels faster and more cheaply than their competitors. The largest Chinese manufacturers have continued expanding module assembly capacity in South-Eastern Asia, in response to the ongoing China-US trade war, plus to avoid US and EU import duties. Good examples included Chinese giants GCLPoly and Longi Silicon Materials which have both announced plans for new production lines in Asia.

Expansions elsewhere included the first solar PV module manufacturing plant in Ghana being opened to serve the West African market. Canadian Solar has commenced module production at a new facility in Brazil. Japanese thin film module producer Solar Frontier has begun commercial production at a new plant. Solarion from Germany has announced plans to expand its Leipzig facility to supply solar projects in Turkey.

However, some other solar PV manufacturers have scaled back expansion plans, closed facilities, changed strategies or restructured so as to adjust to the fast-changing and competitive business landscapes. A good example is that Dow Chemical from the USA has halted production of its solar shingle line. Some big US manufacturers have also announced plans to refocus on their home market with the new US government policies.

Consolidations have also been continuing with downward pressure on prices and the slim margins. These have led to various solar manufacturers, inside and outside of China, to lay off workers and some companies have even failed. In Japan, the number of bankruptcies in solar-related companies has reportedly reached a record high due to fierce competition in a shrinking market. The highest profile insolvency case was that of the US-based project developer SunEdison. After recent rapid growths but substantial debt accumulations, SunEdison had finally filed for bankruptcy protection in 2016.

Mergers and acquisitions, as well as new partnerships, have continued as companies have tried to capture values in project development or to move into new markets. A good example is that the solar PV inverter specialist Ingeteam from Spain had purchased Bonfiglioli's solar PV business so as to strengthen its position internationally in sales, operation and maintenance (O&M). Three Chinese companies including Longi, Trina Solar and Tongwei have agreed to partner together to build a new 5 GW monocrystalline silicon ingot pulling production plant in China.

There have also been good international co-operations amongst solar developers and manufacturers. A good example is that China National Building Materials Group has established a new partnership with the UK solar developers WElink Energy and British Solar Renewables. They have agreed to work jointly to develop new solar energy projects and zero-carbon homes in the United Kingdom.

Falling prices and expanding markets for solar PV have also lured new players to the industry. A good example is that the Apple supplier, Foxconn from Taipei, had purchased the financially troubled company Sharp in Japan, which started making solar PV cells in the 1960s. The US electric vehicle manufacturer Tesla has partnered with Panasonic and acquired US solar installer SolarCity. These are in line with Tesla's corporate plans to establish an integrated solar PV-storage-EV product value chain. Also, four of the world's top wind turbine companies, including GE, Gamesa, Goldwind and Mingyang, have all entered the solar industrial sector in addition to their existing wind renewable businesses.

Electricity utility companies have also been becoming more active in the solar sector. They have participated in the distributed market plus have been constructing and operating large-scale solar PV plants. A good example is that Tata Power Company has acquired a 1.1 GW solar and wind power portfolio from Welspun Renewable Energy in India's largest clean energy deal. The RWE subsidiary Innogy has also acquired solar developer Belectric Solar & Battery in Germany to further its market entry into the EU renewable energy market. EDF in France has acquired installer Global Research Options to expand its US renewable presence.

Fossil fuel oil and gas producers have also moved into the solar energy market. A good example is that Bangchak Petroleum from Thailand has bought SunEdison's solar PV plants in Japan. Coal India Limited, Thai state-owned oil and gas company PTT and Wärtsilä from Finland have all entered into the solar sectors. Oil and gas operator Eni from Italy and Africa's largest oil and gas company Sonatrach from Algeria have both agreed to develop solar projects jointly in Algeria. Statoil from Norway has also invested in the UK solar technology company, Oxford PV.

Investments and financing by various financial institutions have also promoted solar growths in emerging economies and developed countries. Banks, pension funds and mutual funds have all been investing in large-scale solar PV projects and forming new partnerships with solar renewable companies. A good business example is that APG Asset Management, the Netherlands' largest pension fund, has started to invest in solar companies in India. Another example is that the largest US public pension fund has begun to invest in solar farms in California. Crowdfunding has also become an important means for financing new solar projects as well as technology innovations, with various new platforms being launched.

Innovations and technical advances have continued in the manufacturing, product efficiency and performance, installation and O&M areas. These have helped solar developers and companies to reduce costs significantly. In addition, companies have to differentiate themselves, in response to growing demands by customers for increased functionality and rising demands for grid connectivities in some countries. Good solar manufacturer examples included SolarWorld from Germany and REC Solar from Norway who have both upgraded their production lines to the advanced passivated emitter rear cell (PERC) technology. Module manufacturers have also continued increasing the number of busbars to reduce internal electrical resistance, as well as reducing barren spaces on modules to enhance light trapping. Oxford PV has purchased a former Bosch Solar facility to ramp up production of its perovskite technology.

Other key areas of improvements included advancing both materials and self-regulating technologies in order to build higher voltage central inverters. These would help to reduce the balance of systems costs and the levelised cost of electricity (LCOE), as well as improving performance and software to reduce O&M costs. As with solar PV production, inverter manufacturing has been shifting to Asia. As the market matures, the industry is becoming more concentrated, with the top ten vendors accounting for 80% of global shipments. These leading companies include Huawei and Sungrow from China plus SMA from Germany.

Efficiency gains from technological advances have also reduced the number of modules required for a given solar generation capacity which helped to further lower soft costs. Labour and other soft costs of large-scale projects have also been falling due to customised design testing, pre-assembly of systems and advances in racking.

There have also been rising interest in new integrated hybrid renewable projects which have integrated solar PV with other renewable and energy storage technologies. Innovations include integration with wind, natural gas, distributed power management systems, etc. These integrated innovations should help to strengthen a plant's generation profile and improve power supply reliability, plus enable better sharing of resources for construction and maintenance.

Efforts to improve the solar recycling processes have been continuing, although there have so far been relatively small demands for recycling of waste and solar panels. In addition to recycling's potential environmental benefits, the process could yield valuable materials to be sold in the global commodity markets for the production of new solar panels. Australia's Reclaim PV has teamed up with major manufacturers to refine its processes. A US industry programme was launched with the goal of making the national industry landfill-free. Japanese companies NPC and Hamada have established a joint venture with the aim of recycling 80% of the solar panel materials and reusing the rest which would be in line with the Japanese government issued recycling guidelines. The EU has also been regulating solar PV-related waste since 2014.

There has also been steady progress in producing cheaper and more efficient solar technologies. A good example is that solar researchers have been developing materials that would convert a broader spectrum of the sun's light to solar energy. A group from George Washington University, funded by Advanced Research Projects Agency Energy (ARPA-E), has recently reported a new multi-layered device which uses lenses to concentrate sunlight onto tiny solar cells. It could utilise energy from long-wavelength photons that conventional cells cannot. The new solar cell could potentially achieve a higher efficiency of 44.5%, compared with a lower efficiency of 25% of most of the current solar cells. Another interesting innovation is the development of the new liquid solar fuels. A good example is that scientists at CalTech in the USA have been developing "solar fuels" through new processes that mimic photosynthesis. The technology would use a catalytic membrane that absorbs sunlight, CO_2 and water to secrete liquid or gas fuels. One of the more promising solar technologies has been an "artificial leaf" being developed at Harvard University. The new process would employ sunlight-activated catalysts to split water into hydrogen and oxygen. Engineered bacteria would then combine the hydrogen with carbon dioxide to produce liquid fuels. The laboratory results showed that these methods have been working ten times better than an average plant's natural ability to convert sunlight into energy (USA Office, Emerging Science and Tech Trends, 2017).

Concentrating solar thermal power (CSP) developments

Concentrating solar thermal power (CSP) is also known as solar thermal electricity (STE). It has been growing steadily and slowing with global capacity approaching near to 5 GW in various emerging economies and developed countries. Looking ahead, CSP is likely to continue on a growth trajectory, with over 900 MW of new CSP capacity expected to enter operation in the near future.

All new CSP facilities that have come online have also incorporated thermal energy storage (TES). Most of the new CSP plants have been developed with TES incorporated as this will enable the dispatch of solar power at all times. CSP TES integration has been an important innovation as it has helped to improve the competitiveness of CSP, versus other fossil and renewable power sources globally. The integrated CSP TES system is able to improve the flexibility of solar power dispatchability plus ensure a reliable, stable power supply to customers.

Parabolic trough and tower technologies have continued to dominate the CSP market. Parabolic trough systems have represented the bulk of CSP capacity that has become operational as well as most of new planned capacities. Fresnel and parabolic dish technologies are still largely overshadowed, apart from some smaller plants in the development and construction phases.

Around the world, CSP has continued its push into both emerging economies and developed countries that have high direct normal irradiance (DNI) levels together with specific strategic and economic alignments with CSP technology. These strategic drivers will help to maximise the value and benefits of CSP to the country's economic and clean energy developments. CSP has also been receiving increased policy support in countries with limited oil and gas reserves. This should help to promote CSP growth as part of these countries' new clean energy policy plus their plans to reduce fossil consumption and reduce oil imports.

Globally, Spain has remained the global leader in existing CSP capacity, with some 2.5 GW. This is followed by the United States with just over 2 GW. These two countries have collectively accounted for over 80% of the global CSP installed capacities. New CSP market growths have been occurring outside of the traditional markets of Spain and the United States. South Africa and Morocco have been active in adding new CSP capacities. China has also brought new CSP plants online.

In Asia, China has also brought its first 10 MW of CSP capacity online. China's aggressive CSP programme has started to bear fruit in 2016 with the addition of the 10 MW Shouhang Dunhuang facility. In addition, trough, tower and Fresnel CSP capacities of as much as 650 MW are also at varying phases of construction across China. In Asia, apart from China, India was the only country with CSP facilities under construction. India's CSP projects included the 25 MW Gujarat Solar 1 plant and the 14 MW National Thermal Power Corporation's Dadri Integrated Solar Combined-Cycle (ISCC) plant.

In Africa, Morocco continued to be a key country for CSP expansion. Both the 200 MW Noor II parabolic CSP trough and the 150 MW Noor III CSP tower facilities are expected to enter commercial operation soon. These followed the 160 MW Noor I CSP facility which was commissioned in 2015. These CSP plants will bring Morocco's total CSP capacity to over 0.5 GW. South Africa brought its first commercial CSP tower plant online with the launch of the Bokpoort parabolic trough plants. These CSP plants have helped to bring the total installed capacity in South Africa to 200 MW.

In the Middle East and North Africa (MENA) region, construction has continued on Israel's 121 MW Ashalim Plot B CSP tower facility. The 110 MW Ashalim Plot A parabolic trough facility was also under construction. In Saudi Arabia, two ISCC plants have been under construction including the 42 MW Duba 1 facility and the 50 MW Waad al-Shamal facility which will also incorporate advanced thermal energy storage (TES) systems.

In Latin America, construction was halted at Chile's 110 MW Atacama 1 CSP plant due to financial challenges faced by Abengoa, the initial developer and owner of the facility. The 12 MW Agua Prieta II CSP plant in Mexico is scheduled for commissioning.

In the EU, some CSP activities have continued in various European countries. In France, a 9 MW Fresnel CSP facility was under construction in the Pyrenees-Orientales district. In Denmark, a hybrid biomass-CSP facility with 17 MW of CSP capacity was under construction. As a CHP plant, the facility will generate both electricity and low temperature heat for district heating. This would represent an important new application for CSP in countries with colder temperate climates.

Concentrated solar power (CSP) industry developments

Global CSP activities have seen a significant shift from developed countries, especially Spain and the United States, to emerging economies in recent year. These have been driven by the ongoing stagnation of the Spanish CSP market and the slowdown in the US CSP market. There have been ongoing CSP growths in some new markets including South Africa, the MENA region and particularly China. Many emerging economies including Morocco, Saudi Arabia, South Africa and the UAE have also been enforcing local content requirements in their new CSP programmes and plants. At the same time, the CSP industry, despite record efficiency improvements and declining system prices, has been unable to compete with conventional solar PV sector.

These developments have meant mixed fortunes for various CSP companies globally. The CSP industry's largest developer and builder, Abengoa from Spain, has managed to avoid the threat of insolvency when it reached a USD1.2 billion (EUR1.14 billion) restructuring deal with its creditors. The company underwent significant changes, including the restructuring of ownership plus the disposal of their non-core solar PV and wind power assets. Abengoa's rising debt was partially a result of Spanish energy reforms enacted in 2013. These reforms reduced the FITs for CSP facilities in Spain which then led to stagnation of the Spanish CSP market. However, ACWA has continued to grow as a developer, owner and operator. ACWA made strong inroads into the global CSP market, most notably through projects in South Africa and Morocco.

Other top companies engaged in CSP construction, operation and/or manufacturing areas included Rioglass Solar from Belgium; Supcon from China; Acciona, ACS Cobra, Sener and TSK all from Spain; Brightsource, GE and Solar Reserve all from the United States.

The innovative integration of CSP with TES power storage has improved ability for reliable continuous power supply by larger CSP renewable power plants integrated with TES systems. Various CSP TES-integrated facilities have demonstrated their ability to supply power continuously and reliably in the absence of sunlight and even throughout the night. A good example is that in South Africa the newly commissioned Khi Solar One CSP TES facility reached a technological milestone for the region when it completed a 24-hour cycle of uninterrupted solar power generation and supply.

Looking ahead, the bulk of the new CSP facilities globally will include TES or hybridised with other power plants, such as natural gas power plants. A good example is Israel's Ashalim CSP facilities and the ISCC plants under construction in Saudi Arabia.

CSP innovation and cost reduction management

Globally, CSP plant generation costs have varied widely depending on the specific economic characteristics and DNI levels of a given location. In the US market, it has been found that CSP prices have declined in line with the trajectory proposed by the US DOE's SunShot Initiative. The US initiative targeted a decline of 75% in the cost of CSP systems between 2012 and 2020. This has resulted in CSP generation cost coming down to USD0.06 per kWh. Cost declines have also been shown elsewhere globally, especially in emerging economies. Two good examples included a reduction of 30% over two bid cycles in Chile and a reduction of 43% over five bid cycles in South Africa (REN, 2018).

Although CSP costs have seen significant declines globally, CSP deployment has been hampered by a strong competition by a concurrent rapid and substantial decrease in the price of solar PV. These changes have helped to focus CSP developers to maximising values through the integrated application of CSP with TES systems. These CSP TES integrations have enabled CSP facilities to provide dispatchable power continuously globally which have helped to improve CSP competitiveness against other fossil and renewable power generation options.

R&D and innovation in CSP have continued to focus strongly on technological improvements and cost reductions in TES plus cost reductions in key CSP components including collectors. There are also developments in alternative applications of CSP and in better efficiency of the heat transfer process. CSP R&D efforts are being undertaken in various countries including Australia, Europe and the United States.

A good technological innovation example is that in Australia researchers have achieved 97% efficiency in converting sunlight into steam and generated "supercritical" steam at the highest temperatures that has been achieved by non-fossil–based thermal fuels. Pieces of research supported by the EU have yielded advances in thermochemical energy storage and hybridised CSP systems. In the United States, research currently undertaken included new advanced thermochemical storage systems (TES) for CSP, which will offer the possibility of increased energy storage density at lower costs. Another interesting research is the application of supercritical CO_2 which should offer the potential to increase CSP efficiency and reduce further cost.

Whilst CSP power has remained more expensive than wind power and solar PV on a pure generating cost basis, the overall value of CSP with TES can be higher as a result of its ability to dispatch power during periods of peak demands. SolarPACES, an international network of CSP researchers and industry experts, has made a significant progress in quantifying the real value of CSP incorporating TES and standardising yield assessment methodologies required to evaluate new projects. CSP efficiency could also be improved further with the Brayton Cycle which uses air as the working fluid in a gas turbine. This is distinct from the Rankine Cycle, which has been used in existing CSP plants. These CSP Rankine cycle plants had made use of water as the working fluid, in conjunction with a steam turbine. The new Brayton cycle CSP plants should be able to achieve higher operating temperatures, which should then result in higher overall CSP efficiency.

Solar thermal heating and cooling market developments

Solar thermal technology has been used extensively in different regions globally for various heating and cooling applications. These included providing hot water, to heat and cool residential or commercial buildings, to dry products plus to provide heat, steam or refrigeration for industrial processes or commercial cooking. Over the past five decades, the primary application of solar thermal technology globally has been for water heating systems in single-family houses.

The residential segment has accounted for over 60% of the total installed collector capacities. In recent years, the markets have been transitioning to larger-scale systems for water heating in multi-family buildings plus in the tourism and public sectors.

Solar heating and cooling technologies had been sold in over 125 countries globally covering both emerging economies and developed countries. The cumulative capacity of the glazed collectors, including both flat plate and vacuum tube technologies, and the unglazed collectors in operation has increased to over 455 GWth globally. Solar thermal collectors of all types have provided over 375 TWh (1,350 PJ) of heat annually which was equivalent to the energy content of over 220 million barrels of oil but with none of the GHG emissions (REN, 2018).

The top five countries for cumulative solar heating and cooling capacity included China, the USA, Turkey, Germany and Brazil. Amongst the 20 largest markets, significant market growths have been reported in Denmark, Mexico and India. The five leading countries for new installations were China, Turkey, Brazil, India and the United States. The top 20 countries for solar thermal installations accounted for an estimated 94% of the global market. In most of these top 20 countries, the markets have been dominated by the solar thermal flat plate collectors. In China and India, more than half of new additions have been with solar thermal vacuum tube collectors. In the United States, Australia and South Africa, more than half of the new installations were unglazed collectors. Amongst the top 20 markets, vacuum tube collectors have accounted for 75% of new installations with flat plate collectors making up about 20% and unglazed water collectors accounted for the remaining.

China has remained the world's largest solar thermal market despite recent downturns. China's operating capacity was 325 GWth (464 million m^2). This was just over half of its 2020 national target of 560 GWth, which was announced in China's 13th Five-Year Plan for solar applications. The transition in China from small residential solar thermal units to larger projects for multi-family houses, tourism and the public sector has accelerated recently. Larger solar thermal projects have accounted for 68% of China's annual additions in recent years. This trend was supported by increasing demands for centralised solar space heating systems in southern China, where heating systems have been uncommon thus far and where fossil fuels are expensive. The transition was also driven by new China building codes in urban areas, which mandated the use of solar thermal and heat pumps in new building construction and major renovations as a means to reduce local air pollution. A good example is the significant new interest in solar district heating in the Chinese province of Shandong. The local government announced a subsidy scheme in 2016 to support central space heating systems in public buildings, such as schools, hospitals, nursing homes and daycare facilities. One of the first larger solar district heating plants, completed in 2013, was an 8.1 MWth (11,592 m^2) vacuum tube collector system that provides heat for student flats at the Hebei University of Economics and Business.

Turkey's solar thermal market has remained strong, though the formal market remained fairly stable. Residential demands accounted for over 45% of new installations and have been primarily supplied by vacuum tube collectors. Solar thermal capacity in operation has helped Turkey to save around 10% of its annual natural gas consumptions.

Brazil has continued to rank third for new installations and remained the largest solar thermal market in South America. The decrease in Brazil's solar thermal market was relatively small considering the country's ongoing economic problems. These have led to slowdowns of the social housing programme which mandated solar water heaters in new buildings for very poor families. These in turn have resulted in declines in the solar thermal market growths in Brazil.

India continued to grow as the fourth largest market globally with the market bouncing back recently. This has followed a temporary reduction in demands which resulted from the suspension of India's national grant scheme in 2014. The share of imported vacuum tubes grew strongly. This segment included an increasing number of vacuum tubes backed with aluminium mirrors which are the so-called compound parabolic concentrators. They have been used primarily for industrial process heat applications. The growth in India was supported by a national 30% capital subsidy scheme for concentrating solar thermal technologies, which has reduced the payback times to three to four years for manufacturing businesses.

The USA has become the fifth biggest market worldwide. The US market volumes have been declining gradually in recent years. These have been caused by lower oil and natural gas prices plus the increasing focus on solar PV. The USA has continued to be the largest market for unglazed swimming pool systems, followed by Brazil and Australia. The smaller US segment of glazed collectors saw some additions driven by state-level rebate schemes such as the California Solar Initiative plus solar thermal rebates in Massachusetts and New York State, as well as the solar obligation in Hawaii.

The European Union has been the second largest regional market after Asia. The EU's cumulative installed capacity in operation has reached over 35 GWth, which represented around 8% of the world's total capacity. The largest European market has been Germany, followed by Denmark. Other EU markets have been facing serious challenges because of lower oil and gas prices, declining residential demands and reduced interest in solar thermal technology amongst installers. In addition, the EU energy-efficient building regulations have supported the installation of heat pumps in new buildings in Germany and France, which suppressed the markets for solar thermal systems. In Poland, there had been big declines in the solar thermal market. These were caused by a lack of political support for solar thermal and increased competition with hot water heat pumps, which are considered cheaper and easier to install.

However, solar district heating systems in the EU have enjoyed increased attention across Europe, led by Denmark. Denmark has brought into operation 31 new solar district heating plants and systems. The strong market in Denmark was supported by good regulatory framework conditions, including national taxes on fossil fuels, sufficient land for cost-effective ground-mounted collector fields, plus the existence of non-profit, user-owned co-operatives that operate local district heating systems. The Danish Energy Ministry had recently signed a new agreement with district heating companies. The new agreement allowed them to fulfil energy-savings mandates for the period 2016–2020 by extending existing solar district heating plants or by initiating the construction of new facilities. Amongst all existing and new solar thermal plants, Denmark's new installation has been the world's largest solar thermal plant, with 110 MWth (156,694 m^2) of installed capacity, in the town of Silkeborg. The solar district heating plant was commissioned and brought online by the Danish turnkey supplier Arcon-Sunmark after a record seven-month construction. Denmark has also built the world's second largest solar thermal plant which is the 49 MWth (70,000 m^2) district heating field in Vojens.

The successes in Denmark have promoted new project development activities in other central European countries, especially in Germany and Poland. A good example is that Germany's first record-size solar district heating plant, in 11 years, came online in August 2016, when 5.8 MWth (8,300 m^2) of vacuum tube collectors began supplying to the municipal district heating network in Senftenberg. Germany has installed a combined total of 9 MWth (12,921 m^2) in four new systems. These have helped to increase the district heating capacity in Germany to 39 MWth. Spain's plans to install in Barcelona new large-scale solar thermal installations did not materialised. These were mainly due to a lack of affordable space for the collectors in the dense urban area. In total, Europe has been home to 290 large-scale solar thermal systems with a total of 1.1 GWth (1.58 million m^2). These made up around 3% of the total operating solar thermal capacity of the EU region.

The globalisation of solar heating and cooling technologies to emerging economies and developing countries has continued with sales picking up in several new emerging markets. These included Argentina, the Middle East and parts of eastern and central Africa. In Argentina, new solar water heater installations have grown strongly in recent years. A good famous example is that the Argentina President has ordered a new 260-litre solar thermal thermosiphon system to be installed for his Presidential residence in Argentina. Rising electricity prices and solar building obligations have also helped to drive up new demands in these new emerging markets.

Solar thermal technology developments and innovation management

There are interesting R&D efforts into new innovations and developments in solar thermal heating and cooling technologies. One new interesting development for solar thermal technologies is that these are increasingly being considered to provide process heating for industry and manufacturing. Process heating has accounted for around two-thirds of final energy consumption in the industrial sector. Over 50% of the process heat demands have also been in the low- and medium-temperature range, which is normally below 400°C. These will make them suitable for solar thermal technology applications. Hence, solar heating, via CSP and solar sources, could help to replace fossil fuels and other energy sources. This should help to reduce GHG emissions and lower pollution. Good examples of new solar thermal heating applications include solar thermal generated by CSP concentrating collector types such as linear Fresnel, parabolic trough and dish collectors.

There are significant potentials for solar thermal heating applications in various industrial processes globally. Expert assessments for the world market for solar heat for industrial processes (SHIP) showed that over 525 SHIP plants have already been operating globally with over 400 m² of collector and mirror area. These have enough capacity to provide approximately 18 GWh (1 PJ) of industrial process heat worldwide.

However, the application of SHIP to date has so far not been meeting its economic and technical potentials. The key reasons included low fossil fuel prices and lack of supportive policies. For future SHIP market developments, the key enabling conditions should include higher fossil energy prices plus suitable political mandates with relevant policy supports for the use of solar process heating.

The industrial segments with the highest numbers of realised SHIP plants have been in the food and beverage, machinery and textile industries. A good SHIP industrial example is the Amul Fed Dairy in India, which has installed a 561 m² parabolic trough CSP collector to use solar heat to raise steam for milk pasteurisation. Another good example is in South Africa where the Cape Brewing Company has installed a 120 m² flat plate CSP collector to supply solar heat for use in its brewing process.

Another good SHIP application example is in Australia. Good sun conditions for solar concentrating technologies in the Australian desert, coupled with relatively high gas and oil prices, have facilitated the construction of a concentrating solar plant at a tomato farm in the state of South Australia. A mirror field of 52,000 m² has helped to reflect the sunlight towards a CSP receiver which provided solar heat for three different applications. These included the heating of the greenhouses in winter and during cold summer nights, desalinating seawater into potable water for irrigations plus periodically running a steam turbine to produce electricity.

Another good example is in Austria where a record-size process heat system was installed at the automotive consulting company AVL List. It included a new 1,585 m² flat plate collector field which supplied solar thermal energy to meet the heating demands of the factory's test facilities.

It is interesting to note that the mining industries have installed some of the largest SHIP facilities to date. In particular, copper mining and enhanced oil recovery sectors have installed some of the largest SHIP facilities to date. A good example is the Chile mining solar thermal facilities, with 27.5 MWth (39,300 m²) capacity, located at the Gabriela Mistral mine in Chile. Over the first 35 months of its operation, the plant recorded a specific yield of 1,112 kWh per m² despite the operational challenges of the large field's hydraulics and the dusty surroundings.

Mexico also has a good example of a SHIP mining installation. Mexico completed its first solar-heated copper mine project at La Parreña, in the centre of Mexico, in September 2016. The 4.4 MWth (6,270 m^2) facility was designed to provide 58% of the mine's demand for heat.

Solar thermal heating has also been applied in the fossil oil sector for enhanced oil recovery with innovative integrations. A good example is the new 1 GWth solar thermal system for enhanced oil recovery plant in Oman. PDO Petroleum Development Oman, in conjunction with GlassPoint Solar, has been building the largest solar plant in the world in terms of peak energy production. The Miraah Solar Project would be a new 1,021 megawatt solar thermal facility in South Oman. "Miraah" is the Arabic word for mirror. The plant has been designed to harness the sun's rays to produce steam for sustainable enhanced oil recovery in Oman. The full-scale project will comprise 36 glasshouse modules which would be built and commissioned in succession in groups of four. The total project area, including all supporting infrastructure, would span 3 km^2 with an area equivalent to more than 360 football pitches. Construction on the project began in October 2015 with steam generation from the first glasshouse module in 2017. Miraah, when completed, will deliver more energy than any other solar heating plants in the world. This SHIP project is also expected to reduce CO_2 emissions by over 300,000 tons annually which is equivalent to taking 63,000 cars off the road (PDO Petroleum Development Oman, Mirrah Solar Project, 2019).

New innovative integrated solar PV-thermal (PV-T) technologies have also been used to help to capture the waste heat from solar PV modules. These modules would typically only utilise about 12–15% of the incoming sunlight, to provide solar heating for space and water. A good example is that a large-scale demonstration of solar PV-T plant in Switzerland has shown that the system could achieve an annual thermal yield of 330 kWh per m^2 in addition to the annual 163 kWh per m^2 of solar electricity that it produced. France and Switzerland have both installed increasing numbers of new PV-T projects, but with different applications. In France, about 55,000 m^2 of systems have been installed which compromise mostly of air-based PV-T elements for single-family houses. In Switzerland, unglazed water collectors have dominated the solar heating market. They are also increasingly being used in combination with heat pumps to regenerate boreholes over the summer.

Solar thermal cooling applications have also been increasing globally in both emerging economies and developed countries. These have been driven by falling solar PV prices and hotter summer temperatures induced by global warming, especially in the temperate regions in Europe, America and China. As a result, solar cooling systems are being used increasingly for residential, commercial and public buildings. Preliminary findings in Europe showed that multi-usage solar thermal systems that supply hot water, space heating and space cooling could be very efficient. These new multistage solar heating and cooling systems have the potential to cover up to 50% of the total heating and cooling demands of new high-efficient buildings in the region. A good example of the new combined solar heating and cooling operation mode was first demonstrated in 2016 in an office building in Shanghai with a 200 m^2 flat plate collector field and a 23 kW absorption chiller.

There are also growing interest in solar cooling in the Middle East. Increasing demands for air conditioning in the sun-rich countries in the Middle East, combined with financial support from international development agencies, have helped to spread interest in solar heat-driven cooling systems in various Middle East emerging economies and developing regions. A good example is that three new solar cooling systems have been completed in Jordan including the Royal Culture Center, Irbid Chamber of Commerce and Mutah University. During the non-cooling season, these systems can support the buildings' hot water demands which have helped to increase the usable solar yields over the year.

Solar thermal heating and cooling company developments

Solar heating and cooling companies have been adopting their corporate strategies due to changing market conditions. The declining demands from established sales partners and end consumers have led an increasing number of manufacturers of solar collectors and tanks to change their product lines and sales strategies. Many suppliers of solar thermal systems have responded to the rising challenges by taking up new directions and diversifying their portfolios. A good business example is that in Austria several solar collector manufacturers have added heat pumps and solar PV solutions to their product offerings. They believe that these should enable them to provide complete heating system solutions. In China, solar manufacturers have been developing new solar applications such as space heating and cooling, as well as drying of agricultural products.

In addition to focusing on new applications for solar thermal technologies, some suppliers have been developing new business models. A good business example is that in Germany manufacturers of solar thermal systems have provided their potential end consumers with new online sales platforms for heating systems, with or without solar energy. These online platforms will allow clients to provide information about their desired heating systems and then receive a quote or offer directly from the system supplier, bypassing the installer. In Spain, manufacturers have offered loans in partnership with financial institutions so as to promote the sales of their solar systems.

In Europe, manufacturers of air collectors in Germany and Austria have recorded increasing sales, despite the general downward trends in these countries. These growths were supported by cost-effective system solutions combined with high investment subsidies. The strong demands in Denmark have led the market leader Arcon-Sunmark to increase its production volumes to meet the market demands. Arcon-Sunmark has also expanded its business model to China, the world's largest district heating market. It has established a joint venture with China's market leader, Jiangsu Sunrain Solar Energy, to offer new large-scale solar heating solutions to the Chinese market.

To meet the challenges of expanding solar district heating systems to other countries globally, an increasing number of solar manufacturers in Europe have developed mid-temperature flat plate collectors that would employ either a second glass cover or a foil between the absorber and the glass cover. These new generations of collectors have shown good performance even in use with higher-temperature district heating networks.

Most leading solar thermal manufacturers worldwide have been trying to consolidate their leading positions. The largest manufacturers of vacuum tube collectors have been the Sunrise East Group which included the Sunrain and Micoe brands. Other leading manufacturers included Himin, Linuo Paradigma and Sangle. All these manufacturers are based in China. The largest manufacturers of flat plate collectors globally included Greenonetec from Austria, Fivestar from China, Soletrol from Brazil and Bosch Thermotechnik from Germany.

An increasing number of companies worldwide have recognised that solar thermal heating for industrial processes (SHIP) will be an attractive future business area. The main hubs for turnkey SHIP technology development and supply have included China, Mexico, India and Germany. Globally, there are over 70 SHIP-related companies from over 20 countries. Over 40 of these companies have reported that they had already completed various turnkey SHIP reference plants. Nearly two-thirds of the SHIP suppliers have operated their own collector production facilities. The most common collector types have been parabolic trough, followed by flat plate, linear Fresnel and vacuum tube and concentrating dish.

In the solar cooling industry, a key area of focus for most companies has been on reducing costs and improving efficiency. Standardisation of systems has been one of the key approaches used by most companies to reduce the overall investment costs of various solar technologies. This is particularly relevant for solar technologies, such as solar cooling, which have continued to see only small market volumes. Individually, engineered solutions which would normally include a chiller, a collector field, tanks and a re-cooler would generally result in higher costs.

Solar distributed power storage new business developments

With the new innovations and technological advances in solar renewable energy and new distributed power storage systems in recent years, there have been many interesting new developments in distributed solar storage systems and businesses globally.

A good new business example is that GE and BlackRock have launched their new distributed solar and storage business globally. With BlackRock as a partner and with a new focus on project ownership, GE and BlackRock are aspiring to further grow their solar power storage business in future. Over the past four years, a small business unit of GE has been building a growing business around developing distributed solar and solar-plus-storage projects. GE recently announced that it will be growing this business via a partnership and majority investment by the asset management firm, BlackRock Real Assets (WoodMac GTM, GE and BlackRock Launch Distributed Solar and Storage Business, 2019).

BlackRock Real Assets has been primarily investing in utility-scale renewables globally. It has invested some $5 billion in over 250 wind and solar projects with a total generation capacity of over 5.2 gigawatts. As part of its new investment strategy, it has been making strategic moves into the distributed-scale solar project sector in 2019. A good example is its recent investment into the small-scale solar project owner CleanCapital in April 2019.

GE has been having a bumpy journey in its solar renewable energy and power storage businesses. GE initially set up its PrimeStar thin-film solar PV manufacturing business but it later decided to abandon the field by selling it to First Solar. GE then established a new start-up on distributed solar and storage solutions in 2012. It is also still making solar inverters, switchgear and other solar-related equipment. It is also heavily involved in financing and investing in large-scale wind power projects. GE is also amongst the world's leading suppliers of onshore wind turbines and has big ambitions for the offshore wind market. In 2018, GE's energy storage business was transferred to GE Power, whilst the company underwent a broader restructuring that led to the formation of GE Renewable Energy as a standalone business unit based in Paris. The Renewable business unit included all of GE's renewable energy and grid assets, including solar, storage, wind and hydropower. Solar revenue is still only accounting for a tiny fraction of GE's overall renewable business. Onshore wind revenue has been accounting for nearly 90% of revenues of the GE Renewable Energy segment in 2018. Hydropower revenue has been accounting for most of the rest of renewable business incomes.

The new joint GE BlackRock company will be called Distributed Solar Development (DSD). It will be owned 20% by GE Renewable Energy and 80% by BlackRock. The business will focus on a broad range of customers from the commercial, industrial and public sectors. The new investments will allow the new company to expand its current project development work and also own some of the projects that it has been developing.

Distributed Solar Development has developed about 125 projects in 15 states in the USA. It has been working with a variety of solar PV system providers and a set of regional electrical contractors. It has specialised in carport solar PV systems for both carports and on top of a parking deck. About two-thirds of its projects are behind-the-meter. It has also developed rooftop and greenfield projects, as well as front-of-meter, distribution-grid-connected systems.

Battery storage systems are currently making up a small portion of the new company's projects. However, it has been found that a majority of their US West Coast customers and projects have normally included power storage as part of the project scope. These are in line with the boarder growing trends for solar renewable power in these markets.

The US commercial solar market has contracted in 2018 and 2019. It has been largely due to rising market saturation. In addition, the changes to less favourable rate structures and incentive programmes in key states have created additional challenges and hurdles. These US states included California, Minnesota, Massachusetts, New York and New Jersey. However, recent market research has shown that solar distribute power storage developer-owners have been capturing an increasing share of the more challenging market, compared to those developers who have limited their involvement to just acquiring projects. In addition, third-party financed projects have grown from about a third of projects in 2015 to more than half of all projects as of last year.

3 Wind renewable energy growth management

不入虎穴, 焉得虎子
bù rù hǔ xuè, yān dé hǔ zǐ
If you do not enter the lion's den, how can you get the lion's cubs?
Nothing ventured, nothing gained.

Executive summary

Wind renewable power has, with recent technological innovations, become one of the most competitive renewable energy sources against fossil generation routes. Technology developments and cost reductions have made onshore wind power generation cost competitive against fossil power generation. Wind power costs are expected to decline further with future new innovations which should help to improve their competitiveness further against fossil options. These have led to recent strong growths in wind renewable energy applications worldwide. Globally, the total wind energy installed capacity has risen by six times since 2006. The total investments in wind energy installed capacity have risen to over USD330 billion globally. Looking ahead, the installed capacity of wind power should rise further to over 4,000 GW by the end of 2050. Details of wind renewable energy growths and new developments will be discussed more in this chapter together with international examples.

Wind renewable energy growth management

New wind renewable energy applications should help key emerging economies and developed countries to meet their climate change challenges. It should help them to meet the challenges of reducing their fossil fuel consumptions and to lower their environmental pollutions plus meet their Paris Agreement commitments. In recent years, wind renewable energy applications have been growing fast in various emerging economies and developed countries. Wind renewables have benefited from new technology developments and significant cost reductions in recent years. Onshore wind renewable power plants have become cost competitive against fossil fuel power generation options. Offshore wind power projects have also seen record low bid prices globally, especially in Europe. These have help to promote recent strong growths in wind renewable power world-wide. Globally, the total wind energy installed capacity has risen to above 450 GW. This is some six times larger than the global wind capacity in 2006, of 74 GW. The total investments in wind energy projects have risen to over USD330 billion globally which have made wind renewable energy one of the leading renewable energy sectors globally.

Wind power has been playing a greater role in power supplies in many emerging economies and developed countries globally. A good example is that wind energy has been supplying some 11% of the total power demands in EU countries. Over 24 countries around the world have already 5% or more of their annual electricity demands being supplied by wind renewable power. A good example is that in the USA, utility-scale wind power generators have been supplying over 5% of the total US electricity generation capacities. Globally, wind renewable power has been supplying over 4% of the total electricity consumptions worldwide.

Looking ahead, international energy experts have predicted that the installed capacity of wind renewable power could rise further to over 790 GW by 2020 and then increase further to over 4,000 GW by the end of 2050. Technology developments and cost reductions have already made onshore wind power generation to be one of the cheapest electric power generation options and it is cost competitive against fossil power. Looking ahead, wind power costs are expected to decline further with future new innovations which should help to improve wind renewable energy's competitiveness against fossil fuels (REN, Global Status Report, 2018).

Globally, China has been leading with installing new wind renewable energy facilities, despite a significant decline in the country's annual market in recent years. Overall, Asia has represented about half of all the new added capacities, with Europe and North America accounting for most of the rest. New markets for wind renewable energy have continued to be open around the world resulting in wind power being operated in more than 90 countries globally. Future challenges to wind power growths include curtailment, particularly in China, and policy uncertainty.

China has become the global market leader for wind renewable energy. It is followed by the USA and Germany. India has surpassed Brazil to be ranked fourth globally. Other top ten countries globally for new wind renewable energy additions included France, Turkey, the Netherlands, the UK and Canada. New markets for wind renewables have continued to open up elsewhere in Asia and across Africa, Latin America and the Middle East. Good examples included Bolivia and Georgia having installed their first wind plants. The United Kingdom has become a global leader in offshore wind renewable installations. It is followed by Germany, China, Denmark, the Netherlands and Belgium.

International companies have continued to purchase wind renewable power from utility companies and power generators. They have been signing PPAs or buying their own wind turbines for power operations. Their main drivers are to gain access to reliable low-cost wind renewable power and to reduce their

GHG emissions. A good example is that in the USA the cumulative corporate PPA wind renewable power purchases have exceeded 5.5 GW. In Europe, both Sweden and Norway have seen a surge in demands for wind power generation from insurance companies and large corporations.

In recent years, the top wind renewable energy markets globally have contracted due to renewable policy changes and strong competition from solar PV. A good example is that the wind renewable market in China has seen a steady decline since its 2009–2011 highs. Both the UK and US markets have also declined. However, some new wind markets, such as Japan, have started to emerge.

The repowering of wind turbines has become a billion-dollar market globally, particularly in Europe. Most repowering projects have involved the replacement of old wind turbines with bigger, plus more efficient and reliable machines. Some operators have switched their relatively new machines for upgraded wind turbines together with advanced software improvements. Good country examples of repowering activities included Germany, Denmark, the USA, Finland, Canada, the UK, the Netherlands, Sweden and Japan.

The global market for small wind turbine systems has also been growing. These have been used for a variety of applications, including defence, rural electrification, water pumping, battery charging and telecommunications. Experts have estimated that more than one million small turbine units have been operating worldwide. Small-scale wind systems generally are considered to be wind turbines that only produce enough power for a single home, farm or small businesses. The International Electrotechnical Commission has set a limit at approximately 50 kW. The World Wind Energy Association (WWEA) and the American Wind Energy Association have defined "small scale" as up to 100 kW. It is very encouraging to see that in many remote locations, small wind turbines have been increasingly used to replace diesel power generators in recent years. Wind has become a viable and attractive option to supply clean renewable power to remote areas where access to electricity from grids has been difficult. Looking ahead, wind renewable power is expected to continue growing globally but possible policy changes could affect the future market growths for small-scale turbines in different countries (WWEA, Small Wind World Report, 2017).

It is also interesting to note that community and citizen investments in wind renewable power generation projects have been expanding in recent years in different countries globally. A good country example is that in Ontario, Canada, the country has commissioned its first community-owned wind renewable power project into commercial operation.

Wind renewable regional market growth management

Wind renewable energy applications have been growing in various key emerging economies and regional markets globally. Onshore wind has become the most cost-effective option for new grid-based power in many emerging economies and developed countries globally. These included Brazil, Canada, Chile, Mexico, Morocco, South Africa, Turkey, Australia, China, Europe and the United

States. Offshore wind has also been attracting lower tenders and higher interests in many countries. There are also serious challenges for wind power growth on both the onshore and offshore sectors. These serious challenges included lack of transmission infrastructures, delays in grid connections, public concerns, etc. In some countries, curtailment has been a serious issue for wind energy growth. These curtailments have been caused when regulations and management systems have made it difficult to integrate large numbers of variable wind renewable power supplies into existing national grids. A good country example is that the renewable curtailment problems in China have costed Chinese wind renewable industry significant revenue losses in recent years. The details of wind renewable power developments in various key regional markets in Asia, Americas, the EU, the Middle East and Africa will be discussed in more detail below with regional business examples (REN, 2018).

Asian wind renewable market growths

Asia has become one of the largest regional wind energy markets globally in recent years. Half of the newly added wind capacities globally have taken place in Asia. Europe and North America have been accounting for most of the rest. The growths in wind deployment in Asia have been driven by the rising cost competitiveness of wind power and by the need for environmental improvements. In Asia, wind power has become one of the most cost-competitive options for new power generating capacities compared to other fossil power options. Looking ahead, continued wind power growths in some of the largest Asian markets would be dependent on continued future policy supports from the governments of various emerging economies in Asia. These would be necessary to avoid the cyclical or policy-related slowdowns which have been affecting other markets globally.

China has become a global leader in wind renewable power and has accounted for one-third of total global installed renewable wind capacities. However, new wind installations have been declining due to reductions in China's feed-in tariffs (FITs). These FIT declines have also been caused by weaker growths in electricity demands and various grid integration challenges. The top provinces for wind capacity in China included Yunnan, Hebei and Jiangsu. The northern and western provinces in China have been home to a significant portion of China's installed wind power capacity historically. However, new wind installations have also been rising in the southern and eastern regions. These shifts in growths have been driven by new regulations to steer investments away from the high curtailment areas plus to meet the faster electricity demand growths in the southern and eastern regions. Despite the introductions of new regulations by the central government of the PRC on guaranteed annual full load hours for wind energy, curtailment has still remained a major challenge in China. These have been caused by a variety of factors including poor grid connections, lack of transmission infrastructures, slower-than-expected demands' growth and the grid managers' preference for coal-fired generation.

Elsewhere in Asia, India has continued to install new wind power capacities which helped to firm up its fourth place position for total installed wind capacities globally. Turkey has also continued to add new wind capacities making it to rank amongst the top ten countries globally for new capacities. Pakistan, South Korea, North Korea and Japan have also added new wind capacities. Indonesia has also been constructing its first utility-scale wind farm. Vietnam and Australia have also been installing more new wind renewable power capacities.

American wind renewable market growths

The USA has been ranked second globally for new wind renewable power additions and cumulative wind capacities plus for wind power generation. Wind renewable power has accounted for one-fourth of newly installed US power generating capacities. Wind renewable power has been ranked third after solar PV and natural gas, for the gross new generation capacity additions in the USA. Leading US states for wind renewable power included Texas, Oklahoma, Iowa, Kansas, North Dakota, Nebraska, etc. US utility companies have been investing strongly in wind renewable power, with some going beyond the state mandates and based on favourable economics. The increasing cost competitiveness of wind power has also driven a diverse range of new companies to enter the growing US wind renewable market (REN, 2018).

Canada has also continued to add new wind renewable power, albeit growths have slowed down. Wind energy has represented Canada's largest source of new electricity generation for the past decade. The leading provinces with wind renewable energy included Ontario, Québec, Prince Edward Island, etc.

Latin America and the Caribbean have been the next largest region with wind renewable power in the Americas region. Brazil has continued to lead the Latin America region and has also been ranked amongst the global top ten countries in terms of wind renewable capacity. Wind power has been supplying near to 6% of the electricity demands in Brazil. Other countries in the region to add new wind capacities included Chile, Mexico, Uruguay and Peru. Both Chile and Uruguay have passed the 1 GW cumulative wind renewable power capacities in their countries.

European wind renewable market growths

New onshore and offshore wind facilities are being installed in various EU countries, despite some recent slowdowns. New wind renewable power has become the leading new power capacity additions in the EU region, followed by solar PV and then new fossil fuel power capacity at third place. Sixteen EU member states had installed more than 1 GW of wind power in their countries. However, ongoing economic slowdowns and austerity measures, combined with the transition from regulated prices, under FITs, to competitive tenders for new wind projects, have affected EU wind growths (REN, 2018).

Seven EU member states have also set new renewable energy targets beyond 2020 as part of their Paris Agreement commitments. The top five EU markets for wind renewable capacities include Germany, France, the Netherlands, the United Kingdom and Poland. These five markets have accounted for 75% of the EU region's newly added wind capacities.

Germany has become the largest European wind market. Germany's wind boom has been driven largely by the regulatory shift from guaranteed FITs to competitive auctions for most renewable installations since January 2017. Elsewhere in Europe, Russia has also awarded about 700 MW of new wind projects in its first wind power auction in 2016.

Middle East and Africa MEA wind renewable market

In the Middle East and Africa region, there have been growing interests in wind renewable energy. A good example is that Saudi Arabia has commissioned its first utility-scale wind turbine power station and announced a 400 MW tender for a new wind renewable plant.

In Africa, some countries have been added new wind renewable installations. A good example is Kenya's Lake Turkana wind project. The Lake Turkana project with 310 MW wind capacity is the single largest private renewable investment in Kenya's history to date. It will represent approximately 15% of Kenya's generating capacity when completed. It will also become Africa's largest wind farm after completion (REN, 2018).

Wind renewable companies' strategy management

The leading wind turbine manufacturers globally have been enjoying good growths in recent years. These have been driven largely by the increasing cost competitiveness of wind renewable power plants against fossil power plants. There has also been strong competition from low-cost natural gas and solar PV power plants. To improve efficiencies and reduce costs, wind renewable companies have to continue innovating and implementing new cost reduction measures. Most wind turbine manufacturers are located in China, the EU, India and the USA.

The world's top ten turbine manufacturers have been accounting for some 75% of the global wind market. Vestas from Denmark has retaken its leadership position back from Goldwind from China. Vestas has been the most globalised wind supplier internationally, with installations in some 34 countries. GE from the USA has also grown strongly to become one of the top three turbine manufacturers globally. Other leading turbine manufacturers include Gamesa from Spain, Enercon from Germany, Siemens and Nordex Acciona from Germany plus United Power and Envision and Mingyang from China. These leading wind turbine manufacturers have also been sourcing their wind turbine components from many countries globally.

In response to the rising demands for wind power technologies and projects, turbine suppliers and project developers have been expanding globally. Many have been opening new factories and offices around the world. A good example is that Siemens has opened a new wind turbine blade plant in England and has also broke ground on a nacelle factory in Germany. Siemens has also finalised an agreement to build a rotor blade manufacturing factory in Morocco in Africa.

Leading wind companies have also been expanding their scale and global reach through some important merger and acquisition (M&A) activities as further consolidations have continued across the value chain. A good EU M&A example is the merger between Siemens and Gamesa, which has been confirmed and cleared by the EU. This would help to create the world's largest wind power company in terms of capacity in operation. Siemens-Gamesa has also announced plans to purchase from the French nuclear firm Areva its shares in Adwen which is a German company in the offshore wind industry.

Another good M&A example is that Nordex has completed its acquisition of Acciona Windpower, which has good wind positions in emerging markets. This should help the new group to become a major global player. To gain assets upstream, GE has also acquired LM Wind Power from Denmark. It is a leading wind turbine blade manufacturer which has supplied wind turbine blades to most of the world's top turbine manufacturers. Senvion has also acquired the wind turbine blade manufacturer, Euros Group from Germany.

Several state-owned Chinese wind companies have also acquired assets around the world. A good example is that China General Nuclear Power has acquired 14 Irish wind farms from Gaelectric. Electricité de France (EDF) has also become the first European wind operator to enter the Chinese market when it acquired UPC Asia Wind Management.

The wind industry has also shown growing interest in innovative hybrid energy integrations, particularly with solar PV. These new innovative hybrid renewable energy integrations could help to strengthen a renewable plant's generation profile plus enable optimal sharing of resources for construction and maintenance. Hybrid energy projects which have included innovative advanced energy storage technologies have also been developed. These have resulted in wind renewable companies also expanding into other renewable business sectors, especially solar renewable power. A good example is that four of the world's top wind turbine companies, including GE, Gamesa, Goldwind and Mingyang, have all developed new corporate strategies to support their expansion from wind renewables into the solar renewable business sector.

Other wind companies have been developing new hybrid technologies to develop various integrated solar PV-wind hybrid projects. A good example is that Suzlon from India and Gamesa have both announced plans to increase their focus on new wind-solar hybrid developments. Gamesa has also unveiled a new hybrid solar-wind-diesel system, with energy storage for the off-grid sector.

Some leading multinational oil and energy companies have also been adopting new corporate strategy to expand into wind renewable energy. Good examples include Shell, Statoil, Keystone, etc. They have been able to leverage their expertise in offshore oil exploration and development into offshore wind development. A good example is that Shell has been developing offshore wind platforms in various countries globally. DONG Energy has announced that it will be selling its core oil and gas business to focus on offshore wind power. Russian state-owned nuclear company Rosatom has also entered the wind energy market with plans to develop a 610 MW wind project pipeline.

Wind renewable technology innovation management

Wind renewable energy technology has continued to evolve with new innovations. These have been driven by mounting global competitions, plus the needs to improve the ease and cost of turbine manufacturing and transportation. There are also requirements to optimise wind power generation at lower wind speeds. There have also been increasingly demanding grid codes to deal with the rising penetration of variable renewable sources.

The wind turbine manufacturers have been developing new advance materials and designs, as well as improved O&M regimes. In particular, there are new developments for wind turbine blade tips, which normally have to undergo much wear and tear. To reduce the logistical challenges and costs of transport, plus to increase the use of local labour, new innovations have included two-part blades, nesting towers and portable concrete manufacturing facilities for tower construction. A good turbine example is that Siemens had unveiled a low-noise blade add-on, inspired by the silent flight of owls. Vestas has also been developing its new four-rotor concept wind turbine, which aims to reduce transportation requirements and to minimise structural costs.

The digitalisation of wind turbines has been continuing, so as to provide better quality data and access to data. These are particularly important for wind turbine siting and design, performance management, plus the trading and balancing of wind power output. A good digital example is that GE has introduced new software applications for its advanced digital wind ecosystem. Vestas and Envision both have also launched advanced data analytics packages. Goldwind has introduced a 3 MW digital wind platform with smart turbine controls.

To boost wind energy outputs, many wind companies have been adopting the general move towards building larger wind turbine machines. These have included longer blades, higher hub heights and, in particular, larger rotor sizes. These changes have driven the wind capacity factors significantly higher within given wind resource regimes. These have helped to create further opportunities in the established wind markets as well as new ones. A good example is that the average capacity factors for all operational wind farms in Brazil have increased by 2% from some 38% in 2015 to over 40% in 2016, as new wind projects with better technology were brought online.

Globally, various wind turbine manufacturers have also been racing to launch different larger wind turbines. These have included Enercon, GE, Nordex and Senvion for onshore plus Siemens and MHI Vestas for offshore. Increasingly, leading manufacturers have been developing new wind turbine options based on tested and well-proven existing platforms. These have enabled them to more easily develop new wind turbines for specific markets, whilst also minimising development risks and costs.

For offshore wind facilities, the needs to reduce costs through scale and standardisation have driven up the sizes of wind turbines as well as of wind farm projects. Vestas, Siemens, GE and Adwen have all introduced large 8 MW wind turbines for the offshore market. MHI Vestas Offshore Wind has also unveiled an up-rated version of its 8 MW turbine that could achieve a rated power output of 9 MW. The new larger wind turbine's blade swept area will be larger than the London Eye Ferris wheel.

The offshore wind industry has also to meet different technical and logistic challenges from the onshore wind market. Siemens was the leading offshore turbine supplier, accounting for nearly 65% of new added capacities. It was followed by Shanghai Electric Wind Power Equipment or Sewind from China. DONG Energy from Denmark has become the largest offshore wind owner, accounting for more than 16% of cumulative offshore installations in Europe. It was followed by Vattenfall, E.ON and Innogy.

New offshore wind installations have continued to move farther out and into deeper waters. In addition, the average size of offshore wind projects under construction has continued to rise. New wind platform substructures have also been evolving to help to reduce project costs and logistical challenges. Although the majority of turbines installed off Europe have continued to stand on monopiles and jackets, a wide array of other foundation options are also being developed. A good example is that Siemens has been developing a hybrid gravity-jacket concept for offshore wind turbine platforms.

The offshore wind manufacturers have also been continuing to develop floating wind turbines on platforms with anchoring by mooring systems. These have been developed based on the deep water oil and gas drilling rigs plus floating LNG platforms being used in the oil and gas industries globally. A good example is that Japan has added a floating wind turbine platform to its demonstration project off the coast of Fukushima. This has made it to be the largest floating wind project to date. Other projects using floating wind platforms have also been announced or granted consent in various countries. These included projects in South Korea, Ireland, Japan, Scotland, etc.

There have also been new digital system innovations for wind energy. A good example is the DONG Energy's advanced BEACon wind radar system, which has been developed by SmartWind Technologies from the USA. The advanced digital radar system will provide minute-by-minute three-dimensional data of the wind flows through a wind farm over a stretch of sea. The radar can also provide valuable insights on the siting, design and operation of future offshore wind projects (CleanTechnica, Wind Power Radar System, 2016).

There have also been interesting new innovations in the offshore wind farm logistic areas. A good example is that Siemens has launched a new customised transport vessel which would allow for rolling nacelles on and off deck. This would help to minimise the needs for expensive crane operations which should help to reduce logistic costs and lower the total project costs.

Offshore wind renewable market growth management

The economics of offshore wind power have improved far faster than experts have previously forecasted. The offshore wind costs have been driven down rapidly by a combination of factors. These have included the improved economies of scale achieved by larger wind turbines and larger wind projects. The increased competition amongst developers and rising expertise has also help to reduce operating costs. The significant technical improvements with turbines, installation processes, grid connection, logistics plus operational and maintenance strategies (O&M) have all helped to reduce costs and improve competitiveness. In addition, the lower costs of capital which have resulted from the general perception of reduced risks of wind renewable investments in financial markets have helped to reduce the overall new wind renewable project costs.

There have also been good international co-operations on offshore wind projects across country boundaries. A good example is that in June 2016 nine European countries have agreed to co-operate on new offshore wind power developments through joint tenders. Eleven wind companies also signed an open letter calling for a stable legal framework for wind renewable energy growths. They are also aiming to develop various innovations so they can produce offshore wind power more cheaply than coal-fired power generation within the next few years. Looking ahead, they are also aiming to reduce offshore wind costs to less than EUR80 per MWh or USD84 per MWh per project, by 2025.

A good example of international business co-operation on offshore wind is that Shell and CoensHexicon Co. Ltd have signed an agreement to develop, construct and operate a floating offshore wind farm in South Korea. These are in follow-up to the successful development and deployments of various offshore floating oil rigs and floating LNG platforms which have been developed and applied by leading oil and gas energy companies, especially Shell.

Initial project developments have started in early 2019 for the new floating wind farm which will be located circa 40 km off the coast of Ulsan. The two companies have already formed a project company in Busan, called TwinWind Development Co. Ltd. They have successfully obtained a wind lease for the offshore Ulsan region. The collaboration of CoensHexicon with Shell will help to bring together a wealth of complementary skills on offshore wind and offshore resource developments. These should help them to develop and operate a large innovative floating wind farm successfully. The project will include in South Korea serial manufacturing of the patented multi-turbine foundation design developed by Hexicon in Sweden. In addition, Shell's extensive global experience in operating offshore oil rigs and floating LNG platforms in different locations globally will be invaluable.

Swedish Hexicon and South Korean COENS have formed the CoensHexicon joint venture company in year 2018 with an aim to transfer the Hexicon floating wind platform technology to Korea and offer serial production of Korea-manufactured units for new floating wind platforms in the local and international markets. The parties have signed a Memorandum of Understanding (MoU) with the City of Ulsan to build and maintain offshore floating wind farms, as well as to create a local supply chain in South Korea (Offshorewind Biz, Shell and CoensHexicon Offshore Wind Farm, 2019).

Another interesting example of offshore wind development is in Saudi Arabia in the Middle East region. The development of new floating offshore wind farm projects is part of its new 5 gigawatt (GW) wind market concept. These are being implemented in Saudi Arabia by international wind developers. Saipem has just signed a memorandum of understanding (MOU) with the Abu Dhabi-based Plambeck Emirates for the development and construction of a floating offshore wind farm in Saudi Arabia. The 500 megawatt (MW) wind project will commence its development phases via Plambeck Saudi, which is a Plambeck subsidiary company located in Riyadh. Under the signed MoU, Saipem will begin operations after finalisation of the financial agreements at the end of the planning phase. Then a contract will be signed for Saipem to undertake the engineering, design, construction and installation of the entire offshore wind farm project plus provide related services.

4 Hydropower and ocean renewable energy growth management

有其父必有其子
Yǒu qí fù bì yǒu qí zǐ
The son always takes after his father.
Like father like son.

Executive summary

Hydropower renewable energy applications have been important elements in the renewable transformation plans of key emerging economies and developed countries. Hydropower is currently the largest single renewable electricity power generation source globally. Hydropower has been competitive against fossil fuel power generation and is currently providing over 16% of world's electricity generation. Significant new developments are planned for emerging economies in Asia, Latin America and Africa. Ocean renewable energy sources have remained a largely untapped renewable energy source, despite decades of development efforts. Details of hydropower and ocean renewable power developments will be discussed in more detail in this chapter with international examples.

Hydro renewable power growths and developments

New hydropower and ocean renewable energy applications have been important elements of the new renewable energy transformation plans of many key emerging economies and developed countries. These clean renewable power applications should help the emerging economies and developed countries, with the appropriate hydro and ocean resources, to meet their twin challenges of reducing fossil fuel consumptions and of lowering their environmental pollutions.

Hydropower is currently the largest single renewable electricity power generation source globally. It has been supplying over 16% of global electricity generation and 70% of all renewable electricity generation globally. Hydropower has been successful in meeting the cost competitiveness challenges from fossil power generation routes. Hydropower generation is currently providing over 1,000 GW of installed electricity generation at competitive prices in both emerging economies and developed countries globally (REN, Global Status Report, 2018).

Significant new hydropower developments are being planned for emerging economies in Asia, Latin America and Africa. Asia has the largest unutilised hydropower potential of over 7,000 TWh/year globally. The emerging economies in Asia are the likely leading markets for future new hydropower developments. At the same time, there are also significant public environmental and political challenges to these new hydropower projects.

The leading countries for cumulative hydro capacity globally included China, Brazil, Canada, the United States, Russia, India and Norway. Together, these countries have represented about 63% of the total installed hydro renewable capacities globally. China has become the global leader in new hydropower capacities and was followed by Brazil, India, Angola and Turkey. Other countries that had added significant hydropower capacities included Iran, Vietnam, Russia and Sudan (REN, 2018).

Hydropower developments have remained relatively strong across various emerging economies in Asia. A good example is Vietnam which had completed the new 260 MW Trung Son hydropower plant. This new hydropower plant is intended to provide flood protection and meet irrigation needs as well as to generate hydroelectricity to promote local economic developments. The project has been designed to minimise its potential social and environmental impacts. It is also Vietnam's first large-scale hydropower project to receive funding from the World Bank.

India has also brought into commercial operation some new hydropower capacities. However, nearly half of all the large-scale hydropower projects in India have been facing delays or other challenges. In Pakistan, the new 147 MW Patrind hydropower plant has been owned and developed by parties with commercial interests from the Republic of Korea. The project had been awarded certified emission reduction credits under the Clean Development Mechanism (CDM). This is in line with Korean efforts to promote CDM projects abroad (REN, 2018).

Russia has also been one of the top countries for hydropower capacity globally. Russia has recently seen a net five-year growth in installed hydropower capacities. Most of the newly added hydropower capacities in Russia have been tied to the inauguration of the 320 MW Nizhne-Bureyskaya hydropower plant in the Russian Far East. This is the region where a majority of Russia's new hydropower projects under construction are located. Following a flood in the Amur River basin in 2013, the design of the plant was modified so as to cater for improved flood controls.

In North America, the USA continued to be ranked third globally for installed hydropower capacities. However, recent new hydropower expansions in the USA have been relatively modest. In Canada, the Upper Lillooet River Hydro Project with two run-of-river hydropower facilities has been completed in British Columbia.

In Latin America, Brazil has continued to be the largest hydropower producer. Brazil has also been ranked second globally for new hydropower installations. The construction of the new 11.2 GW Belo Monte hydropower project in Brazil has faced various setbacks due to serious concerns about its potential social and environmental impacts on the local indigenous communities. Brazil's hydropower output has also declined in 2017 due to climate-induced extreme droughts in various parts. These declines in hydropower outputs have led to a national surcharge on electricity rates plus an increase in electricity imports from neighbouring countries.

Bolivia has just completed its largest hydropower plant to date. It is the multipurpose 120 MW Misicuni hydropower plant. This hydropower plant is representing 7% of the total country's power generation capacity. Its water reservoir will also serve to improve local municipal water supplies. Peru and Colombia have also expanded their hydropower portfolios.

In the Middle East region, Iran and Turkey have been adding new hydropower capacities. In Iran, the new 450 MW Rudbar hydro project was completed. This new project is in line with Iran's new national energy plans to reduce electricity generation from fossil fuels plus to lower emissions and pollutions. This Iran hydropower project has been funded largely by Chinese interests as part of China's Belt and Road initiative (BRI). Turkey has also been expanding its hydropower capacity. In 2017, hydropower generation in Turkey contracted to 12.7%, due to climate-induced severe droughts (REN, 2018).

In Africa, Angola has made significant progress in two large new hydropower projects. The Laúca hydropower project brought online two of its 334 MW turbines. These large hydro projects are part of the Angola government's national drive to increase its electrification to 60% across the country by 2025. Côte d'Ivoire has also inaugurated its largest hydropower project, which is the 275 MW Soubré hydropower project. This is part of the government's new energy plans to double its generating capacity by 2020. This should improve the country's electrification rate whilst diversifying its electricity and energy mix away from the dominance by natural gas with increasing shares of hydropower and renewables in its electricity mix. Sudan has also inaugurated its new 320 MW Upper Atbara and Setit Dam hydropower project. This hydropower project is linked to an agreement which will allow Saudi Arabia to cultivate land in Sudan within the vicinity of the dams. There have been considerable public objections with thousands of displaced local families complaining about the government's lack of commitment to compensate them for farmland lost to the project. The tensions, between Ethiopia and its downstream neighbours Sudan and Egypt, have persisted over their serious concerns about the potential impacts of Ethiopia's Grand Renaissance Dam on water flows in the Nile. The dam has also raised serious concerns about restricted sediment flows, which could potentially exacerbate the relative sea-level rises in the Nile delta (DW, Nile dam project, 2019).

Hydro renewable energy storage developments

Hydropower energy storage technologies have been applied in many emerging economies and developed countries to optimise hydropower supply and generation to improve fits with market requirements. The traditional hydropower energy storage approach has been to use reservoirs for balancing variable renewable electricity generation and for managing water supply. Pure hydropower pumped storage plants, involving reservoir schemes, are more of a means to store hydro energy and will normally involve conversion losses. A good example is the pumping of water uphill to a storage reservoir during low-power demand periods, such as during nighttime. The water pumping power could be by renewable or non-renewable generated electricity. Then the water from the reservoir can be released downhill to generate electricity during peak demand periods. Pumped storage hydropower schemes have traditionally played important roles in balancing grid power supplies and in the integration of variable renewable hydropower energy resources. A good example of a hydropower-pumped storage system is the Cruachan Hydropower Station that has been installed and operating in Scotland, UK. The Cruachan Power Station, together with the Cruachan Dam, is a pumped-storage hydroelectric power station located in Argyll and Bute, Scotland. The hydropower scheme can provide 440 MW of clean hydropower electricity and has a capacity of 7.1 GWh.

China has been the global market leader for installed pumped hydropower storage capacities. China's hydropower development plans have sought to optimise the potential capacities and values of pumped storage in hydropower generation. This has also help to balance China's overall renewable power supplies with wind power and solar PV generation. Switzerland and Portugal have been following China in the application of pumped hydropower installations globally (REN, 2018).

Hydropower energy storage capacities have long been critical components of the modern hydro renewable energy infrastructure. These hydropower storage systems have helped to support power generation at peak hours and storage at low demand hours. These should then help to improve the overall reliability and efficiency of hydropower renewable systems. Hydropower reservoirs can be designed to passively store energy by reducing outputs during low electricity demand periods. It will normally utilise natural or pumped water flows to raise the water levels and energy potentials in the reservoir, thereby achieving effective energy storage. Conversely, pumped storage can be used to directly absorb surplus power off the grid to pump water to storage. These innovative combinations should then allow the hydropower plant to generate the maximum amount of clean electricity supplies for the grid, at peak demand hours.

The growing penetration of new hydropower variable renewable energy (VRE) schemes has raised interests in additional hydropower electricity storage capacities. Pumped storage hydropower has been the dominant form of large-scale hydropower energy storage schemes traditionally. It has accounted for an estimated 96% of global energy storage capacity. Global hydropower pumped storage capacity has been rising in recent years. New hydropower storage capacity has been installed in China, Portugal and Switzerland.

A good example of a modern hydropower energy storage scheme is located in South China in Shenzhen. China has recently completed the first 300 MW of a 1.2 GW hydropower storage plant in the fast growing Shenzhen city. This is China's first large-scale pumped hydropower storage facility, which has been built within a modern urban environment.

In Europe, three mixed pumped hydropower storage plants have also recently entered service. Each of these has incorporated an open-loop system which would combine pumping capacity with conventional hydropower generation from natural flows. A good example is the Veytaux hydropower plant in Switzerland which was originally built in 1971. In 2017, its capacity was doubled with the addition of two 120 MW generators. The expanded hydropower plant can pump water from Lake Geneva to the Hongrin reservoir which is 880 m higher in altitude with a hydropower generation capacity of 420 MW.

Another good example is Portugal's 780 MW Frades II and 263 MW Foz Tua pumped storage plants which have both entered service in 2017. The two variable-speed 390 MW pump turbines of Frades II are the largest of their kind in Europe. They can respond faster and better to changing electricity grid demands than conventional turbines with fixed speed controls. In addition, they should be more stable against voltage fluctuations and drops. Many projects in Europe have also been incorporating variable-speed turbines for improved flexibility and for providing wider operating ranges. These should help to accommodate the rising penetration of variable renewable energy (VRE) in Europe and globally.

Climate change and global warming have led to more extreme drought incidents globally, especially in Europe and Africa. A good drought example is the severe drought induced by global warming in Portugal in 2017. This extreme drought incident highlighted the importance of pumped storage and hydropower reservoir system. These systems have helped to provide reliable hydropower energy supplies which contributed to stabilising electricity supplies and prices during emergency situations. In addition, the reservoirs provided supports for stable water supplies during severe drought periods. Subsequently, Portugal has begun to consider interconnecting its various dam infrastructures and increasing the storage capacity of existing dams.

Hydropower companies' renewable strategy plans

Globally, the hydropower industry and many of its leading companies have implemented new corporate strategies to promote innovations and technical advances. Many companies have adopted these as their top corporate strategic objectives and priorities. They hope that continued improvements and innovations will help them to achieve sustainable hydropower business growth and developments globally. In addition, the ongoing modernisation and digitalisation of existing and new hydropower facilities have been high priorities for many hydropower companies globally.

The World Bank and the hydropower industry both have also affirmed their ongoing commitment to the responsible development of hydropower projects globally, both large and small. Historically, the World Bank has been a significant funder of hydropower projects in developing countries and emerging economies. The World Bank has stressed the potentials for hydropower to provide significant development benefits to different emerging economies. It has stressed that hydropower projects should be installed in a socially, financially and environmentally sustainable way. The World Bank Group's International Finance Corporation (IFC) has also declared that it is imperative for sustainability that there should be appropriate consideration of the environmental and social risks at the early stages of hydropower project planning. IFC has stressed that integrated planning should also allow for broad economic benefits beyond hydropower energy generation alone.

The World Bank has also included climate change resilience as a key consideration in its project assessments globally. The World Bank has set out new guidelines which have been designed to ensure that both the existing and future hydropower projects will be resilient to climate-related risks. These climate risks would include physical, operational and economic risks. These risks could pose serious threats to the viability of hydropower infrastructures. A good example of the potential risks includes dramatic shifts or extreme variability in hydrological conditions which could be caused by extreme droughts induced by global warming and climate change. In addition, there could be serious related social and environmental risks, such as flooding damages, major climate migration, etc.

In 2017, the World Bank and IFC worked with the Myanmar and Laos PDR governments to integrate strategic environmental and social assessments into their country-wide evaluations of water resources and hydropower developments. Both Myanmar and Laos, together with Cambodia, China, Thailand and Vietnam, have been sharing the hydropower resources of the Mekong River which flows through all these countries. New large hydropower projects have altered the river flows significantly and have raised serious concerns about the potential environmental impacts on the aquatic ecosystems, agriculture and fisheries in the downstream regions along the Mekong River.

The Hydropower Sustainability Assessment Protocol, introduced in 2011, has gained prominence as a global standard for evaluating hydropower projects from inception to construction and operation. In 2017, three project assessments have been published under the Protocol. All these have covered hydropower projects to be implemented in Europe. A good example is the post-installation evaluation of the 690 MW Kárahnúkar hydropower project in Iceland. This hydropower project was completed in 2007. It was Iceland's largest and most controversial hydropower project. There were a lot of environmental concerns on the loss of wilderness areas to land inundation by several hydropower storage reservoirs and to potential changes in river flows. The assessment showed that the hydropower plant met various standards of best practice across most of the topics assessed (IHA, Hydropower Sustainability Assessment Protocol, 2015).

In late 2017, Sustainable Energy for All (SEforALL) and the International Hydropower Association (IHA) signed an important agreement to develop the concept of a Hydropower Preparation Facility. They believed that this should help national governments, in both emerging economies and developed countries, to better prioritise potential hydropower projects, in accordance with their sustainability assessments, before putting these projects out for competitive tendering by the private sector. Both organisations believed that these assessments and screenings should help to identify the most viable hydropower projects in the context of sustainability and local needs. In addition, SEforALL and the IHA expected that these preliminary screenings should improve the prospects for project funding, by reducing the high upfront costs and risks associated with early-stage preparations of hydropower projects (IHA, SEforALL and IHA, 2017).

The leading hydropower companies have also been undertaking modernisation and digitalisation of their existing and new facilities. The digitalisation of hydropower facilities has become an essential modernisation effort on existing hydropower plants. In addition, digitalisation has become an essential design and construction element of new hydropower projects. These have involved the implementation of advanced digital simulation, process monitoring and control technologies. These would allow the plant operators to better observe and respond to various aspects of plant operating conditions in a more efficient manner. These should contribute to meeting the objectives of improved efficiency of operations and maintenance, greater plant reliability, plus more flexible integration with the operations of other generating and storage facilities, including VRE.

Many of the leading hydropower technology companies have continued to develop and expand their digitalisation capacities. A good example is Voith Hydro from Germany which had introduced a new digital augmented virtual reality (VR) application. The new VR application will enable remote visualisation and analysis of hydropower plant conditions. These new digitalisation features should also help to optimise the repair and service planning of the hydropower plant. Another good example is that GE from the USA has also used computer-generated digital simulations of hydropower plant components along with actual measurements to identify potential plant weaknesses. These should help to provide real-time recommendations on potential corrective actions. Andritz from Austria has also started to offer a digital solution for enhancing operation and maintenance of hydropower plants. The new system should help engineers to better decide on when to refurbish hydro plant components and operators to better optimise specific hydropower plant operations.

The leading hydropower companies have also been working hard to improve their business performances amidst the difficult market conditions. GE's renewable energy business unit has continued to show growing revenues. This was due in part to higher hydropower-related sales. In comparison with other renewable powers, hydropower has contributed only one-tenth of the revenues that GE has generated from wind power. Andritz Hydro has also reported that the market conditions have been difficult. In particular, the low electricity prices and low energy prices have made the hydropower market conditions more difficult. These difficult market conditions have resulted in moderate investment activities amongst various power companies that own and operate hydropower facilities. There has also been a continued decline in new orders and sales, particularly for hydropower plant upgrades. Voith Hydro has also reported that fewer contracts are being awarded than expected in recent years and new orders have been declining.

Leading hydropower companies are hopeful that pumped hydropower storage schemes may continue to be a good growth area. They are anticipating positive impacts on orders from growing demands for pumped storage facilities in emerging economies. A good example is that they are expecting strong hydropower orders from China, where several pumped storage facilities are being considered in the China national hydropower project pipeline.

Ocean renewable energy growth management

Ocean renewable energy has remained a largely untapped renewable energy resource, despite decades of development efforts. Most of the current ocean renewable operating capacities have been represented by two tidal barrage facilities. Ocean renewable energy technologies had been deployed in open waters with the application of both tidal stream and wave energy technologies. New ocean renewable capacities that are coming online have mostly been launched in the waters of Scotland (REN, Renewables report, 2018).

Open-water technologies, such as tidal stream and wave energy converters, are generally in an earlier stage of development. Various ocean open-water renewable prototypes have been deployed but these are still in the development stages.

Tidal stream technologies are probably closer to technological maturity than the open-water technologies. These have shown a significant convergence around the use of horizontal-axis turbines, combined with a variety of mooring techniques. A good ocean tidal example is that the first ocean tidal turbine arrays with a cluster of multiple interconnected turbines have been deployed in 2017 (MRC, State of the Sector Report, 2018).

However, ocean wave energy technology developments have shown very little technological convergences. These were due in part to the diversity of the wave resources in different locations globally. In addition, the complexity of extracting energy from waves has added to the technological and operational challenges. Ocean wave energy converter demonstration projects have mostly been in the pre-commercial stage. The developments of various ocean thermal energy conversion and salinity gradient technologies have so far been in the developmental stages and are quite far away from commercial deployment. Only a few pilot projects have been launched. Experts have estimated that there are currently over 90 tidal energy technology developers around the world. About half of these are focusing on horizontal-axis turbine developments. At the same time, over 200 companies have been developing wave energy converters of various types. The point-absorber devices have generally become the most common development approach adopted by most companies and developers.

Scotland has continued to be the centre for ocean tidal energy developments. A good ocean tidal example is Scotland's MeyGen tidal stream energy project which has just completed the initial leg of its first phase. All four 1.5 MW horizontal-axis turbines have started to deliver power to the grid in early 2017. The developers of MeyGen have received full consent to expand the project up to 86 MW. It is expected that the installation of the expansions will continue into 2019/2020.

Another good example of an ocean pilot project in Scotland is that Nova Innovation from the UK has installed in the Shetland Bluemull Sound a third

100 kilowatt (kW) direct-drive turbine. This was the world's first grid-connected tidal array. It had secured EU funding supports for its innovative ocean energy technology with an EU grant of EUR19.3 million (USD23.1 million). Some of the EU funding should support expansion of the Bluemull Sound array to six turbines. It is generally expected that this should provide enough insight into various operational performances so as to reduce the costs of future ocean tidal energy generation. These should help to boost the confidence of potential investors in future ocean tidal energy projects. The ongoing Brexit developments have introduced uncertainties on future EU funding, in the case that the UK completes its exit from the EU.

In France, the ocean tidal turbine developer Guinard Energies had also undertaken a demonstration of its 3.5 kW P66 turbine. Its designs of the tidal turbine have aimed to simplify installation and maintenance in isolated areas. The design has also included innovative hybrid renewable energy applications together with solar PV and storage batteries.

There have also been various wave energy pilots and demonstration projects being undertaken in several emerging economies and developed countries. These included China, Spain, Sweden, etc. China has redeployed the 100 kW Sharp Eagle wave energy demonstration project with upgrades. This project should allow it to better serve the power requirements of remote islands. Spain has undertaken tests of a new ocean wave air turbine made by Kymaner from Portugal. Spain has undergone tests at the Mutriku wave power plant in the Bay of Biscay. These devices have been designed to harness wave-driven compressed air with an innovative technology known as an oscillating water column.

Some environmentalists have also raised various serious environmental concerns as some ocean renewable energy technology developments have been moving closer to commercialisation. These serious environmental concerns mostly covered the potential impacts on marine life and ecosystems by the new ocean renewable power turbines.

Ocean experts have, based on current experience and knowledge, advised that the deployment of single devices would appear to pose very small risks to the marine environment and ecosystems. In reality, there will need to be much more actual operating experience with larger commercial arrays so as to better assess and reveal any risk that they might poise to marine life. More research, data collection and sharing will be required to establish the risks more accurately, so that realistic accurate risk assessments on the marine lives in the sea can be undertaken. These should be important prerequisites for the assessment and approval of future ocean renewable projects.

Ocean renewable energy government support developments

The global developments of the ocean renewable energy markets have been highly dependent on government policy supports, in both emerging economies and developed countries. International co-operations have also played important roles in research and developments. There have also been considerable challenges for developers to obtain suitable financing for new ocean renewable projects. The key reason is that the ocean renewable industry has been characterised by relatively high risks with big upfront development costs. In addition, the rising requirements for various planning, approval and licensing processes in relevant countries globally have added to additional pressure and hurdles.

Government supports for ocean renewable energy developments have been critical in different countries. These supports have included direct government funding, research grants or infrastructure supports. These have been critical elements in supporting ongoing ocean energy developments. A good example is that in Europe various project and research funding opportunities, including MaRINET2 and FORESEA, as well as the availability of marine testing facilities, have been made possible by regional, national and local government supports. More details of both of these programmes and their implications are described below.

The EU MaRINET2 programme has been supported by the European Commission's Horizon 2020 programme. Since 2017, the project has been awarded some EUR3.5 million (USD3.8 million) to provide free access to ocean renewable power testing facilities to almost 100 developers and users. These have provided important boosts to ocean wave, tidal and offshore wind developments plus supported new projects heading towards commercialisation. The transnational nature of the initiative has meant that projects from some 14 EU countries, as well as Australia, Canada, Norway and the USA, have been able to accelerate their technology developments at various advanced testing facilities across Europe (Marine Energy, Third MaRINET2 Call, UK 2019).

The EU FORESEA programme was launched in 2016 to provide competitive funding opportunities to ocean energy technology companies to test their new devices. Various funding sources have helped companies to test their ocean renewable devices under real sea conditions at various test centres in France, Ireland, the Netherlands and the United Kingdom. FORESEA stood for Funding for Ocean Renewable Energy through Strategic European Action project. The project partners included the European Marine Energy Centre, SmartBay of Ireland and SEM-REV of France. FORESEA has enabled the demonstration of various innovative marine renewable energy technologies under real sea conditions. These should help these new technologies to accelerate their development progress towards commercialisation faster. In addition, it should help to leverage the appropriate investments required to take these new technologies to market. Various ocean renewable test centres have been supported by the European industry association Ocean Energy Europe which is based in Brussels (Dutch Marine Energy Centre, FORESEA Funding Ocean Renewables, 2019).

In Scotland, the local government has established Wave Energy Scotland in 2014 as a subsidiary of the Highlands and Islands Enterprise of the Scottish government. This is to ensure that Scotland will maintain a leading role in ocean renewable energy developments and implementation. Since its establishment, it had awarded some GBP 28 million (USD37.8 million) to 62 ocean renewable projects in 11 countries. All these ocean renewable projects have focused on various key components, such as novel wave energy converters, power take-off devices (PTOs), structural materials and manufacturing processes, and control systems.

In the USA, the US government's Department of Energy (DOE) has been working with the Oregon State University on finalising its plans for the Pacific Marine Energy Centre South Energy Test Site, which is planned to be completed by 2021. After completion, it should have space to accommodate 20 grid-connected wave energy converters. The US DOE has also announced an additional USD12 million funding in 2017 to promote the advancement of wave renewable energy developments in the USA. It has allocated funding supports to four ocean renewable projects. Two of the ocean renewable projects will test and validate wave energy converters in open waters. The other two ocean renewable projects being funded will address early-stage development challenges.

In China, the Chinese government authorities have also released several edicts on ocean renewable energy and technology innovations. These included the 13th Five-Year Plan on Ocean Energy together with new national ocean renewable energy targets. The Chinese government has announced a new ocean energy capacity target of 50 MW, which authorities aspire to be installed by 2020. They have also highlighted specific national targets for ocean energy developments. These included the development of new ocean renewable demonstration and testing facilities together with the construction of various island projects.

The European Commission had also published an EU report in 2017 titled "Renewable Energy in Europe." The report helped to shed more light on the reasons for past failures in ocean energy development. It highlighted various lessons that might be drawn from these developments for future improvements. The EU report had called for establishing more covenants and co-operations between the ocean renewable energy industry and the public sector. The key focuses should include better co-ordination and evaluations of ocean renewable technology developments in the EU. In addition, there should be improved EU certification, performance guarantees, standardisation and accreditation of various ocean renewable technologies. The report has also proposed a more consistent policy framework and alignment of public funding activities. It has proposed the establishment of a staged support structure for future ocean renewable developments. The proposed structure will include strict conditions together with performance criteria to assess ocean technological and sectoral readiness. These should all help to provide a more selective and targeted support for ocean energy developments in the EU (EU EEA, Renewable energy in Europe Report, 2017).

5 Geothermal renewable energy growth management

善有善报,
Shàn yǒu shàn bào,
Kind deeds will normally generate good rewards.
What goes around comes around.

Executive summary

Geothermal renewable energy has grown globally especially in various emerging economies in East Africa, Central America, the Caribbean and the South Pacific. Over 80 countries, adjacent to the Pacific Ring of Fire or East African Rift, have been developing various new geothermal renewable resources which could potentially double the global geothermal power generation capacity. Looking ahead to 2020–2025, experts have estimated that the total geothermal renewable investments could reach some USD9 billion globally. There are considerable challenges for new technology advancements so geothermal renewables could become more cost competitive against fossil energy options. Details of the geothermal renewable developments in various emerging economies globally will be discussed more in this chapter with international examples.

Overviews of geothermal renewable developments

Geothermal renewable energy has been growing globally in recent years to reach over 12 GW of installed capacity globally. Various emerging economies in East Africa, Central America, the Caribbean and the South Pacific have become some of the countries with the fastest growing geothermal renewable energy applications worldwide. The UN Intergovernmental Panel on Climate Change, UN IPCC, has estimated that the global geothermal power potential could be over 200 GWe. Currently, only a small fraction of that total geothermal renewable potentials available have been tapped or developed for various technical and commercial reasons.

Over 80 countries, adjacent to the Pacific Ring of Fire or East African Rift, have been actively developing various new geothermal renewable energy resources. There are also developments of over 700 possible geothermal sites globally which could possibly double the global geothermal renewable power generation capacity in the near future.

Looking ahead to 2020–2025, experts have estimated that the total investments in geothermal renewable power projects globally could rise to some USD9 billion. These new investments will have to overcome considerable technical and commercial challenges. These challenges include the need for more technological innovations together with major new cost reductions so as to transform geothermal renewable power to become more cost competitive against other fossil energy options, such as coal, oil or gas (REN, Global Status Report, 2018).

Geothermal renewable energy developments have been facing various serious challenges globally. These included the inherent high risk of geothermal renewable energy exploration and project developments. There are also additional challenges in the lack of cost competitiveness of expensive geothermal energy relative to the lower costs of natural gas. In addition, there are serious challenges in finding suitable project financing for geothermal renewable projects. Despite these, some good progress has been made with new geothermal renewable projects in various key markets in emerging economies. Good geothermal renewable project examples included Indonesia and Turkey which have both added about 200 megawatts (MW) of geothermal renewable capacity in recent years.

Global geothermal renewable developments have seen measured progress in some key markets globally. Geothermal renewable power installations have provided both clean electricity and thermal energy services for heating and cooling applications. A good geothermal example is that in 2016 the estimated electricity and thermal output from geothermal sources was 567 PJi (157 TWh). The split between geothermal electricity and thermal outputs was approximately in equal shares of 50/50. Some geothermal renewable power plants have been producing both electricity and thermal outputs for various heating and power applications globally.

Globally, the countries with the largest numbers of installed geothermal renewable power generating capacities included the USA, the Philippines, Indonesia, New Zealand, Mexico, Italy, Turkey, Iceland, Kenya and Japan.

In Asia, the Philippines is second only to the USA for total geothermal renewable power capacities in operation. However recently, there has been little new geothermal renewable capacities being brought online. Philippine's Geothermal Industry Association has called for its government to consider granting suitable FITs for geothermal renewable power. These will be similar to those FITs already granted to other renewable energy applications. These should help to spur the development of more challenging low-temperature expensive geothermal energy resources. These low-temperature geothermal resources might require deeper drilling and the application of the binary-cycle technology. These should increase the development risks and costs plus raise the ultimate cost of the geothermal energy produced.

The Asian Development Bank (ADB) has announced plans to back the issuance of the first Climate Bond in Asia and Oceania. The ADB has issued a 75% guarantee of principal and interest on a USD225 million bond. These bonds are specifically to support the refurbishment of the Philippines' Tiwi and Mak-Ban geothermal facilities.

Indonesia has been adding new geothermal capacities and had started commercial operations at its 110 MW Sarulla geothermal plant, which is one of the largest geothermal renewable plants in the world. The design of the Sarulla geothermal plant is notable for being a combined-cycle operation. The conventional flash turbines have been supplemented with a binary system so as to extract additional energy from the post-flash turbine steam. These improvements have helped to maximise the total energy extraction and efficiency of the geothermal plant. The existing installed geothermal capacities in Indonesia have been estimated to be only representing less than 6% of Indonesia's total geothermal renewable power potentials. To promote further geothermal growths, the Indonesian government has announced plans to mitigate the risks of exploration and development with new digital mapping of the country's geothermal resources. In addition, the Indonesian government has been considering a feed-in tariff (FIT) for new geothermal renewable energy supplies. These should help to provide a more predictable fixed supply price for geothermal energy. These should further reduce risks for new geothermal renewable projects and geothermal developers in Indonesia.

In Japan, the progress on geothermal renewable development has been mixed so far. The Japanese government has to deal with competing desires to develop viable clean energy alternatives to fossil and nuclear fuels. There are also strong public concerns about the potential environmental and safety consequences. Many hot spring resort owners and local governments in Japan have also expressed serious concerns that the development of new geothermal power projects could put their traditional businesses at risk. To alleviate these concerns, the Japanese national government has established an expert advisory committee in 2016 to provide detailed information on geothermal energy development to local governments. The Japanese government also announced plans to cover some of the initial costs of geothermal exploratory drilling and data gathering. These should help to address and reduce the development risks for new geothermal projects. A combination of higher geothermal feed-in tariffs (FITs) and an exemption from having to prepare environmental impact assessments for small geothermal projects, which are of capacity less than 7.5 MW, have promoted interests in the development of new small-scale geothermal renewable power projects in Japan. A good example is that a small geothermal facility in Tsuchiyu in Japan was completed in 2015, and at least one small ORC generator came online in 2016. However, Japan currently has no large-scale geothermal renewable project under active development.

In China, the central government has planned to increase the sustainable use of geothermal renewable energy in various Chinese cities. These should help to reduce the serious local air pollutions and greenhouse gas emissions. China's current geothermal renewable power capacity has been developed mostly in Tibet. China's 13th Five-Year Plan (FYP) for geothermal energy has called for an additional new 500 MW geothermal renewable capacity in the 2020–2025 period. China geothermal companies have also been partnering with international geothermal project developers. These new partnerships should help to better develop new geothermal projects in China with the latest international technologies and best practices. Details of some new Chinese geothermal developments will be discussed in the China geothermal case study at the end of this chapter (PRC, 13th FYP, 2016).

Malaysia, unlike many other ASEAN countries, has still no geothermal plant in operation. It is currently constructing a new 30 MW geothermal renewable plant in the state of Sabah, on the island of Borneo. To support its new geothermal energy developments in Malaysia, the Malaysian central government has been setting up a new National Geothermal Resource Centre. It is hoping that this will help to create a new platform for collaboration by local geothermal project developers with international companies. In addition, the Centre should help to bring together stakeholders and specialists in geothermal energy to promote sharing of knowledge and best practices (REN, 2018).

In the Middle East, Turkey has been implementing new geothermal renewable applications. A good example is that Turkey has opened 20 new geothermal plants in recent years. With so much new additional geothermal capacity coming online, Turkey has seen continued rapid growth in clean electricity generation from geothermal renewable energy. Experts have estimated that clean electricity generation from geothermal renewable energy has risen to supply some 25% of Turkey's total electricity demands. All the new geothermal plants have the binary Organic Rankine Cycle (ORCii) units, with capacity of up to 25 MW each. Turkey has also been developing new geothermal projects with the conventional flash turbine technology which is suitable for the country's remaining high-temperature geothermal resources. A good example is the new 70 MW Unit 2 of the Kizildere III geothermal plant in Turkey. It has combined a 51 MW flash-steam turbine to harness high-pressure steam with a 19 MW binary-cycle unit to maximise the recovery of usable energy from the flash turbine's exhaust stream.

In Africa, Kenya has been active in developing and applying geothermal renewable energy. Kenya's total installed geothermal capacity reached 690 MW in 2019. A good geothermal example is that Kenya has completed a new 29 MW addition to their Olkaria III geothermal complex. This has increased the facility's total geothermal capacity to 139 MW.

Ethiopia has been sharing the rich geothermal resources of the Great Rift Valley with Kenya. Limited developments in geothermal renewable have occurred to date. The Ethiopian government is promoting new future geothermal developments. It has signed a 500 MW power purchase agreement PPA for the first phase of the Corbetti geothermal project. The project has been planned to be developed and built in two stages within the next eight to ten years. The International Finance Corporation (IFC) has been working with Ethiopian government to enact suitable new regulations to facilitate the engagement of more private investors in new geothermal projects. The Ethiopian government has also reclassified geothermal resources as renewable energy. This should help geothermal energy users to grant exemption from the royalty payments which would be exacted under the Ethiopia's mining laws, for extracting mineral resources.

In America, the USA has been the global leader in geothermal energy applications. However recently, the USA has seen little net increases in geothermal renewable capacity. The USA has about 0.8 GW of ongoing geothermal projects which are likely to be operational by 2020–2021. There are another 0.9 GW of geothermal projects which are under development with the potential to come online if some small hurdles could be overcome. However, progress has been reported to be slow and constrained by an unfavourable regulatory environment and by strong competition from lower priced natural gas supplies.

In Latin America, Mexico has been building new geothermal energy facilities. A good geothermal example is that a new 25 MW condensing flash unit has been added to the Domo San Pedro geothermal plant in Mexico. The net additions have helped to bring Mexico's total geothermal capacity to about 950 MW. This geothermal plant has been the first private geothermal project in Mexico. Mexico has also awarded three additional exploration permits to private Mexican companies under the country's new Geothermal Energy Law. The government has enacted the new law so as to better manage and control the exploration and use of geothermal resources in Mexico.

In the Caribbean, many of the Caribbean islands are volcanic with good geothermal resources. New local geothermal facilities will also help them to reduce their costly fossil fuel imports. Some Caribbean government has been working with international funds on financing their new geothermal projects. A good example is that the Abu Dhabi Fund for Development has announced a new loan to St Vincent and the Grenadines for the construction of a new 15 MW geothermal power plant. This is expected to reduce local power generation costs and should create new local jobs plus improve the reliability of local electricity supplies.

New Zealand has also signed a new geothermal partnership agreement with the Commonwealth of Dominica. It will support the construction of a 7 MW geothermal plant on the island. Plans also are under way to expand an existing 10 MW plant on the island of Guadeloupe.

In the EU, Croatia has initiated the construction of its first ever geothermal power project in 2016. The new 16 MW binary plant will utilise the 170°C geothermal brine and steam geothermal supplies from the Pannonian basin. This basin is one of the key geothermal areas in Europe.

Geothermal renewable direct use developments

Geothermal renewable direct use capacities have been growing by an annual average rate of 6% in recent years. Direct geothermal heat consumptions have been growing by a lower annual average rate of 3.5%. The differences in the geothermal renewable usage rates could be explained in part by the rapid growths in geothermal space heating. The annual growth rate of over 7% has exhibited below average capacity utilisation. Direct geothermal uses would include deep geothermal resources, irrespective of scale. These are distinct from the shallow geothermal resource utilisations which are specifically for use of ground-source heat pumps.

The single largest direct use geothermal application has been estimated to be swimming pools and public baths. These are followed by space heating, including district heat networks. These two broad markets have accounted for around 80% of both direct geothermal use capacity and consumption. The remaining 20% of the direct geothermal use capacity and heat outputs have been for other applications including domestic hot water supply, greenhouse heating, industrial process heat, aquaculture, snow melting, agricultural drying, etc. (REN, GSR, 2018).

China has been utilising the largest amount of direct geothermal heat globally. Other leading country users of direct geothermal heat included Turkey, Iceland, Japan, India, Hungary, Italy, the USA and New Zealand. These countries have accounted for approximately 70% of direct geothermal use globally.

In China, the development of geothermal capacities for heating has been growing. Experts have estimated that the direct use of geothermal energy has covered slightly more than 100 million square metres (m^2) of heated space in China. The central government in China has announced plans for significant increases in geothermal renewable heating developments. It expects that the sustainable use of geothermal renewable resources should help to reduce air pollution whilst also protecting water resources in various cities in China. Under the China 13th Five-Year Plan (FYP), China has planned to increase the direct use of geothermal heat by another 400 million m^2 by 2020 (PRC, 13th FYP, 2016).

In the EU, several European countries have added new geothermal direct use capacities through the continued expansion of geothermal district heating. The main EU geothermal markets have been in France, the Netherlands, Germany and Hungary. A good geothermal renewable example is that between 2012 and 2016, 51 new or renovated geothermal district heating plants have been completed in the EU. In 2016, Europe had more than 260 geothermal district heating systems, including co-generation systems. These geothermal district heating systems have a total installed capacity of approximately 4 GWth.

A good example of a recent EU geothermal project is a 20 MWth geothermal plant for district heating in the city of Munich. The plant is the latest of many small-scale geothermal facilities in Bavaria, Germany. These geothermal plants have been using relatively low-temperature geothermal resources, often to produce both heat and power for local consumption.

In France, geothermal district heating has grown in Paris with significant developments of these systems in recent years. The growth of geothermal district heating systems has also extended beyond the Paris metropolitan area. A good example is that in early 2017 the city of Bordeaux has issued a contract to develop geothermal resources to serve the heating requirements of some 28,000 homes in Bordeaux. The use of geothermal heat in the French industrial sector has also been growing. A good example is that a new 24 MWth enhanced geothermal plant has been opened in Rittershoffen, in the Upper Rhine Valley. The plant became France's first high-temperature (higher than 150°C) geothermal facility supplying industrial process heat. The geothermal heat was extracted from a 170°C underground aquifer at a depth of 2.5–3.0 km below the surface of earth. The Rittershoffen geothermal project has benefited from lessons learned from the nearby pioneering enhanced geothermal system (EGS) power plant at Soultz-sous-Forets.

Overviews of geothermal renewable companies

Various geothermal companies in emerging economies and developed countries globally have to face many challenges in developing their geothermal projects. These included the inherent high risks of geothermal exploration and project development. Improved enterprise risk management systems have to be implemented by project developers to mitigate against exploration and project risks. There have also been difficulties in finding suitable project loans and financial sponsors. In addition, there have been significant cost competitions from lower-cost natural gas supplies. These have all led to higher commercial and technical challenges and risks for most geothermal project developers.

Despite these challenges, various geothermal companies have continued to made progress with new project developments in key markets in both emerging economies and developed countries globally. There have also been encouraging developments by geothermal industrial leaders which have cemented new international partnerships with various local partners to tackle new geothermal opportunities globally.

The lack of clear international geothermal resource assessment standards globally has also constrained the wider development of geothermal energy around the world. To help to address these challenges, new geothermal specifications have been developed under the UN Framework for Fossil Energy and Mineral Reserves and Resources. The framework's objective has been to harmonise different standards for reporting geothermal resources so that these would be in line to other resource-extractive industries worldwide. These new standards should be beneficial for the geothermal investors, regulators, project developers and the general public.

The development of the geothermal industry has also been very sensitive to global trends in fossil fuel pricing and consumptions. These could have major positive and negative impacts on geothermal developments globally. The recent declines in oil and gas prices globally have resulted in more cost pressure on reducing geothermal generation costs. At the same time, the new energy policies enacted in many emerging economies and developed countries have reduced fossil fuel consumptions as countries have promoted clean energy applications. The lower oil and gas consumptions have in turn led to reductions in global demands for drilling rigs for new oil and gas explorations. These could provide positive effects for the geothermal industry by reducing the geothermal exploration drilling costs and the development costs of new underground geothermal fields. However, the lower fossil fuel prices, especially the low natural gas prices recently, have also reduced the competitiveness of geothermal heat and power versus traditional fossil generation options.

It is interesting to see that some leading traditional oil and gas companies have also broadened their business portfolios into geothermal renewable resources. These have made good business sense as many skills and competences are transferrable, especially in the areas of drilling and resource exploration. At the same time, the shift by fossil fuel companies into geothermal and renewable sectors should help them to reduce their GHG emissions plus promote their public image on sustainability.

A good example is Chevron Corporation of the USA which has become one of the world's largest operators of geothermal renewable facilities. It has built up geothermal operations in developed countries and emerging economies, such as the Philippines and Indonesia. However, the recent difficult geothermal business conditions have led Chevron to announce its intention to sell its geothermal assets in Indonesia and the Philippines. These would include the Darajat and Salak geothermal fields in Indonesia and the Tiwi and Mak-Ban geothermal plants in the Philippines (Chevron, 2010).

There have also been some interesting geothermal M&A activities in different countries. A good example is the purchase of the Indonesian geothermal plants (637 MW in total) by a consortium of holding companies in the Philippines and Indonesia. The deal was completed in April 2017. The planned acquisition of the remaining geothermal assets (747 MW in total) is pending for regulatory approvals.

Some top geothermal technology providers have also been forming different strategic partnerships in recent years to develop new geothermal technological innovations or jointly pursue different geothermal projects. A good geothermal partnership example is that Ormat Technologies of the USA and Toshiba Corporation of Japan have formed a new strategic agreement in 2016 to jointly integrate Ormat's binary technology and Toshiba's flash technology into a new geothermal combined-cycle configuration with technological innovations.

These new international geothermal partnerships have helped various companies to win geothermal projects globally. A good partnership example is the Mitsubishi Hitachi Power Systems Joint Venture Ltd. The new joint venture company was formed by the 2014 merger of the thermal power divisions of Mitsubishi and Hitachi. The new partnership enabled the company to win a new order for a 55 MW geothermal turbine project in Costa Rica. The partnership was also supported by Japan's International Cooperation Agency which helped to pave the way for Japanese companies working on new geothermal projects in key markets globally, through low-interest loans for exploration and development.

Geothermal technology developments and innovations

Various technology advances and innovations have been taking place in different geothermal renewable areas. A good geothermal innovation example is the Icelandic Deep Drilling Project. It has recently achieved a significant milestone for the geothermal industry with the completion of its 4,659-m-deep borehole on the Reykjanes Peninsula. The drilling of the deep well has resulted in successful discovery of hot supercritical fluid at a high temperature of 427°C. These super-critical fluids have promising characteristics for high-temperature geothermal renewable thermal energy generation. The key objective of the project was to investigate the feasibility of finding and utilising supercritical hydrothermal fluids for geothermal heating. Advanced geothermal computer modelling work has suggested that these supercritical fluids might have ten times the power output of a conventional geothermal well. These should lead to improved economics and reduced environmental impacts for every unit of geothermal renewable energy produced (REN, 2018).

Another exciting new technological development has been in new technical advances to allow the reinjection into geothermal wells both carbon dioxide (CO_2) and hydrogen sulphide (H_2S) for sequestration in mineral form. Together, CO_2 and H_2S could comprise more than 80% of the off-gas emissions at some geothermal plants. These new developments should help to reduce emissions plus promote the integration of carbon capture and storage (CCS) with geothermal renewable developments. A good CCS geothermal example is the Iceland CarbFix project. It has been found that more than 95% of the injected CO_2 has become bound as carbonate minerals within a period of two years. This was much faster than was previously predicted. Alternatively, CO_2 could be, after separation from the other gases, supplied to local commercial company operations, such as greenhouses and algae producers. These should promote the integration of geothermal energy with carbon capture utilisation (CCU) developments (REN, GSR, 2018).

As the CO_2 concentrations in geothermal gases could be significant, there have been some environmental concerns about the potential greenhouse gas impacts of open-loop geothermal power generation. The atmospheric emission rates would be dependent on local geology and operating conditions. A good example is that CO_2 emissions from geothermal power plants in California have been significantly lower per kilowatt-hour (kWh) than those emissions from an equivalent coal or natural gas-fired plants. Experts have estimated that emissions could have been at less than 0.2 kg per kWh from open-loop flash steam geothermal plants and about 0.03 kg per kWh for open-loop dry steam geothermal plants.

In Turkey, studies have also found that a typical open-loop 50 MW geothermal plant could emit some 1 kg of CO_2 per kWh, or approximately 1,200 tons per day. This was probably due to high levels of dissolved calcite in the geothermal reservoirs in Turkey. In some instances, the CO_2 emissions from geothermal power generation plants in Turkey might be twice of those from equivalent coal-fired power plants. It has been postulated that these might place future geothermal projects in Turkey at odds with the environmental criteria of development agencies, including the developing criteria for green bonds. Further research efforts are being undertaken to study potential means to capture the CO_2 emissions from Turkey's geothermal plants for commercial uses.

In the US state of Utah, the world's first geothermal-hydro renewable hybridisation plant was established. Enel S.p.A. (Italy) started operating a hydro-generator in a geothermal injection well during 2016. The 25 MW Cove Fort geothermal plant captured the energy of the geothermal brine flowing back into the earth which helped to increase plant's efficiency.

In North Dakota of the USA, a first-of-its-kind geothermal power project with integrations with fossil productions has been launched recently. The geothermal plant would be utilising the hot water that has been produced naturally from petroleum production wells, so as to co-produce electricity. The large number of oil- and gas-producing wells at the site could help to provide potential large energy production potentials.

Research has also continued in the field of enhanced or engineered geothermal system (EGS). A good example is that in the USA, government-funded research works on EGS have been undertaken with the aim of achieving commercial, cost-competitive power production. In addition, the shale gas fracking techniques and expertise gained in the recent US shale gas exploration and production operations could also help EGS developments. The key common feature amongst all the most productive geothermal regions of the world has been their naturally occurring hydrothermal activity. These are characterised by the availability of high heat, geothermal fluid and permeability.

Enhanced geothermal systems (EGS) have been identified as a key to expanding the potential of geothermal heat and power production worldwide. EGS can be used to achieve economical geothermal production elsewhere or to enhance production at existing geothermal locations. The fracturing of subsurface rock formations could help to create the required improved permeability to form a more productive geothermal reservoir. In other instances, adequate permeability might exist in hot sedimentary aquifers, but fracturing might be needed to ensure adequate well productivity (Lu, A global review of EGS, 2018).

A good EGS project example is the Rittershoffen project in France. The project has been a thermal application but it has been used to generate electricity with the use of binary-loop technology. Stand-alone closed-loop binary cycle power plants could avoid significant venting of CO_2 and other pollutants from the geothermal fluid. In a binary plant, the geothermal fluid heats and vaporises a separate working fluid that has a lower boiling point than that of water. The fluid would then drive a turbine for power generation. Each fluid cycle is closed, and the geothermal fluid is reinjected into the heat reservoir. The binary cycle should allow an effective and efficient extraction of heat for power generation from relatively low-temperature geothermal fluids. The ORC binary geothermal plants would use an organic working fluid, and the Kalina cycle would use a non-organic working fluid. In conventional geothermal power plants, geothermal steam is used directly to drive the turbine.

China geothermal heating project case study

In China, the development of geothermal renewable energy for heating and electricity generation has been growing. The central government of the PRC has announced plans to significantly increase geothermal renewable energy developments in China. Under the 13th Five-Year Plan of China, it has announced plans to expand the direct use of geothermal heating by another 400 million m^2 by 2020. It believes that the sustainable use of geothermal resources will help to reduce air pollution and lower emissions plus reduce fossil fuel consumptions. In addition, it could help to protect water resources and reduce fossil fuel imports. To meet their new geothermal growth targets, Chinese geothermal companies have also been partnering with leading international geothermal companies on different projects.

An important new geothermal Sino-foreign partnership is the Icelandic-Chinese Joint Venture that has been established by the Arctic Green Energy Corporation (AGE) and Sinopec Star, which is called the Sinopec Green Energy Geothermal Company Limited (SGE). The new joint venture aims to expand geothermal district heating services in China with their combined expertise and network. SGE was established in 2006 and has grown to be the world's largest geothermal district heating company in terms of service area. It is a joint venture between AGE and Sinopec Star of the Sinopec Group, which is also known as China Petrochemical Corporation. AGE is based in Iceland and is a leading global developer and operator of renewable projects, including geothermal technology and energy efficiency projects. The key mission of AGE is to export Icelandic expertise in geothermal and renewables to fast growing countries in Asia, especially China.

In a groundbreaking deal in 2018, the Asian Development Bank (ADB) provided loan facilities of $250 million to the new Icelandic-Chinese Joint Venture, Sinopec Green Energy Geothermal Company Limited (SGE), formed by Arctic Green Energy Corporation (AGE) and Sinopec Star (ADB, ADB Signs Landmark Project, 2018).

In China, the traditional coal-based power and heating plants have been some of the major causes of air pollution in the country, especially for the Beijing-Tianjin-Hebei region. New goethermal renewable district heating systems should help to extract clean thermal energy from underground geothermal wells so that these could be delivered to households and business through dedicated district heating system pipelines. This should offer a clean renewable energy alternative which is sustainable, stable and cost competitive to fossil sources, including coal and gas. The new geothermal systems would have zero emissions, and could be integrated into existing networks to replace heat sources.

The ADB which is based in Manila has the mission to reduce poverty in Asia and the Pacific through inclusive economic growth, environmentally sustainable growth and regional integration. The ADB was established in 1966 and is owned by 67 member countries with 48 from the Asia region. The ADB has considered the new China geothermal project to be a landmark renewable project for Asia. It believed that geothermal district heating could help to provide millions of citizens in Asia-Pacific with safe and stable heating whilst dramatically reducing air pollution and greenhouse gas emissions. Geothermal heating will also help the emerging economies in Asia to reduce their reliance on fossil heating and power generation. It should help them to lower GHG emissions whilst reducing oil and gas imports into the emerging economies in Asia-Pacific.

The funding from the ADB would enable both AGE and SGE to significantly expand their geothermal operations. These should contribute to China's fight against air pollution whilst providing much needed clean heating to the Chinese cities. These new geothermal applications should also help to reduce oil and gas imports into China. There are also plans to replicate these successful collaborations across Asia and Central Asia (ADB, ADB Signs Landmark Project, 2018).

Other leading Chinese state-owned enterprises (SOEs) have also shown interest in geothermal energy developments. A good example is that the largest oil company in China, China National Petroleum Corp (CNPC), has started testing for geothermal energy resources. It had conducted a pilot test of geothermal power generation in Huabei, which is in the Hebei province of China. Two testing wells have met the low- and moderate-temperature requirements for geothermal power generation. These pilot tests have provided the basis for establishing future geothermal power plants and for future large-scale development of geothermal resources in the region. The significant amount of oil and gas drilling expertise that CNPC has built up from its vast oil and gas operations in China and overseas should help CNPC to accelerate its new geothermal exploration and business developments.

6 Biofuel and biomass renewable growth management

美名胜过美貌
měi míng shèng guò měi mào
A respected brand name is always better than just beautiful packaging.
Good reputation lasts forever.

Executive summary

The use of biomass and biofuel renewable energy has been growing globally, despite a number of serious challenges. These challenges included low oil and fossil fuel prices plus policy uncertainty in some key markets. Biomass consumptions for renewable power generation and biofuel consumptions in the transport sector have both been forecasted to increase significantly in the coming years. Looking ahead to 2020, biomass renewable power generation is likely to rise to nearly 200 billion kWh, which will be over three times the 60 billion kWh capacity in 2008. However, there are also considerable environmental and supply chain challenges. Details of new biomass and biofuel developments will be discussed more in this chapter together with international references.

Overviews of biomass and biofuel renewable growths

Biomass and biofuel renewable energy applications have both been growing fast in emerging economies and developed countries globally. Despite various serious challenges, biofuel and bioenergy productions have continued to increase in various countries, especially in emerging economies. The serious challenges have included strong competitions by low fossil fuel prices, especially the low oil and gas prices. In addition, there have been serious policy uncertainties in some key markets in different countries globally.

In recent years, bioenergy and biofuel productions have continued to grow in emerging economies and developed countries. Biomass consumptions for clean renewable power generation and biofuel production for the transport sector have both been forecasted to increase significantly in coming years. Looking ahead to 2020, biomass renewable power generation has been forecasted to rise to nearly 200 billion kWh. This will be over three times the biomass renewable capacity of 60 billion kWh in 2008. The majority of new biomass power, estimated to be over 165 billion kWh, will likely to come from wood and other biomass sources. At the same time, there are also considerable environmental and biomass supply chain challenges, especially on increased particulate emissions (REN, Renewables Global Status Report, 2018).

Bioenergy developments and deployment activities have continued spreading into new regions and countries. These are particularly noticeable in the emerging economies in India and Asia plus Africa. Bio-heat energy production has grown slowly whilst biopower production has increased more quickly. There has been rapid growth of biopower in the developed countries of the European Union (EU) and in the emerging economies of Asia. A good country example is that biopower generation has risen particularly sharply in the Republic of Korea.

Global biofuel and ethanol productions have been experiencing stable growths. There have been record production levels in the USA and Brazil, together with sharp increases in biofuel production in both China and India. There have also been new biofuel initiatives in Africa, notably in Nigeria and South Africa. Global production of biodiesel has recovered after recent falls. There have been particularly strong growths in both Indonesia and Argentina. The production of hydrotreated vegetable oil (HVO) has also increased in recent years.

There has also been continual progress in the commercialisation and development of advanced biofuels in some key countries. There have been expansions in the capacity and production of biofuels by both thermal and biological routes. Good biofuel production examples included the announcement of new biofuel plants in both China and India. These have helped to broaden the geographical spread of biofuel facilities and applications globally, especially in the emerging economies.

The use of biogas and biomethane in the transport sector has also grown recently. It has been due largely to significant growths in the USA, which has been stimulated by their Renewable Fuel Standard RFS. New conversion processes for the production of advanced liquid biofuels have also been maturing rapidly (REN, 2018).

There are many pathways by which biomass feedstocks can be converted into useful renewable energy. A broad range of wastes, residues and crops grown for energy purposes can be used directly as biofuels for heating and cooling or for electricity production. Alternatively, they can be converted into biogas or liquid biofuels for transport fuel applications or as replacements for fossil fuels and petrochemicals. Many bioenergy technologies have become well established and fully commercialised. New biofuel conversion processes have also been maturing rapidly (REN, 2018).

In the meantime, there have also been rising global and regional environmental concerns on biomass and biofuel developments. In particular, there are rising concerns on the environmental and sustainability aspects. The ongoing discussions about the sustainability of bioenergy, biomass and biofuel have led to regulatory and policy uncertainties in some key markets. These have resulted in a more difficult investment environment for biomass and biofuels in some markets. In other markets, bioenergy consumption and investment in new capacities have been supported by government policy and new energy policies (Sustainable Energy for All, 2015).

Biomass renewable heating markets

Biomass in many different forms, including the solid, liquid or gaseous forms, has been used to produce thermal energy for residential and industrial heating applications. Solid biomass has been burned directly in both traditional stoves and more modern appliances so as to provide heat for cooking. Biomass has been providing renewable thermal energy for residential heating and water heating. It can also be used on larger scales to provide heating for industrial and commercial premises. Biomass can be used to provide either low-temperature thermal energy for heating and drying applications or high-temperature process heat. Various forms of biomass thermal energies could also be co-generated to produce electricity via combined heat and power (CHP) systems. Bio-heat energy can also be distributed from larger production facilities by district energy systems to provide heating and cooling to residential, commercial and industrial customers.

The traditional uses of biomass for generating heat have involved the burning of wood biomass or charcoal as well as animal dung and other agricultural residues. These have traditionally been burnt in simple but inefficient stoves or burning devices. In recent years, there have been significant improvements in developing more advanced and cleaner burning stoves for both homes and industrial applications.

The consumptions of fuel wood for traditional biomass energy uses have been remaining relatively stable since 2010. Globally, some two billion cubic metres (m^3) of fuel wood have been used annually, which is equivalent to some 15 EJ of heat energy. The largest shares of fuel wood, dung and agricultural residues have been consumed in the emerging economies of Asia, South America and Africa. The production of fuel charcoal for use in cooking in the urban areas has also increased. In recent years, the charcoal growth rates have slowed down with various new municipal environmental and pollution guidelines issued by different municipal governments, in various emerging economies and developed countries, so as to reduce environmental pollution.

The growth of bioenergy for heating has also slowed down in recent years. Bioenergy uses in industry have also not increased in recent years. The main bioenergy industrial uses have been in various bio-based industries, such as the pulp and paper, timber, and food and tobacco sectors. The cement industry has also been using larger volumes of waste biofuels.

The principal regions for industrial bioenergy and bio-heat applications have been the emerging economies in Asia and South America. In Asia, bioenergy applications have included bagassei, rice husk, straw and cotton stalk applications. In South America, particularly in Brazil, biomass from agricultural and wood residues has been used to produce bio-heat for the food, tobacco, and pulp and paper industries. Bioenergy from bagasse has also been used in the sugar and alcohol industries.

North America has been the next largest user of bioenergy after Asia and South America. In Canada, 22% of all industrial heating has been provided by bioenergy. A good example is the use of bioenergy heating in the pulp and paper industry. Looking ahead, there have been some signs of reduced bioenergy uses in North America. At the same time, there are also signs of stronger growths in Asia. These are reflecting changes in production patterns in various key industrial sectors, especially in the pulp and paper sector.

In the buildings and residential sectors, the USA has been the largest consumer of modern biomass for residential heating. The US market for wood biomass and pellet boilers has remained stable, despite the strong competition from the low fossil fuel prices. Europe has been the largest consumer of bio-heat by region worldwide. EU member states have promoted renewable heat in order to meet their mandatory national targets under the EU Renewable Energy Directive. Germany, France, Sweden, Italy, Finland and Poland have been the largest producers and users in Europe. In Eastern Europe, the market for bioenergy in district heating has continued to grow. A good example is that in Lithuania wood chips have overtaken natural gas as the major fuel for district heating schemes. It is important to note that in the EU the increased uses of residential bioenergy, in particular wood pellet burning, have also led to rising environmental concerns. The key reasons are that these applications have contributed to rising atmospheric pollutions, especially in increased particulate emissions.

Biogas has also been used in both industrial and residential heating applications. In Europe, biogas has been used increasingly to provide heating for buildings spaces and industry processes. Biogas has often been applied in conjunction with electricity production via CHP systems. Asia has led the world in the use of small-scale biogas digesters to produce gas for cooking and water and space heating. A good biogas example is that around 4.9 million rural households have been operating village-scale biogas plants in India. These biogas plants have been fuelled mostly by cattle dung and agricultural wastes.

Bio renewable power market growths

Global biopower green electricity generation capacities have been growing steadily. The leading countries for green electricity generation from biomass included the United States, China, Germany, Brazil, Japan, India and the United Kingdom.

In Americas, the USA has remained the largest producer of green electricity from biomass sources. In recent years, the overall US biomass electricity generation capacities have fallen in recent years. A key reason is that existing generation plants have faced increasing price competitions from alternative renewable generation sources under the Renewable Portfolio Standards (RFS) in a number of US states. However, the total US biopower capacity in operation has reportedly increased by 0.5 GW with the installation of 51 small-scale biopower generation plants.

In Europe, the growth in bio-electricity generation from both solid biomass and biogas has been continuing. These increases have largely been driven by the EU Renewable Energy Directive. Germany has become EU's largest producer of green electricity from biomass. The UK's biopower capacity has also increased. These were mainly due to growths in larger-scale generation plants and to a continual growth in biogas productions for electricity. In Poland, capacity auction schemes have been introduced with dedicated tranches for municipal solid waste (MSW) plants.

In Asia, the biopower capacity in China has increased in response to the revised clean energy objectives in the 13th Five-Year Plan. The combustion of municipal solid wastes (MSWs) and agricultural wastes has accounted for most of the biopower generation in China. In Japan, biopower capacity and generation have both risen strongly. These have been driven by bioenergy being included in the Japan feed-in tariff (FIT) scheme. Japan's imports of wood pellets for direct combustion and for use in co-firing installations have also grown rapidly. In the Republic of Korea, bioenergy generation has risen by over 40% in recent years. These increases have resulted from the Korean government efforts to reduce coal burning in electricity generation. The government reduced coal firing by introducing innovative co-firing with biomass. India's biopower capacity has also increased with both higher on-grid and off-grid capacities.

In Latin America, Brazil has been the largest overall consumer of biopower and green electricity in the region. Brazil's bioenergy power capacities have been growing steadily in recent years. Over 80% of the biomass-based electricity generation in Brazil has been fuelled by bagasse. These have been produced in large quantities in sugarcane production. Their uses in biopower production have helped to minimise biological waste and are in line with circular economy developments in Brazil.

Biofuel renewable transport market growths

Global biofuel production growths have been closely tracking the biofuel demands in various emerging economies and developed countries. The USA and Brazil have remained the largest biofuel producers amongst different countries. Among them, they have accounted for 70% of all biofuels produced globally. Other key biofuel consuming countries included Germany, Argentina, China and Indonesia. Globally, it is estimated that 72% of biofuel production has been for fuel ethanol, 23% for biodiesel and 4% for hydrotreated vegetable oil (HVO) (REN, 2018).

The USA and Brazil have been leading the global production of biofuel and ethanol. The United States (USA) and Brazil have been maintaining their leading roles in global ethanol biofuel productions. China, Canada and Thailand have been the next largest biofuel producers globally.

The US biofuel and ethanol domestic demands have been supported by the annual volume requirements under the Protection for US Environmental Protection Agency (US EPA) final Renewable Fuel Standard (RFS2) allocations. The ethanol productions in Brazil have fallen slightly. Canada, which has been ranking fourth globally, has also shown some biofuel production declines in recent years.

Asia has been the third largest regional producer of ethanol globally. China has become Asia's largest ethanol producer. It has also risen to the third place globally for ethanol production, after the USA and Brazil. About 99% of the ethanol produced in China has been based on conventional starch-based feedstocks. In China, all the ethanol production and distribution has been controlled by Chinese state-owned oil companies. In addition, only state-approved companies can carry out biofuel blending plus receive relevant government incentives and subsidies. China's biofuel policies have focused mainly on ethanol production. An E10 biofuel mandate has been put in place in four provinces and 27 cities. Outside of these government designated areas, biofuel production has been largely constrained. Historically, no biofuel blending has been allowed to take place outside of the designated areas. These limitations have been eased recently and this should promote biofuel growths in China. In addition, some government grain stockpiles, previously designated for food uses, have been released by government authorities for ethanol production in China. These are in line with the Chinese government plans to boost domestic ethanol productions, so as to reduce the overseas imports of crude oil and oil products.

Elsewhere in Asia, ethanol productions have also increased in Thailand and India. These have mainly resulted from government encouragements with stronger policy support in the form of biofuel mandates in both of these developing countries.

Europe has become the fourth largest ethanol-producing region after North and South America plus Asia. France has been Europe's largest biofuel producers. However, ethanol productions have fallen recently, mainly due to poor grain harvests which have mainly been caused by climate-induced droughts.

Biodiesel productions have been more geographically diverse than ethanol productions. Biodiesel productions have taken place in many countries. The leading countries for the production of fatty acid methyl ester (FAME) biodiesel included the USA, Brazil, Indonesia, Germany and Argentina. The USA is leading with 18% of global production. Brazil is second with 12% global share. Then Indonesia, Germany and Argentina each have about 10% share.

The US biodiesel production has risen in response to improved opportunities for diesel within the RFS2. Canada biodiesel productions have also risen. By contrast, biodiesel productions in Brazil have fallen despite an increase in the blending mandate. The reductions in Brazil had probably resulted from a decline in diesel consumptions, linked to a reduced level of business activities and increased environmental drives. In Argentina, biodiesel productions have recovered after recent falls. These recoveries have mainly resulted from increased domestic demands plus improved market prospects in the USA and Peru. European biodiesel productions have also declined. Germany is the largest European producer, followed by France, Spain and Poland. In Asia, Indonesian biodiesel productions have risen. These increases have resulted from a number of new government measures aimed to stimulate the domestic market and to make Indonesia the region's largest biodiesel producer again. China's biodiesel productions have also fallen due to reduced diesel fuel uses and an absence of widespread blending mandates.

The global productions of hydrotreated vegetable oil (HVO) have grown in recent years. Most of the HVO productions have been concentrating in the Netherlands, the USA, Singapore and Finland. HVO biodiesel is a form of renewable diesel that has been produced from vegetable fats and oils. Unlike regular biodiesel, hydrogen is being used as a catalyst in the manufacturing processes of HVO, instead of methanol.

The global production and consumption of biogas have continued to grow in recent years. In particular, the growth of biomethane as a clean transport fuel has continued to increase. A good example is that in the USA, biogas consumption has grown nearly six-fold between 2014 and 2016. The conversion of biomass to biomethane was stimulated by the 2014 EPA ruling on the RFS2. This has helped to increase the incentives for biomethane by promoting it to an advanced cellulosic biofuels category. As a result of these substantial growths, the United States has overtaken the other key markets globally, including both Sweden and Germany, for the application and use of biomethane in transportation.

The aviation transport sector has accounted for over one-tenth, around 11%, of the total energy used in transport globally. In 2016, the use of biofuels in aviation has moved from a theoretical concept to a business reality for a few airlines. A number of significant agreements for the provision of aviation biofuels have been signed in 2016. Some of these aviation fuel agreements are likely to have potential values of over USD1 billion. In addition, there has been ongoing development work on new electric aeroplane prototypes for short-range electric flights plus new solar powered planes (IRENA, Biofuels for Aviation, 2017).

In 2017, the International Civil Aviation Organization (ICAO) announced in 2017 that a landmark GHG emission agreement has been signed by 66 nations, which together accounted for 86% of the global aviation activity. These countries have jointly agreed to mitigate and reduce greenhouse gas emissions in their aviation sector. They have planned to start the first phase of their planned joint GHG emission reductions in 2021. The new agreement will support the production and use of sustainable aviation fuels. These new clean aviation fuels are likely to include new aviation biofuels, which will be produced from biomass and different types of waste by advanced biofuel manufacturing processes being developed by leading companies globally (IRENA, Biofuels for Aviation, 2017).

The shipping transport sector globally has been consuming less than one-tenth, around 7%, of the total energy used in the transport sector globally. The International Maritime Organization (IMO) has agreed to implement a new 0.5% sulphur cap in ship bunker fuels globally by 2020. This new sulphur cap will have serious implications on limiting the burning of heavy sulphur fuel oil in ships. This in turn will have big impacts on oil refinery operations and fuel oil bunker sales globally. The new cap will contribute to GHG emission reductions and climate change improvements. These new caps should increase interests in renewable energy and cleaner fuel applications in shipping. These could include liquefied natural gas (LNG), biofuels, and solar and wind energy applications in ships. In theory, clean renewable energy applications, including wind and solar energy, could be incorporated directly into shipping applications, but these would probably need more developments. A good shipping example is the research and development of new wind energy-assist technologies for ships, particularly in the use of modern wind turbines and advanced sail designs. For ship propulsion, the use of biofuels, biogas or other renewable-based fuels, including hydrogen, is also being investigated but this will need further developments. A good example is the deployment of LNG-fuelled ships in Australia which may also offer opportunities for biogas applications (Seatrade, IMO 2020 Sulphur Regulation, 2018).

Overviews of bioenergy renewable companies

The bioenergy and biofuel industries comprised a wide range of international and local companies. These would include feedstock suppliers and processors plus firms that would deliver biomass to end users. In addition, there are manufacturers and distributors of specialist biomass harvesting, handling and storage equipment and machineries. There are also manufacturers of appliances and hardware components designed to convert biomass to useful energy carriers and energy services. Details of the key bioenergy companies active in various solid, liquid and gaseous biomass markets will be discussed in more detail in this chapter below together with international business examples.

Overviews of solid biomass industry and companies

A very diverse range of companies have been involved in the delivering, processing and using of solid biomass to produce renewable heat and green electricity globally. These could range locally from the informal supply of traditional biomass, to the locally based supply of smaller-scale heating appliances. On larger scales, these could include the regional and global players involved in large-scale district heating plus power generation technology supply and operations.

The global markets for wood pellets in industrial applications, especially for power station uses and heating uses, have continued to expand. The leading countries with wood pellet biomass applications included Denmark, Japan, Korea, Italy, Germany, Sweden, etc. Some large-scale pellet biomass plants have been designed to provide supply chain security to major industrial users.

A good example is the Drax biomass power plant in the UK. The Drax power station is a large biomass and coal-fired power station located in North Yorkshire, England. It is designed to burn biomass with the co-firing of petcoke and wood pellets. It has been designed with 2.6 GW capacity for biomass and 1.29 GW capacity for coal. The Drax power plant has been gradually upgraded and its coal burning units have been converted to burn biomass feedstocks. Drax is already the biggest decarbonisation project in Europe after conversion of its three coal burning units to biomass burning units. More conversions are being undertaken so that Drax is on course to stop coal burning before the UK government's 2025 deadline (Drax, 2018).

In general, most of the wood pellet industry has historically been comprised of independent wood pellet producers. These have been mainly based around logging and saw mill operations. There have also been some signs of industrial consolidation globally.

There have been ongoing debates about the sustainability of biomass applications, especially around the large-scale use of pellets derived from wood. This has continued to be a controversial environmental issue and has caused serious public concerns in different countries. The European Commission (EU), in its new EU Renewable Energy Directive launched in November 2016, has stated its intention to reinforce mandatory sustainability criteria for bioenergy and biomass. The EU has proposed to extend the scope of their directive to cover solid biomass and biogas for heating and cooling plus electricity generation. These mandatory criteria have previously been applied only to biofuels. Various EU member states could also introduce criteria for their biomass heating and electricity sectors. Two good country examples are that both the United Kingdom and Denmark have introduced new criteria for their own heating and electricity sectors (EU, Renewable Energy Directive, 2016).

An important new bioenergy technological innovation is the torrefaction of wood. This innovation will enable the production of wood pellets with a higher energy density. It should result in a biomass feedstock which will be compatible with furnace systems that have been designed for coal burning. The energy density of the renewable bio-coal pellets would be similar to thermal coal products. The new bio-coal pellets could be used directly in traditional coal-fired plants instead of fossil coal, without the need for significant investments in plant modifications and associated infrastructures. The major climate change benefit is that the carbon dioxide emissions would be mitigated when fossil coal is replaced by bio-coal pellets in thermal power stations. In addition, the energy density of the new bio-coal pellets would be significantly higher than that of white pellets or wood chips. This would also mean that the logistic costs per ton for transportation and storage should be significantly lower. This would also help to reduce the overall carbon footprints for bio-coal versus fossil coal. Bio-coal pellets are also water-resistant plus could be stored and handled using existing fossil fuel coal infrastructure. Although the commercialisation of the technology has been slower than expected, some promising developments have occurred. A good example is that Airex Energy from Canada has started producing torrefied pellets at its Becancour plant in Canada, with a capacity of 15,000 tons per year. The Finnish company Biopower Oy has invested USD74–84 million (EUR70–80 million) to build a new bio-coal plant in Mikkeli, Finland. Its new bio-coal plant will be producing 200,000 tons of bio-coal pellets annually (Mining.com, Scandinavian Biopower, 2016).

Various major solid biomass developments in the emerging economies and developed countries of Europe, Asia and America will be discussed in more detail below with international business examples.

In Europe, Latvia is Europe's largest wood pellet producer with exports to Denmark, the UK, Sweden and Italy. Another good pellet manufacturer example is Graanul from Estonia and it has 11 pellet plants located across Estonia, Latvia and Lithuania.

In Europe, there have also been encouraging trends to convert traditional large-scale coal power station capacities to burning biomass wood pellets. A good conversion example is that in Denmark a 360 MW unit of a coal-fired power plant in Aarhus has been converted from coal to run on wood pellets. The converted biomass renewable energy station would be supplying biomass-based renewable heat to more than 100,000 homes and green electricity to about 230,000 homes in Denmark. In the United Kingdom, Drax has received the European Commission's approval to convert a third unit of its coal-fired plant to run on wood pellets. Drax has been importing wood pellets from the USA to run its plant.

In Asia, wood pellet biomass imports to both Japan and the Republic of Korea have been rising in recent years. These have resulted from the rapidly increasing use of biomass for co-firing with coal in their power generation plants. A good import example is that Japan has been importing 300,000 tons per year of industrial pellets. The majority, about 70%, has come from Canada, along with 600,000 tons of palm kernel shells from Vietnam and other South-Eastern Asian countries.

In America, the USA has been the largest exporter of wood pellets globally. Most of the US pellet exports have been sold to the UK Drax power plant. Canadian pellet exports have also risen and these have mostly been exported to Asia.

Liquid biofuel renewable industry and companies

Two leading countries for biofuel production and uses have traditionally been Brazil and the USA. Liquid biofuel productions have also been concentrated amongst a small number of large industrial players with dominant market shares. These would include leading ethanol producers such as Archer Daniels Midland ADM, POET and Valero in the United States plus Copersucar, Oderbrecht and Raizen in Brazil. A number of large international oil and energy companies have also been developing biofuels. Good examples included Shell, Neste and UOP. Leading companies from bio-based industries have also been engaged in developing and producing new biomass-based fuels. A good example is UPM from the pulp and paper sector.

In the marine sector, there has been rising interests in biofuel applications for shipping. An important initiative has been established in the Netherlands to develop sustainable biofuels for marine applications. A good shipping example is that the Maersk Shipping Group from Denmark has been testing biofuels and other alternatives in its larger ships. It also has a dedicated container ship for the purpose of testing biofuels derived from a wide variety of sources. In Italy, ENI has been producing biodiesel which has been prepared using its eco-fining process for the Italian navy's offshore patrol vessel Foscari (REN, 2018).

In the aviation sector, there has been rising interest in the development of aviation biofuels. The aviation biofuel quantities have remained relatively small and have mostly been used for demonstration purposes. The American Society for Testing and Materials (ASTM) had also certified two additional technology pathways to produce bio-jet fuels. These have helped to bring the total certified aviation biofuel pathways to five. Several aircraft manufacturers have been instrumental in the development of bio-jet fuels, including Airbus and Boeing. In addition, a number of air carriers and airlines worldwide have started to use biofuels. These have included Aeromexico, Alaska Airlines, British Midland, FedEx, Finnair, Gol, KLM, Lufthansa, Qatar Airways, Scandinavian Airlines (SAS), Southwest Airlines, United Airlines, etc. Several voluntary initiatives at the local and regional levels have sought to establish new bio-jet supply chains at various specific airports. A good example is the supply of bio-jet fuel to Arlanda airport in Stockholm, Sweden by SkyNRG and Air BP.

The US Air Force has also continued to actively develop bio-aviation fuels for defence purposes. It is working with a number of companies to establish new secured aviation biofuel production facilities. In the USA, the AltAir Renewable Jet Fuel Project in the US city of Los Angeles has begun producing "drop-in" biofuels via Honeywell UOP's Renewable Jet Fuel Process in a retrofitted part of an existing oil refinery. The plant, which uses vegetable oils, animal fats and greases as feedstocks, is capable of producing 2,500 barrels (0.15 billion litres) per day of bio-jet fuel.

New international trade patterns for ethanol and biofuels have also been developing. These have been driven in part by the rise in both biofuel demands and new biofuel productions in different countries. Details of biofuel developments in various key emerging economies and developed countries will be discussed below with international business examples.

In Asia, China has become a major importer of ethanol from the United States in recent year. A good example is that the US ethanol exports to China have risen about 2.4-fold in recent years. However, these US exports to China might change and reduce with the ongoing trade tariff war between the USA and China. Indigenous Chinese biofuel productions have also increased. These have largely been derived from China's high stocks of grains. China has recently introduced an import tax on ethanol to support domestic production and has also started to export ethanol to some Asian markets.

There have also been rising international co-operations between Chinese and US biofuel companies. A good example is that DuPont of the USA has signed a licensing agreement with the New Tianlong Industry Company Ltd, in China, to construct China's largest cellulosic ethanol manufacturing plant, which will be located in Siping City. However, these good ongoing technological co-operations might also be affected by the ongoing US–China trade war.

In India, the India Glycols company has opened its first cellulosic plant in Kashipur. The new plant will be running on wood chips, cotton stalk, cane bagasse, maize stover and bamboo. A new Memoranda of Understanding (MOU) relating to five additional new cellulosic ethanol plants has also been finalised.

In Thailand, Toray and Mitsui from Japan have announced their plans to build a new large-scale biofuel plant which will be based on the conversion of sugar bagasse to ethanol.

In Latin America, Brazil has been the leading biofuel manufacturer globally together with the USA. Argentina has been a rising biofuel supplier with its significant biodiesel production capacity. Since 2010, Argentina has been supplying biofuel to markets in the EU as well as in the USA, Peru and other countries. Despite growing domestic demands and rising exports, Argentina's biodiesel manufacturing capacity has been underutilised. It has been running at 40–55% capacity levels only since 2013. These have been mainly caused by the EU imposing a heavy import tax on Argentinian biodiesel exports to the EU.

In Africa, there have been rising interests in biofuel production and applications in various African countries. A good example is that the Nigerian government has recently developed and launched a new national biofuels strategy in 2016. Despite significant attempts by some African countries to develop and enact new biofuels strategies, the overall development of biofuel production in Africa has been slow. One of the key hurdles has been problems in accessing appropriate international biofuel technologies by local African biofuel companies. Some promising new developments have occurred recently. A good example is that the Nigeria National Petroleum Corporation (NNPC) has announced plans to set up a new bio-refinery which will use agricultural products to produce bioethanol and other biofuel products. Union Dicon Salt has also agreed to a joint biofuel project with Delta State from Nigeria. They are planning to jointly plant 100,000 hectares of cassava and to build an ethanol processing plant which will produce 22,000 litres a day biofuel along with starch products. Biofuels Nigeria has also been planning to build a new biodiesel plant in Kogi State using jatropha as feedstock. In South Africa, Ethala Biofuels had announced plans for a sweet sorghum bio-refinery project which will produce ethanol and other products.

In North America, the USA has been one of the leading biofuel producers globally along with Brazil. US biofuel companies have become some of the largest, leading biofuel companies globally. A good example is the US Renewable Energy Group, which has 14 production sites in the United States and Germany. Its total cumulative biodiesel production had exceeded two billion gallons (7.6 billion litres) in 2017. It has also announced plans for the construction of several additional new cellulosic ethanol manufacturing plants. These should help to extend its geographical coverage of biofuel production beyond the USA and Europe.

In Canada, Enerkem had commissioned a commercial-scale biofuel plant in Edmonton in Canada, based on the gasification technology and ethanol synthesis technology. The new Edmonton biofuel plant will be using 300 tons per day of sorted recycled municipal waste to produce bio-methanol.

In the EU, Italy's Beta Renewables has been operating the Crescentino cellulosic ethanol plant in Italy. It has also been cooperating in various joint-venture biofuel projects in the United States, Brazil, China and the Slovak Republic with international partners.

In Finland, BioTech Oy has been developing advanced ethanol production plants in Pietarsaari and Kajaani. These biofuel plants should be able to produce 50 million litres each of advanced ethanol per year using softwood sawdust, recycled wood and other forestry wastes and residues.

Biogas renewable industry and companies

Most biogas productions globally have been taking place in the United States and Europe. Most of the biogas has been based predominantly on the collection of landfill gases. The biogas productions in Europe have also been based on the anaerobic digestion of various bio-wastes. These should include agricultural wastes, animal manures and increasingly the digestion of recycled domestic wastes from urban cities. Good biogas examples included the new biogas productions in Sweden and the United Kingdom. Other regions, including Asia and Africa, have also been building new biogas plants using advanced new biogas technologies. The growth rates of biogas in emerging economies have been higher than developed countries.

The expanding markets for biogas and biomethane globally have also stimulated rising commercial activities worldwide. A good biogas example is that in response to the recent growth of biomethane as a transport fuel in the USA under RFS2, BP has announced that it would be acquiring from Clean Energy Fuels its bio-methane business for USD155 million (EUR147 million).

In Europe, the bio-waste management firm Suez had acquired a 22% stake in biogas producer Prodeval. Suez is attracted by the new technology that Prodeval has developed using an advanced high-performance membrane purification process for biomethane production. Meanwhile, strong growths in the market for biogas facilities have also led to the Danish supplier and builder of biogas systems, Xergi, being named as one of the fastest growing businesses in Denmark.

In Asia, many Indian companies have been modifying their industrial processes to produce biogas. These have been driven in part by the new strict water quality standards from the Indian government which will limit the release of effluents into waterways in India.

In other parts of Asia, there have been similar growing trends to produce and use biogas generated by treating liquid effluents and wastes. A good example is that in Malaysia Green & Smart Holdings has started operations of its first biogas-based power plant with a 2 MW capacity. The biogas plant has been operating based on palm oil mill waste effluents. It has been generating green electricity and exporting the green electricity to the Malaysian national grid.

In Africa, biogas production has also continued to expand in various African countries. The expansions have been driven largely by biogas productions from municipal and agricultural wastes. A good example is that in Kenya the country's first biogas-powered grid-connected CHP plant commenced power generation at a commercial farm. It has been producing 2 MW of electricity plus enough heat to cultivate 704 hectares of vegetables and flowers. It has also been supplying surplus green electricity power to 5,000–6,000 rural homes nearby. In

South Africa, the renewable energy developer New Horizons had partnered with the local gas firm Afrox, to operate an energy-from-waste biogas plant near Cape Town. The new plant will cost some USD29 million (ZAR400 million) and will generate green electricity from waste.

Biogas human waste developments and innovations

There are a lot of research and developments being undertaken in biogas production from human waste. These new innovations and developments could help to reduce the global human waste problems whilst generating clean electricity and heat for local communities.

An interesting biogas pilot programme is being undertaken in South Australia. It has been designed to use biogas from human waste to generate green electricity and heat. New technological innovations have enabled the pilot plant to take biogas from a waste treatment plant and store it as latent heat in molten silicon at a temperature of 1,414°C. Afterwards, the green renewable energy will be recovered to generate heat or power for the local community in South Australia (ABC News, Australia Biogas Human Waste 1414 Pilot Plant, April 2019).

The new biogas from human waste plant was developed by a new Australian start-up called 1414 Degrees. The South Australian government provided the start-up with a $1.6 million grant for its new technology development and commercialisation. The initial loan was made through the Renewable Technology Fund, a programme of the former Weatherill Labor government. The South Australian Energy Minister has said that the pilot programme is a tremendous technological breakthrough which fit in well with their government's priority of producing cleaner, more reliable and affordable electricity for local communities in South Australia.

The 10-megawatt hour biogas pilot plant will provide green electricity and heat to the local South Australia Water Board. It will start with a trial at Glenelg's Waste Treatment Plant.

Bioenergy renewable and green agriculture developments

There are great potentials for green agriculture to contribute to the generation of clean renewable energy, including biofuels, biomass, biogas, etc. At the same time, agricultural production systems have also been big consumers of energy. So renewable energy applications for agriculture should be an important new green energy option. It could help to reduce agricultural energy consumptions and provide clean agricultural energy in both emerging economies and developed countries.

The Integrated Food Energy Systems (IFES) have been developed to address these issues by simultaneously producing food and energy. There are generally two different approaches. The first approach is to combine food and energy crops on the same plot of land, such as in agroforest systems. A good agroforest example is the planting and growth of trees for fuel wood and charcoal. The second type of IFES is the use of by-products or residues to produce useful products or energies. Good examples include the production of biogas from livestock residues, animal feed from by-products of corn ethanol or bagasse for energy as a by-product of sugarcane production for food purposes (Wang, Climate Change and Clean Energy Management, 2019).

A good example of an IFES application is biogas in Vietnam. Vietnam has embarked on an integrated land management scheme, following land rights being granted to individual farmers. This is supported by the Vietnamese Gardeners' Association (VACVINA). It has tried to combine gardening, fish rearing and animal husbandry so as to make the optimal use of the land. Traditional fuels such as wood and coal for cooking have become increasingly scarce and contributed to deforestation. The biogas project has adopted a novel approach to address both energy issues and environmental concerns simultaneously. Biogas digesters would use animal waste to generate energy, whilst the slurry would be used as a fertilizer to improve soil quality. A customer must have at least four to six pigs or two to three cattles which would provide the required amount of animal dung feedstock to the digester. They would pay the total installation cost for the digesters to the local service providers. The farmers would then operate the biodigester using instructions provided by them. These systems should then produce enough daily biogas fuel for cooking and enough renewable power for lighting uses.

The Integrated National Green Regimes (INGR) has been used to promote renewable developments, with key agricultural production systems being operated as part of the national or regional green agendas. A good example is biofuel productions in Brazil. Brazil has become the world's largest biofuel market. Brazilian ethanol from sugarcane is a renewable fuel that is cost competitive against fossil oil fuels for transport applications in Brazil. Ethanol production is more economical in Brazil than in the United States due to several factors. These included the superiority of sugarcane to corn as an ethanol feedstock. Brazil's large unskilled labour force have also supported the labour-intensive sugarcane production requirements. Whilst the USA and Brazil have produced about the same volume of ethanol, the USA has used almost twice as much land to cultivate its corn for ethanol as Brazil has done to cultivate sugarcane. Brazil launched its National Alcohol Program, Pró-Álcool, in 1975 as a nation-wide programme. It was financed by the government with the objective to phase out automobile fuels derived from fossil fuels in favour of ethanol produced from sugar cane.

Brazil's 30-year-old ethanol fuel programme is based on the most efficient agricultural technology for sugarcane cultivation in the world. It uses modern equipment and cheap sugar cane as feedstocks. The residual cane-waste, bagasse, is used to generate heat and power. These have resulted in very competitive generation costs with efficient energy balances. There are currently no longer any light vehicles in Brazil running on pure gasoline. Since 1976, the Brazilian government has made it mandatory to blend anhydrous ethanol with gasoline, at blending ratios up to 22%. In Brazil, sugarcane and ethanol are being produced on an integrated basis. The option to produce more or less of each product is controlled by the relative pricing and market demands. Some experts have suggested that the successful Brazilian biofuel ethanol model is sustainable only in Brazil. These successes have resulted from a unique combination of cheap labour, advanced agri-industrial technology and enormous amount of arable land available. Brazil's ethanol infrastructure model has also required huge taxpayer subsidies and government policy supports over decades, before it became viable.

Biofuel and bio-chemical developments and innovations

There is a lot of development work being undertaken to use renewable bio-feedstocks from agriculture and waste sources to make biofuels, bio-chemicals and bio-naphtha via various new innovative processes. The use of biomass for bio-naphtha or bio-chemical production should help to reduce fossil fuel consumptions whilst supporting new green chemical productions. Bio-naphtha is essentially a paraffinic hydrocarbon which is similar to the traditional fossil-based light naphtha. Bio-naphtha could be converted in a conventional refinery or petrochemical complex into a whole host of new green bio-chemical products including bioethylene, biopropylene, isomerate, reformate, light olefins or aromatics.

These new bio-chemical processes should also help to minimise carbon emissions in comparison to the traditional petrochemical processes based on fossil fuel feedstocks. The carbon dioxide released during the energy conversion of biomass by these new processes, such as combustion, gasification, pyrolysis, anaerobic digestion or fermentation, should circulate through the biosphere. Then it should be reabsorbed in equivalent amounts of biomass through photosynthesis.

Various new technological and process innovations are being developed for the production of bio-naphtha from various agricultural biomass, wastes and renewable fractions. Some of these processes would involve the combination of bio-refining together with a traditional steam cracker. Bio-refining would catalytically convert the triglycerides and/or fatty acids from fats, algae and vegetable oils to a high-quality synthetic paraffinic kerosene (SPK) or biodiesel and a renewable bio-naphtha in three steps.

In the first step, the raw bio-feedstocks are treated to remove catalyst poisons and water. In the second step, the fatty acid chains are deoxygenated and transformed into mainly paraffins in a hydrotreater. For most bio-oils, fats and greases, the hydrotreater liquid products should consist mainly of C15-C18 paraffins. In the third step of the process, these long straight-chain paraffins are hydrocracked into shorter branched paraffins. The hydrocracked products should fall mainly into the kerosene and naphtha boiling ranges.

There are also high-temperature thermo-chemical processes to convert the renewable bio-feedstocks to biofuels or bio-chemicals such as via pyrolysis and gasification or low-temperature enzymatic processes. Currently, these processes are more expensive and not cost competitive compared to the conventional fossil fuel-based processes.

Another new process would involve the hydrolysis of biomass to oligosaccharides using a benign green liquid acid. Then the oligosaccharides are deoxygenated with hydrogen to light naphtha (C5/C6 paraffins). The bio-product would then be separated using a phase separator and the water recycled to the hydrolysis reactor.

A good bio-naphtha and bio-chemical business example is the new Ikea Neste commercial pilot plans. In follow-up to their new partnership established in 2016, Finnish oil producer Neste and the Swedish furniture retailer Ikea have announced joint plans for commercial pilot plant production of bio-based polypropylene. This will be the first large pilot scale production of renewable polypropylene (PP) globally. They should also be able to produce renewable polyethylene PE. The pilot test plant is planned to be started up in 2019/2020. The feedstock will be bio-naphtha which will be a by-product generated in the production of renewable diesel from agricultural waste and recycled used cooking oil at Neste's refinery at Rotterdam, the Netherlands. The bio-naphtha will be processed in a cracker to make bioethylene and biopropylene which could have a renewable content of as much as 50%. The bioethylene and biopropylene grades produced in the pilot facility can be processed with the same machinery converters which have been used to manufacture conventional chemical plastics. Currently, there is a serious economic problem for this production process as the bio-naphtha is more than twice as expensive as the fossil fuel-based naphtha petrochemical feedstocks. So further developments and cost reductions would have to be undertaken so as to improve the efficiency and economies of the process. Initially, Ikea has planned to use the new bio-plastic in a few of its products, such as storage boxes. By 2030, Ikea has been planning that all its plastic products and furniture sold in its stores should be made of recycled or renewable bio-plastic materials (Plasteurope, Ikea NESTE, 2018).

China's biofuel and biomass renewable market case study

In China, biomass and biofuel developments have been key elements of the government policies and plans in both the 12th and 13th Five-Year National Plans. The major biomass and biofuel growth areas have included the production of ethanol, second-generation biofuels and energy produced from organic feedstock sources. However, these are in the initial phase of developments and have been facing challenges from lack of supporting infrastructures.

The bioenergy and biofuel sectors in China have been at the nascent stage of developments. There have also been growing interests in these sectors from leading industry players. Various future investment options have been considered and there may be rapid future investment growths (IEA, The Potential of Biofuels in China, 2016).

In terms of bioenergy potential, China's future biomass supply is expected to be doubled by the end of the next five years. Looking ahead, future biomass supply could even triple by the end of the next 15 years. The Chinese government has set new targets in its 13th Five-Year Plan so that by the end of 2020–2025, the total installed biomass power capacity should reach over 20 GW across China. Chinese government agencies have also stipulated that Chinese companies should be developing biomass energy and other renewable energy resources under the key principle of orderly development, based on local conditions and comprehensive utilisation, with all relevant factors taken into consideration.

These new government policies should promote biopower generation using crop stalks, grain-processing residues and bagasse as biofuel feedstocks. These should be particularly applicable in the major producing areas of grain and cotton in China. In forest covered areas in China, the government is planning to develop wood biomass power generation but there should also be careful consideration on environment and sustainability impacts. In urban areas, it is planning to promote more green electricity generation by using more urban waste incineration and collecting more landfill gases for biogas applications.

China also plans to speed up the construction of biogas systems, including biomethane, supply systems, in various eligible regions. The building of various new production bases of biomass and biofuels would be heavily influenced by local conditions. The development of biodiesel and industrial cellulosic ethanol is the priority areas of focus. Ethanol production has remained quite a small area of investment in China. The key reason is that the first generation of ethanol productions has mostly used feedstocks that would compete with food supplies. However, the new second generation of biofuel production will be using non-food feed sources. These should provide greater potentials for biofuel productions and developments in China.

China has also been promoting the use of biofuel in its large jet fuel market. The China Civil Aviation Administration has announced plans to use 12 MMTPA of aviation biofuels by 2020–2025. This would constitute around 30% of China's total jet fuel market consumptions.

In addition, China has started investing in biomass energy that could be produced from feedstocks such as corn stocks, wheat stocks and gutter oil. China has also been examining the usage of different grasses and algae strains which are fast growing and will not compete with food sources.

The leading Chinese National Oil Companies (NOC), including Sinopec and CNPC, have also recognised the potential values of biofuel and biogas developments in China and globally. A good strategic development direction is that if the Chinese NOC could produce sufficient aviation bio-jet fuels in China, then they may be able export these to overseas aviation market. These might help them to achieve some new sustainable global leadership positions in the competitive aviation fuel market.

A good business example is that the China National Petroleum Corporation (CNPC) has built a new bio-refinery capable of producing 60,000 tons of biofuel annually. Details of the new biofuel and biogas strategies and developments for each of the leading Chinese NOCs will be discussed in more detail below with relevant business examples.

Sinopec biofuel and biomass renewable developments

Sinopec has established a completely new low-carbon energy business unit with a new value chain covering R&D, industrial production and marketing. The

Sinopec management has developed new business plans to build up its low-carbon energy capacities by 2020–2025. The Sinopec management believed that these new strategic developments should complement its main oil and gas business operations plus contribute to the longer-term sustainable development of their company in China and globally. The substitution of traditional fossil fuels with biofuel and bioenergy should also help to produce Sinopec to reduce their GHG emissions and improve their environmental performances.

Sinopec Corp had started to undertake R&D of cellulose ethanol technology and microalgae biodiesel technology over ten years ago, since 2007. In terms of cellulose ethanol technology, Sinopec has been developing new second-generation biofuel technologies to produce ethanol from cellulose, including crops straw, forestry processing waste, biogases, etc.

Sinopec has also been developing new microalgae biodiesel technologies. Microalgae are a kind of lower grade plant which could absorb CO_2 through cell photosynthesis. The microalgae will convert light energy into fat, starch and other carbohydrate, and then release oxygen O_2. Sinopec Corp has been cooperating with the Chinese Academy of Sciences to engineer new microalgae strains and to develop new sets of microalgae biodiesel technologies.

Sinopec has also been pioneering new bio-jet fuel developments in China. A good example is that in 2013 an Airbus powered by Sinopec's independently developed jet biofuel had made a successful first test flight. More developments would be required in China to generate new bio-jet fuel products, using animal and plant fats and oils as feedstocks, so that these bio-jet fuels would meet the international jet fuel requirements. China has become the fourth country globally to have its own independently developed production technology for bio-jet fuel. The other three countries include the United States, France and Finland.

Sinopec has become China's first SOE to have an independent bio-jet fuel production technology and a mass production capacity. Compared to traditional petroleum-based jet fuel, the bio-jet fuel should help to reduce carbon dioxide emissions. After the successful airworthiness flight, Sinopec has accelerated the commercial production of its bio-jet fuels from renewable resources including primarily coconut oil, palm oil, jatropha seed oil, linseed oil, algae oil, waste cooking oil, animal fat, etc. A good example is that the Sinopec Hang Zhou Refinery has successfully produced the first bio-jet fuel from palm oil and waste cooking oil.

CNPC biofuel and biomass renewable developments

The CNPC management has announced plans to make investments of up to RMB 10 billion (USD1.5 billion) in new clean energy developments by 2020. The new investments also included biofuel and biomass developments. A good example is that CNPC had in 2007 entered into several framework agreements with China's State Forestry Administration and several local governments, including Sichuan, Yunnan and Shandong, to develop biomass energy and biofuels. It has also planned to generate bio-diesel and ethanol using non-grain crops.

CNPC has established the Jilin Ethanol Fuel Co. Ltd, which is a joint venture between CNPC (55%), Jilin Grain Group (25%) and COFCO (20%). The joint venture has been producing 500,000 million tons per annum of ethanol biofuel and ethyl acetate each. CNPC has set up 88 ethanol gasoline blending centres. It has also upgraded over 5,500 filling stations in nine provinces and cities. CNPC has also produced bioethanol with sweet sorghum straw. It has constructed and inaugurated a demonstration project to produce 3,000 tons per annum of bioethanol from sweet sorghum straw in Dongtai of Jiangsu province. CNPC has also been collaborating with various provincial governments in the development of bioethanol fuel and associated manufacturing facilities.

CNOOC biofuel and biomass renewable developments

CNOOC has established a new subsidiary for clean energy developments. The CNOOC New Energy Investment Co. Ltd is a wholly owned subsidiary of CNOOC. It was founded in 2007 with a registered capital of RMB 80 million (USD13 million). The new company's major new business focuses would include the exploration, development and utilisation of renewable and clean energies. These would include wind power, coal-based clean energy (coal gasification, coal to liquids and coal to chemicals), biomass energy, solar power and Li-ion power battery.

The new company was set up by CNOOC in order to promote renewable energy developments and to develop its new strategic emerging clean energy businesses. It has also been monitoring the investment trends of competing international oil companies in its new clean energy and renewable energy developments.

CNOOC has been actively involved in bioenergy and biofuel developments. A good example is that the CNOOC Biolux Company and Hainan Biomass Energy and Chemicals Company have generated over 189,200 tons of biological oil fuel or biofuel. CNOOC has also been developing advanced biodiesel production at a FAME biodiesel processing facility. The FAME biodiesel plant has the world's highest production capacity for a single facility, with a design capacity of 270,000 million tons per annum.

CNOOC has established its new biofuel joint venture with international partners. The Biolux (Nantong) Bioenergy Protein Feed Co. Ltd is the joint venture of CNOOC New Energy Investment Co. Ltd with Austria's BIOLUX Biofuel Biotreibstoffproduktions-und Handels GmbH. The registered capital of CNOOC Biolux is USD52 million, with a total investment of USD112 million. Shareholder's equity shareholding has been agreed to be 74% equity for CNOOC, and 26% equity for Austria Biolux. The CNOOC Biolux project has been designed to produce FAME biodiesel with raw bio-feedstocks such as cottonseeds. The project will use the new technology of esterification, which is one of the most advanced in the world. It will also produce valuable by-products like biological protein feed, medium products, high-quality glycerine, etc.

7 Renewable policy development management

求人不如求己
Qiú rén bù rú qiú jǐ
It is better to rely on yourself rather than depend on the help from others.
If you want things to be done well, then do it yourself.

Executive overviews

Many governments and countries around the world have realised the importance of enacting new renewable energy policies and supports so as to promote clean renewable energy growths in their country and to compile with their Paris Agreement commitments. A good example is that China has issued "The Thirteenth Five-Year Plan for the Development of Emerging Industries of Strategic Importance" to encourage the development of clean renewable energy across China. Details of various new clean renewable energy policy developments in different emerging economies and developed countries plus their potential implications will be discussed further in this chapter with country examples.

Clean renewable energy policy overviews

New clean energy policies and revised energy targets have been developed and adopted in various emerging economies and developed countries globally, as part of their drives to reduce fossil fuel consumption and to compile with their Paris Agreement commitments. Many governments have also recognised the importance of developing and implementing a range of new support policies to promote clean renewable energy applications in their countries.

Most countries have been supporting renewable energy development and deployment directly through a mix of policies enacted at the national, sub-national and local levels. These would normally include establishing a range of renewable energy targets together with supporting policies. These should help to attract new investment in renewable plus drive deployment and foster innovation. In addition, these should encourage greater flexibility in energy infrastructure and improve energy security plus support the development of enabling technologies such as energy storage (REN, Global Status Report, 2018).

In 2016, at the 22nd Conference of the Parties (COP22) in Marrakesh, Morocco, more than 100 countries had officially committed to join the Paris Agreement. At COP22, the leaders of 48 developing countries which constituted the Climate Vulnerable Forum (CVF), including COP22's host nation of Morocco, also committed to work jointly towards achieving 100% renewable energy in their respective nations. In addition, a new 20-country coalition launched the Bio-future Platform which is dedicated to promoting the use of biofuels in the transport and industrial sectors.

Many countries and governments have been building on the momentum created by the landmark Paris Agreement of the United Nations Framework Convention on Climate Change (UNFCCC). Over 100 countries have developed and communicated their first Nationally Determined Contributions (NDCs) as part of their Paris Agreement commitments. A total of 117 NDCs have been submitted by end of 2016, largely from countries that have formalised the commitments made in their Intended Nationally Determined Contributions (INDCs) which were submitted prior to the Paris Climate Conference. Amongst the 117 NDCs submitted, 55 had included new targets for increasing renewable energy applications. Another 89 had made reference to boarder clean renewable energy applications.

Various governments have applied a broad range of policy options to support clean renewable energy applications. These included feed-in tariffs (FITs), tendering, competitive bids, net metering and fiscal incentives. These new policy supports should help the transition from fossil fuels to clean renewable energy sources in various countries. Other key developments, including renewable technology advances, reducing renewable costs and rising penetration of renewables in many countries, have also contributed to the fossil to clean energy transformations. Looking across the different sectors, most policy supports have been focusing on the power sector as these have represented the biggest energy users. Policy support for the transport sector, especially electric cars, has also been developing fast in many countries. Policy supports for renewable technologies in the heating and cooling sectors have also been developed in some countries, albeit at slower paces.

Policies targeting broader environmental concerns or other energy resources may also affect the renewable energy market growths. A good example is the carbon pricing policies, including carbon taxes or emissions trading systems. If these have been designed effectively, then these should incentivise renewable energy deployments by increasing the comparative life cycle costs of fossil fuels with higher GHG emissions. In some countries, continued fossil fuel subsidies by some governments have continued to be hurdles to clean renewable energy growths and reductions in GHG emissions.

Many governments globally have been introducing new supporting policies and targets for clean renewable energy applications in the power, transport, heating and cooling sectors. Different renewable target and policy options will be discussed in more detail in the different sections below with industrial examples.

Renewable regulatory policy developments

Many governments globally have enacted new climate policies and regulatory measure on the deployment of clean renewable energy and power in their countries as part of their Paris Agreement commitments. In addition to regulatory policies, many countries have provided public funds through grants, loans or tax incentives to help to drive green finance and investment growths to support various new clean renewable energy deployments.

One of the most commonly applied renewable policy measures has been the Renewable Portfolio Standards (RPS). These RPS have been applied in various countries globally but the pace of their implementation has been slowing noticeably in recent years. At the national level, little new RPS policies have been introduced. At the sub-national level, RPS trends have been more dynamic. A good example is that in the United States 29 of the 50 federal states, including the District of Columbia, had set up new RPS targets within their states.

In addition to regulatory policies, several countries have provided public funds through grants, loans or tax incentives to drive and support new investments in renewable energy deployment. A good example is that India has launched a 30% capital subsidy for rooftop solar PV installations. Its new solar support programme was backed by USD750 million (INR50 billion) of funding. Its plan was to support installation of 4,200 MW of new solar PV capacity in India.

Another good country example is that the Republic of Korea has pledged to invest USD36 billion in clean energy by 2020. The Korean government is targeting 79% of its new green finance fund for the deployment of new renewable energy projects and 11% for new energy storage projects (REN, Global Status Report, 2018).

Many governments have also introduced and applied various new policy incentives for renewables. A good example is Sweden which has removed its tax on solar production so as to help to promote green finance and investments in renewables, in order to reach its national target of 100% renewable electricity by 2040.

Many renewable incentives and subsidies have also been reduced or eliminated in recent years in response to tightening fiscal budget constraints. A good example is the Netherlands which has plans to phase out its renewable subsidies over the coming decades. Another example is the United States, which had rolled back its supports for a number of renewable technologies previously supported by the US Production Tax Credit. These supports have helped to drive significant renewable technological innovations and improvements in recent years. These in turn have resulted in significant renewable cost reductions, especially for solar and wind, which have helped to make renewable technology more cost competitive against fossil fuels.

Governments have also been adopting various new policies to support the development of domestic renewable energy supply chains and manufacturing capacities. A good example is that Iran has established a 35% premium in its FITs for solar and wind power plants which have been built with high domestic contents. Another good example is Turkey which has introduced a premium of up to 50% higher tariffs under the country's wind power FIT if all the wind turbine components have been made in the country. Turkey has also imposed a 50% tariff on foreign solar panel imports to encourage the manufacturing and deployment of domestic solar panels.

Various governments globally have introduced new local sourcing policy requirements for new renewable orders and tenders. These are to stimulate the growth of their domestic renewable manufacturing industries. Many governments have also increased their mandatory requirements for local contents and sourcing, say up to 50–75%, as part of their economic policy to boost domestic renewable manufacturing. A good example is that in Turkey a new local content requirement has been applied for the first time as part of its tender specifications for the new Karapinar Solar PV project. It is anticipated that Turkey will require 75% of the module components for new renewable installations to be manufactured locally. Another good example is that the Indian government has launched a new government renewable investment fund of USD3 billion (INR210 billion), together with new government incentives. This is to support the development and growth of the emerging domestic solar panel manufacturing industry in India.

Policy makers have also been expanding policy supports for renewable deployments specifically for low-income communities in their countries. A good example is that the US federal government has launched an initiative to promote solar power deployment and energy efficiency improvements for low- and moderate-income Americans families in 2016. Most of the US policies targeting low-income populations have occurred at the sub-national level in the United States. A good example is the programmes to expand access to renewable energy for low-income communities in California, Massachusetts and the District of Columbia in the USA. New York has also established a USD3.6 million fund to support solar PV deployment for low-income communities. Illinois has enacted the Future Energy Jobs Bill, which promotes solar PV deployment for low-income communities.

Latin American government has also introduced new policies and funding supports for renewables. A good Latin American example is that Mexico has also instituted a USD106 million renewable funding initiative which is supported by the International Finance Corporation (IFC). The new renewable fund will help to finance the construction of solar-powered energy-efficient houses for low-income communities in Mexico.

Clean renewable energy policy target developments

Many governments and countries have established new policy targets for clean energy and renewable energy to promote clean energy and renewable energy growths in their countries so as to meet their Paris Agreement commitments. These new policy targets included new government policies and codified plans accompanied by quantifiable metrics and compliance mechanisms. Various new policy targets have focused on reducing fossil fuel consumptions plus promoting renewable applications, such as renewable power generation, so as to stimulate economy-wide renewable energy consumptions.

Globally, over 170 countries have established new clean energy and renewable energy targets to promote renewable energy growths. The majority of government renewable targets have been focusing on renewable energy uses in the power generation sector. Some 90 countries have set new clean energy and renewable targets to increase clean energy and renewable energy shares in their primary energy mixes. Over 45 countries have established clean energy and renewable targets for the heating and cooling sectors. Over 40 countries have established clean energy and renewable targets for clean transport energy usages. Many countries and governments have also enacted additional fiscal incentives or public finance mechanisms to support clean energy and renewable energy applications in various sectors (REN Global Status Report, 2018).

Globally, there have been some good policy co-operations between countries on renewables. Several joint renewable commitments by different countries have been made at the regional and international levels. A good example is the 100% renewable electricity commitments made by the 48 CVF member countries, including many emerging economies, at COP22. Globally, there is a growing list of countries committed to achieving a 100% share of renewable energy in the electricity power sector. These covered many emerging economies and developing countries, which included Africa countries such as Cabo Verde, Morocco, Nigeria and South Africa plus Latin American and the Caribbean countries such as Argentina, Aruba, Cuba, Jamaica and Mexico.

New or revised renewable targets have also been established at the sub-national or provincial level in some countries. A good example is that ten provinces in Canada have each set their own renewable energy targets. Alberta in Canada has announced a 30% renewable electricity target by 2030. Massachusetts in the USA has also established new targets for installed power capacities.

The EU has also proposed a new 2030 Clean Energy Framework under which renewable energy will account for at least 27% of total energy consumption in its member states. In addition, the EU has stipulated a target of a 27% improvement in energy efficiency together with a new target to reduce greenhouse gas emissions by 40% in 2030 (EU, 2016).

In Americas, Canada, Mexico and the USA have previously agreed to a joint transnational deal to source 50% of the region's electricity from non-carbon and clean energy sources by 2025. With various new administrations in these countries, there have been some uncertainties if these previously agreed joint clean energy deals and deployment targets would still be supported.

In Asia, various emerging economies and developing countries have been active in launching new renewable targets or revising existing ones. Various targets for renewable energy shares or installed capacity targets have been published and enacted in different countries in Asia. Good country examples included India, Malaysia, the Republic of Korea, Singapore, Taiwan, Thailand and Vietnam.

China's latest 13th Five-Year Plan has also stipulated an overall national target goal to increase renewable power capacity to 680 GW by 2020. This should then push renewable power to account for over 27% of the total power generation in China. China's Five-Year Plan on Ocean Energy has also established a new national target of achieving a total cumulative capacity of 50 MW of ocean energy by applying new tidal, wave and temperature gradient technologies by 2020 (China 13th Five Year Plan, 2016).

In the clean transportation section, a number of new renewable transport targets have also been established by different countries globally. A good example is that in Finland a new biofuel target was set for 30% biofuel blending and 40% renewable transport fuel use by 2030. In Norway, a goal was set for 20% biofuel use in transport fuels by 2020.

Renewable-enabling technology innovation policy overviews

Many countries have been developing and enacting new policies to promote innovations in clean renewable energy technologies and associated enabling technologies. Innovations in various renewable-enabling technologies have led to significant renewable cost reductions over recent years. These have helped to promote the greater uptakes of renewable energies in different sectors in recent years. Significant new innovations have included advanced energy storage systems, digital distributed power management systems, heat pumps and electric vehicles (EVs).

Innovations in renewable-enabling technologies have helped to create new markets for renewable energy applications in many sectors including building, industry and transport. A good example is that the rising electrification of motor vehicles is not only reducing local air pollutions but creating other benefits. These included the development and application of advanced renewable power charging technologies for electric vehicles (EVs). These have helped to reduce fossil fuel usages in the transport sector. These have also led to reductions in vehicle emissions which have helped to improve air qualities in cities, along with expanding renewable deployment.

Another good example of enabling technology is the heat pumps. These have allowed renewable power to substitute fossil fuels in new smart buildings and for industrial heat applications. There are also new heat pump innovations which have promoted greater integration of electricity and thermal applications in buildings and industries plus low-carbon transportation and energy storage. A good example is that in Europe new heat pump innovations have enabled the total installed heat pump capacities to increase and reached over 75 GWh.

Enabling technologies are also helping to better accommodate the rapidly growing shares of variable renewable electricity supplies. Electricity power and grid systems have always required improved flexibility to accommodate the ever-changing electricity demands, system constraints and supply disruptions. The growing shares of variable renewable power generation supplies will require additional flexibility from many of the national grid systems. The development of advanced digital decentralised power management systems has helped to increase the connectivity of variable renewable power supplies to national grids. These new advanced digital systems could also be integrated with new energy storage solutions. These technological innovations should help to better balance grid-connected renewable energy supplies against fluctuating energy demands. Distributed renewable power systems have also facilitated new off-grid renewable energy deployments globally, especially for remote rural villages.

These innovative clean power distributed supplies with energy storage could help to provide new affordable electricity power supply to over one billion people globally who currently do not have any reliable electricity access and supplies. A good example is that these new distributed renewable power systems with energy storage and digital distributed power management systems have been used to provide the supply of clean renewable energies to remote rural communities, in emerging economies in Asia and Africa, which previously have not had reliable electricity supplies from their national electric grids.

Globally, the development and deployment of new renewable-enabling technologies such as energy storage and smart grid systems have also drawn increased policy focus from policy makers at the national and state/provincial levels. To promote the advancement of these renewable technologies, many governments have been adapting new mechanisms, which have previously been used for the promotion of fossil power generation technologies. These would normally include a mix of incentives and regulatory support together with newer mechanisms. A good example is that Germany has enacted a programme of USD31.5 million (EUR30 million) in 2016 to provide loans and grants to support new residential solar PV systems in combination with new battery energy storage systems.

Innovations in new energy storage enabling technologies have also continued to receive strong policy supports from different governments globally. A good example is that Sweden has announced new supports for new energy storage and smart grid technologies. It has established a new investment fund of USD5.5 million per year (SEK50 million/year) for new energy storage systems and a new investment fund of USD1 million per year (SEK10 million/year) for smart grids. They have also enacted an initial outlay of USD2.75 million (SEK25 million) to support new renewable energy storage innovations in Sweden.

Renewable energy efficiency improvements

Globally, there is general recognition that improvements in energy efficiency and energy savings are very important for climate change and clean renewable energy management. Many governments and companies have recognised that additional energy savings can help to reduce fossil fuel consumptions plus promote renewable energy applications. Many governments have enacted new energy efficiency targets and policies. These have led to continued investments in energy efficiency improvements and renewable applications. These have included incremental investments in energy efficiency in building, industry and transport sectors. A good example is that the global energy efficiency and renewable investments have increased significantly to over USD200 billion per year.

Energy efficiency improvements have been more marked in the developing and emerging economies in comparison to developed economies. A key reason is that most of the emerging economies have been growing faster than developed economies and have greater scopes for improvements. In addition, the developing economies have more opportunities for energy efficiency improvements than developed economies, such as with the construction of new buildings and infrastructures.

Different countries have enacted appropriate energy efficiency targets and new policies so as to provide drivers for energy efficiency improvements. An increasing number of countries have set new energy efficiency targets plus adopted new energy efficiency policies and standards. Innovations in energy improvement technologies and financing have also played important roles in the improvements. A good example is the introduction of new financial incentives to channel additional funding towards energy efficiency by different countries.

Global renewable electricity power policy overviews

Globally, the electricity power generation sector has continued to be the prime area of focus for renewable energy policy support in both emerging economies and developed countries. This is mainly due to its large size plus its big impacts on countries and communities. Feed-in tariffs (FITs) have remained the most widely utilised form of regulatory support for the renewable power sector. In addition, various tenders, including competitive bidding or auctions for renewable energy, have been fast becoming the most rapidly expanding form of support for renewable energy project deployments. Tenders have fast become the preferred policy tool by various countries to support the deployment of large-scale utility projects. Their improved transparency, governance and management efficiency aspects have been attractive to governments plus stakeholders from both the public and private sectors (REN, Global Status Report, 2018).

Good country tender examples included Malawi and Zambia who have both held their first renewable energy tenders. China has also tendered 5.5 GW of renewable capacity recently as part of its 13th Five-Year Plan for renewable investments. Some countries, including Poland, Greece and Slovenia, have adopted hybrid policy schemes that have supported small-scale renewable projects through FITs and larger renewable projects through competitive tenders.

Decision makers in many countries have continued to favour using various policy tools to facilitate the integration of variable renewable generation into their national energy systems. Many countries have introduced new support mechanisms and revised existing policies in their efforts to respond to the changing political, societal and market conditions and demands. Feed-in policies, including feed-in tariffs (FITs) and feed-in premiums (FIPs), have traditionally been the most prominent form of regulatory policy support for renewable power promotion by different governments. Recently, many countries around the world, including some in Europe and Asia, have started to shift away from these policies. For large-scale project deployments, some countries have replaced these feed-in mechanisms with auction-based procurement. Feed-in tariff (FIT) policies have continued to remain in force in many countries for the deployment of small-scale utility installations.

Policy makers have continued to adjust their FIT rates as the technologies become more cost competitive. The European Commission (EC) approved revisions to several feed-in mechanisms proposed by its EU member countries. These changes have often included the adoption of market premiums for large-scale projects. The EU has also announced plans to remove priority dispatch rights for new renewable energy projects.

In Asia, several countries have reduced their feed-in rates. A good example is China which has reduced its FIT rates by 13–19% for solar power. At the same time, China has kept its distributed generation FIT rates unchanged. Another good example is Japan which has reduced its solar FIT rates by 11% for 2016. Looking ahead, Japanese government is studying plans for further FIT rate cuts of 20% or more in the next three years.

In Africa, modifications have also been made to the feed-in policies in various African emerging economies and developing countries. A good example is Ghana which has announced plans to update its solar PV FIT rates. Kenya has announced its intention to transition away from FITs to tendering. Egypt has announced a new phase of its FIT programme, including requirements for 30% of financing for solar PV projects and 40% of financing for wind power projects to come from Egyptian sources.

Looking ahead, tendering via competitive bidding or auctions for renewable energy will likely become the most rapidly expanding form of support for renewable energy project deployment in emerging economies and developed countries globally. These have also become the preferred policy tools by various governments to support the deployment of large-scale renewable projects. Public and private sector stakeholders have preferred the tender approach due to its improved transparency, better governance and higher management efficiency aspects. Most new renewable energy tenders have been held for solar PV projects, and to a lesser extent for wind and geothermal power projects.

Asia has been home to some of the largest renewable tenders by capacity recently. A good example is that China has tendered 5.5 GW of renewable energy capacity in 2016. This was a significant increase from 1 GW of renewable capacity that was offered for tendering in 2015. India has also held a tender for the deployment of 1 GW of new solar PV capacity. Indonesia has also held a tender for 680 MW of new geothermal capacity spread across six local regions.

Tenders and FITs have also increasingly been implemented alongside one another. In Europe, this has been driven by the EU State Aid guidelines, which have led to policy changes in EU member countries. They are attempting to meet the new requirement to shift towards tendering for new larger renewable projects. A good example is that Poland's Renewable Energy Law has replaced the existing green certificate scheme with a mix of tenders for large-scale projects and feed-in payments for small-scale projects up to 10 kW. National solar PV tenders have also been held in France and Germany. The Netherlands has held solar power tenders and two rounds of offshore wind power tenders.

In Africa, Nigeria has adopted new renewable policies which are similar to the multi-pronged approach established in Europe. The Nigerian government has introduced a new tender system for renewable projects larger than 30 MW whilst also formally retaining its FIT rates first announced in 2015. Both Malawi and Zambia have held their first renewable energy tenders in 2016. Malawi has held tenders for four solar PV plants with a cumulative capacity of 70 MW. Zambia has held solar tenders for a total of 100 MW of solar projects. These have resulted in a record low solar bid price for Africa at USD0.06 per kWh for a 25-year solar power PPA.

In the Middle East and North Africa (MENA) region, Morocco has called for tenders totalling 1 GW for its large-scale renewable energy projects. Elsewhere in the MENA region, the Palestinian Energy Authority has launched its first tenders in 2016. It is aiming to boost its installed solar PV capacity by as much as 100 MW. Saudi Arabia has also launched a 100 MW solar PV tender as part of its new Saudi Vision 2030 national plan. Iraq has also just announced a tender for a 50 MW solar PV project (Saudi Arabia, Vision 2030, Riyadh, 2016).

In Latin America, Argentina has held its first tenders under its RENOVAR programme. It has awarded 2.4 GW of renewable energy in 2016 together with a green investment fund to help secure renewable investments. Chile has held its largest power auction to date to supply 12,430 GWh of renewable electricity annually for 20 years. This should meet about one-third of Chile's total future clean energy needs. Wind power received 40% of the available capacity in the auction together with the world's lowest price for solar PV generation at USD29.10 per MWh.

In Central America, El Salvador has launched tenders for 100 MW of solar power capacity and 50 MW of wind power capacity. Additional tenders and auctions have also been held in Guatemala, Honduras, Panama and Peru. Mexico has selected 23 bidders to develop its USD4 billion new clean renewable power projects. These new renewable projects are mainly in the solar PV and wind power sectors.

Global renewable heating and cooling policy overviews

Globally, many countries have developed and enacted new policies to promote renewable heating and cooling growths plus to meet their Paris Agreement commitments. Many governments have applied renewable mandates and incentives to support renewable heating and cooling developments. Policy makers have also used various financial incentives in the form of grants, loans or tax incentives to promote the deployment of renewable heating and cooling applications and technology developments. In addition, some countries have enacted new renewable heating and cooling policies which are designed to promote advanced technological innovations and renewable energy applications.

A good example is that several countries including Bulgaria, Chile, Hungary, Italy, the Netherlands, Portugal, Romania, the Slovak Republic and the USA have enacted new or revised financial support mechanisms for renewable heating and cooling applications. South Africa has undertaken competitive bidding for its long-delayed solar water heater supply, delivery and warehousing tender. Despite these positive developments, the renewable heating and cooling sectors continued to face various policy uncertainties in many countries where more work will be required (REN Global Status Report, 2018).

As in the renewable electricity power sector, many governments have been promoting renewable heating and cooling applications through a mix of government targets, regulatory policies and public financing. Most government supports for the renewable heating and cooling sector have been provided through financial incentives in the form of grants, loans, rebates or tax incentives aiming at increasing deployments. In some cases, these policies have also incentivised further innovations and technological development. Some countries have also adopted regulatory mandates, which often include enactment through building codes or via the inclusion of renewable heating and cooling requirements in their RPS policies.

There has also been application of targeted mechanisms to overcome specific technical barriers to the promotion of renewable heating and cooling in the industrial sector. A good example is the application of specific R&D policies to promote new renewable technological developments to meet various industrial consumer technical standards on temperature, pressure, quantity etc.

Europe has been the largest producer of renewable heat worldwide. The EU had continued to be a global leader in the use of government policies to advance the deployment of renewable heating and cooling technologies. A good example is that the European Parliament had adopted a resolution on renewable heating and cooling following the EU publication of "An EU Strategy on Heating and Cooling." It was designed to promote the adoption of energy efficiency measures and to provide a framework for policy makers to better integrate renewable heating and cooling into their building, industry and electricity sectors. The EU resolution called on EU member states to phase out their older, inefficient, fossil fuel-based boilers. In addition, the EU recommended the adoption of new financing support mechanisms for renewable heating deployments. Two good EU country examples included Bulgaria and Hungary. Bulgaria had re-launched an EU energy efficiency loan scheme, which was supported by the European Bank for Reconstruction and Development. It provided supports to a wide range of efficiency improvements and new solar water heaters. Hungary had also expanded policy supports to its renewable heating and cooling sectors through two rounds of tenders. They offered new preferential loans in support of new municipal renewable heating and cooling projects (EU, An EU Strategy on Heating and Cooling, 2016).

Despite these positive developments, there have been some policy uncertainties in several other countries in Europe. A good example is that the United Kingdom had released plans in early 2016 to remove solar thermal support from its RHI in an effort to "promote value for money." However, it later reversed this action under pressure from various industry groups. In Northern Ireland, the non-domestic RHI was heavily criticised for over-subsidising fossil fuel uses. These led to them being closed to new applications from February 2016 onwards. In Switzerland, there have been delays in its cantons adopting the national building energy regulations which included a 10% renewable requirement for heating system retrofits. In addition, some cantons have been forced to end the Swiss Harmonised Incentive Model, which included incentives of up to 20% for the total investment cost of new solar thermal systems. This was mainly due to competing municipal financial priorities.

Africa has been one of the most active regions globally in new renewable heating policy. South Africa has tendered bids for its solar water heater supply, delivery and warehousing systems. Lesotho, Mozambique and Zimbabwe have continued to develop new policy for renewable heating, following the examples of Namibia and South Africa.

In Asia, India has enacted new loan incentives to help solar process heat developers to finance the upfront costs of solar heating project developments. The new policy builds on an existing 30% subsidy available to developers later in the project development cycle with preferential rates for the deployment of solar thermal systems.

In Americas, the USA has extended its tax credits for solar thermal heating systems through to 2021. The USA had also awarded research grants through its SunShot Initiative to six renewable R&D projects which will investigate ways to reduce the costs of concentrated solar power CSP collectors and the thermal energy they would generate. The new research should increase the attractiveness of renewable process heating in the USA. The federal tax credit for biomass stoves in the United States was allowed to expire at the end of 2016. New York State has extended its Clean Heating Fuel Tax Credit which helped to incentivise the use of biodiesel in heating oil through to 2020. In Latin America, Chile had extended to 2020 its tax credits for commercial solar thermal system installations.

Cities and municipal renewable policy overviews

Globally, the energy consumptions by major cities, in both emerging economies and developed countries, have been rising. An important city energy development is that the share of the world's energy consumption by cities has risen to 65% of the global energy demands recently. This has represented an increase of over 140%, up from their 45% share in 1990. Hence, renewable policy developments by cities and municipalities have major impacts on global renewable developments, especially for the emerging economies.

Globally, many countries have committed to achieve a 100% renewable energy target at a national level. The numbers of major cities around the world committing to 100% renewable energy targets or transitioning to 100% renewable energy in their electricity uses has been continuing to rise. Good examples included the Australian Capital Territory, Calgary in Canada, Tokyo in Japan,

Cape Town in South Africa and New York in the United States. These cities have all established significant and ambitious renewable targets and clean energy transition plans.

Municipal policy makers have been playing increasingly important roles in promoting the use of renewable energy in their cities. In the first place, more and more local policy makers have been setting new targets and enacting new policies to advance renewable applications in their cities. Secondly, the rising city populations and increasing urbanisation have resulted in greater energy demands, especially for renewable energy services in municipalities. Thirdly, many cities have been promoting the use of clean renewable energy through the use of their unique purchasing and regulatory authorities.

Leading cities around the world have been collaborating to achieve their renewable energy and climate mitigation goals. A good example is the C40 Cities initiative which has brought together the leaders of 90 world's largest cities, so they can discuss and launch pathways for cities to meet the goals of the Paris Climate Agreement. The Covenant of Mayors for Climate & Energy has attracted another 600 members in 2016, especially from emerging economies. This has increased the total number of signatories to more than 7,200 communities with a combined population of 225 million citizens around the world, covering both developed countries and emerging economies. Specific cities globally have also committed to increase their energy efficiency and renewable energy deployments so as to reduce their emissions by 40% by 2030. With the cities globally accounting for some 65% of the global energy consumptions, these improvements by the leading cities will have major impacts on global energy improvements and rising renewable deployments.

At the COP22 meeting in Marrakech in late 2016, local and city leaders from 114 countries globally, covering both developed countries and emerging economies, have jointly launched the Marrakech Roadmap for Action. This should help to mobilise the financing needed to make renewable energy infrastructure investments in cities around the world. At COP22, a new Covenant of Mayors in sub-Saharan Africa was launched to catalyse municipal-level action on energy access and climate change mitigation and adaptation in Africa. At the Habitat III conference in late 2016, some countries around the globe adopted the New Urban Agenda. This should help to establish a roadmap for guiding sustainable urban development over the next 20 years. These initiatives have helped cities around the world, especially those in the emerging economies, to develop and adopted their own unique commitments and strategies for renewable energy deployment (UN, COP22 Marrakech Roadmap for Action, 2016).

It should be recognised that each major city around the world has a unique pattern of energy use and residential profile. These will create their own unique challenges and opportunities for the city policy makers. A good example is that major cities such as New York in the United States, London in the United Kingdom and Seoul in the Republic of Korea have been using much of their energy in their buildings and transport sectors. However, other major cities in Asia, including Shanghai in China and Kolkata in India, have large industrial sectors which have been accounting for the majority of their energy uses (REN, Global Status Report, 2018).

Globally, the number of major cities which have committed to transitioning to 100% renewable energy in total energy use or in their electricity sector has continued to grow. Good city examples included the Australian Capital Territory which had set a goal of 100% renewable energy by 2020. In the USA, Boulder in Colorado, Salt Lake City in Utah, St Petersburg in Florida, and San Diego and San Francisco in California have all adopted new city targets to achieve 100% renewable energy. Some leading cities have claimed that they have already achieved their 100% clean renewable energy goals. Good examples included Burlington and Vermont in the USA plus more than 100 communities in Japan.

Some other leading cities globally have also been studying how they can move towards 100% renewable energy. A good example is that Los Angeles, the second largest US city, has directed its municipal utility companies to investigate how they can reduce their fossil fuel consumption and transition onto 100% renewable electricity.

Some leading cities globally have committed to new energy transformation targets with partial renewable energy transitions. Good examples included Tokyo in Japan which has committed to meeting 30% of their future electricity demand with renewables by 2030. In South Africa, Cape Town and the Nelson Mandela Bay Metropolitan Municipality have both set new goals to source up to 20% and 10% of their renewable electricity, respectively, by 2020, so as to increase their clean energy uses and improve energy security.

Some leading cities have established new targets for renewable energy storage. Good examples included New York City, California and Massachusetts in the USA which had established new city targets for renewable energy storage. New York City in the USA had set new renewable targets to have 1 GW of solar power capacity by 2030 and 100 MWh of energy storage by 2020.

A number of cities have established their renewable energy targets through the carbonn Climate Registry (cCR). This is a new global platform which had been designed for cities to publicly and regularly report their climate actions. The cCR had registered over 230 renewable energy city targets including 36 commitments to 100% renewables, from various major cities in developed countries and emerging economies.

Municipal government leaders have various specific powers that they can use to promote renewable energy applications and purchases. Good examples included the specific municipal authorities to set local building codes, mandate the use of solar water heaters, enact new energy efficiency standards and new city regulations plus mandate the collection of energy sector data, improve future city energy plannings, etc.

Many municipal and city agencies have been making use of their purchasing and regulatory authorities to accelerate renewable deployments within their jurisdictions. Government purchasing authorities have the power to procure renewable power and equipment for municipal applications. Good examples included the installation of new solar panels on municipal buildings plus the phased changing out of public transportation bus fleets to clean fuel buses or electric buses in many cities in emerging economies and developed countries globally.

Two good city examples are Santa Monica and San Francisco in the USA. Santa Monica in California, USA had mandated the installation of solar PV roof-top systems for all new buildings. They have also passed a new city regulation which required all new single-family homes to qualify as zero net energy homes. This meant that these new homes should only consume as much energy as they produce, resulting in net energy outputs. San Francisco in the USA had man-dated the use of solar energy, covering both solar PV and solar thermal heating systems, for all new commercial and residential buildings. It had become the largest city in the United States, as well as the first city in California, to institute a municipal mandate on the deployment of solar thermal systems.

Some cities have linked renewable energy to their district heating and cooling networks. A good example is that Oslo in Norway has committed to phasing out fossil fuel heating in homes and offices in favour of renewable heating systems by 2020. New York City in the USA has mandated the blending of biodiesel into heating oil with rising shares to 2034. The shares of biodiesel have increased from 2% in 2016 to 5% by October 2017, and will be required to increase to 10% by 2025 and 20% by 2034. New York City has also, via the NYC Retrofit Accelerator, encouraged fuel switching away from natural gas for heating and hot water generation to favour heat pumps and biofuel applications. In addition, the NYC officials have been providing relevant information to consumers plus providing access to both public and private financing for renewable applications.

In the municipal transport sector, many cities have also been applying their power to accelerate the transition of their transportation systems to clean re-newable low-carbon transportations. A good example is that Oslo in Norway has pledged to power all its public buses with renewable energy by 2020 as part of the city's "climate budget." Reykjavik in Iceland had set a goal to fuel all the public and private vehicles in the city with renewable energy by 2025. Sacra-mento County in California had begun fuelling its liquefied natural gas trucks with biogas. In Mumbai in India, the ethanol import tax was eliminated in an effort to better align with its desires for increased national ethanol use and to reduce environment pollutions in the city.

In the municipal aviation transport sector, there have been various develop-ments in bio-jet fuels. A good example is that Seattle's publicly operated Seattle Tacoma Airport in the USA has become the first airport in the world to provide airport-wide access to bio-jet fuels.

Renewable policy case study: UK clean energy policy and energy transformation

The United Kingdom (UK) has enacted and implemented various new climate change and clean energy policies. These have resulted in significant energy trans-formation in the UK from fossil fuel to clean renewable energy over the last ten years. A good example is that a decade ago, coal-fired power plants have generated almost a third of the UK's electricity. Under various new government energy policies, there have been large reductions in electricity generation by coal in the UK. In the first half of 2019, coal-fired power stations have only provided 3% of UK's electricity requirements. In 2019, the UK also reached a record stretch of consecutive 18 coal-free days which ended on 4 June. These coal-free days in the UK have effectively prevented 5 million tons of carbon dioxide from being emitted into the atmosphere (*Guardian*, UK, June 2019).

Looking ahead, experts have predicted that the UK will be left with only five remaining coal-fired power plants by 2020. These major reductions in coal-fired power plants are in line with the UK government plans to phase out all coal-fired power generation by 2025.

In the same period, clean renewable energy has gone from supplying just 2% of the UK's power to a fifth, about 25%, of all electricity produced. This represented a significant increase, of about ten times growth, for renewable energy applications. The UK National Grid is also spending around £1.3 billion a year (USD1.63 billion/year) to adapt the UK national electricity grid network to accept variable renewable energy electricity supplies from renewable power generators.

Zero-carbon energy sources have been predicted, by energy experts, to overtake fossil fuels as the UK's largest electricity source over a full calendar year. Energy experts have said that 2019 will likely be the first year that fossil fuels would make up less than half of the electricity generated in the UK. This has mainly resulted from a dramatic decline in coal-fired power generation, together with rising renewable and low-carbon energy consumptions.

Looking ahead, UK homes and businesses will be relying more on clean electricity generated by wind farms, solar panels, hydropower and nuclear power reactors in future. So the predicted "landmark energy tipping point" by the end of 2019 will be a particularly important achievement by the UK government new energy policies and energy transition plans for the UK to become a net-zero carbon economy by 2050 (*Guardian*, UK, June 2019).

8 Smart city renewable development management

逆境出人才
Nì jìng chū rén cá
Difficult situations force people to rise to the challenges.
Crisis breeds wisdom.

Executive overviews

Climate change and global warming have posed essential and major challenges to leading cities around the world. Different extreme weather events induced by climate change and global warming have caused serious damages and disruptions to major cities, especially those in emerging economies. These events include hurricanes, typhoons, extreme heat summers, freezing cold winters, extreme heavy downpours, flooding and droughts. In addition, the rising urbanisation, population growths and increasing pollutions have put more pressures on cities globally. As a result, new green smart city designs and transformations, with clean renewable energy applications and energy-efficient green buildings, have been important priorities for leading cities globally. These various new smart city developments with renewable energy integrations will be discussed further in this chapter, together with city examples.

Climate change threats and challenges to global cities

Climate change and global warming have serious implications for all the major cities around the world, especially for those in the emerging economies. Some of most serious negative impacts and damages on leading cities around the world have been caused by the various extreme weather events induced by climate change and global warming. These have included hurricanes, typhoons, extreme heat summers, freezing cold winters, extreme heavy downpours, flooding and droughts. These extreme weather incidents have caused serious damages to various cities across the world with heavy financial cost damages, especially those in emerging economies.

In addition, climate change and global warming have led to rising sea levels globally. Scientists have measured that the average sea levels around the world have risen by about 8 inches or 20 cm in the past 100 years. Looking ahead, climate scientists are expecting sea levels to rise further at faster rates in the next 100 years. These will be driven by climate change and global warming causing the accelerated melting of the polar ice caps and sea warming. Ocean scientists have conservatively estimated that sea levels globally could potentially rise by a further 1–4 feet, or 30–100 cm by 2100. These high sea level rises will be large enough to flood many coastal cities plus various small Pacific island states, such as Vanatu. Examples of cities facing serious flooding risks in developed economies included Boston, New York, Hilton Head, Miami, London, Hong Kong, etc. Major cities in emerging economies facing serious flooding risks include Bangkok, Jakarta, Manila, etc. These cities have all been forecasted to experience much more frequent and serious flooding risks by 2100.

Looking ahead to 2050 and 2100, many coastal and low-lying cities around the world will be seriously affected by rising flooding risks and incidents. These cities will have to invest heavily on various flood defences, such as seawalls and catchment ponds, so as to survive and control these potential serious flooding events.

Major cities around the world are also going green and actively transforming their energy mix as part of their commitments to the Paris Agreement. Many leading cities globally have been transforming their total energy mixes and energy consumptions away from fossil fuels to use more clean renewable energies, such as solar, wind, hydro, bioenergy and geothermal. These clean renewable energy applications will help these cities to better meet their rising future energy requirements generated by their growing populations and economic growths. In addition, these clean energy transformations should help these cities to reduce pollution and greenhouse gas emissions plus minimise their climate change and global warming impacts. Some of the top green cities in the world included Copenhagen in Denmark, Amsterdam in the Netherlands, Stockholm in Sweden, Vancouver in Canada, Curitiba in Brazil, Reykjavik in Iceland, London in the UK and San Francisco in the USA. Looking ahead, experts have forecasted that over 100 cities across the world in both developed countries and emerging economies, ranging from Addis Ababa to Auckland, will be using more than 70% renewables in their future energy mixes (ADB, Green Cities, 2012).

Many governments and cities have recognised the serious threats of climate change and global warming. They have agreed to work together to achieve their Paris Agreement commitments. They have also agreed in the COP24 meeting in 2018 to try to limit their emissions so as to reduce global warming to below 2°C and then further to 1.5°C as proposed in the IPCC 1.5C report. In line with these new global consensus and agreements, many city leaders and municipal governments have been improving their environmental management and setting new firmer emission reduction targets plus enacting new municipal renewable policies.

A good example is that in the USA, some 58 cities and towns, including Atlanta and San Diego, have committed to move to 100% clean energy in future as part of their climate change and clean renewable energy drives. Meanwhile,

Burlington in Vermont has claimed to be the first US city to get its energy from entirely renewable sources. Another good emerging economy example is in Latin America where almost half of Brazil's major cities have been powered entirely by hydropower and clean renewable power sources.

There are large variations in how various cities, in developed countries and emerging economies, are transforming their energy mixes with renewable energy applications. A good example is that most of the 100 leading cities in North America, which have been reporting their energy mixes, have been shown to be using less than 70% clean renewable energy in their city's energy mix. However, some of the leading cities in emerging economies have already been using more than 70% renewable energies in their energy mixes. Another good example is that a majority of Latin American cities, which have been reporting their energy mixes, have reported that they have already passed the 70% threshold and are using more than 70% renewable energy in their energy mixes.

Energy experts analysing these different city energy transformation trends have found that many leading cities in the developing world and emerging economies have been actively supporting their clean energy transformations by capitalising on their local natural resources and maximising renewable energy applications. The pioneering clean energy transformation activities in these major cities in the emerging economies have been largely driven by local economic needs plus the political commitments of their local and national governments.

Climate change and global warming are also imposing serious challenges to the availability of clean renewable energies to different key cities of the world. A good example is that in Latin America the production of green electricity from hydropower has been changing drastically between years due to the extreme droughts being caused by climate change in some key Latin American regions. These serious droughts have seriously affected the functioning of some hydropower plants. Looking ahead, cities in the emerging economies, especially in Latin America, have to further diversify their energy mixes into different clean renewable energy sources, including solar, wind, hydro, geothermal, bioenergy, etc. This should then help to provide more sustainable and continuous clean power generation, which should then help to provide good energy security for their local population whilst maximising renewable applications and minimising environmental pollutions (CDP, Global City Report, 2016).

Smart low-carbon green city global developments

Globally, there has been rising urbanisation in recent years, leading to almost half, about 50%, of the world's population now living in urban cities globally. Looking ahead to 2050, experts have projected that the city populations globally could rise significantly to 75% of total population. These are driven mainly by high rural to urban migrations and high urbanisation rates.

City planners globally have been advocating that it would be important to design and transform current cities to become smarter low-carbon cities with renewable applications and green environment to better accommodate the rising city population, in both the developed countries and emerging economies, on a sustainable basis. It is also important to retrofit and improve older cities so that they can become smart low-carbon cities. The potential key challenges and improvements required for smart low-carbon cities are discussed below (BBC, Future cities, 2013).

Smart city researchers in leading institutes globally have been working together via various international alliances on new smart city designs. A good example is the Imperial College London Digital City Exchange. Its research of leading cities globally has shown that many large cities worldwide will soon be reaching breaking points. The serious problems that many leading cities of the world are facing have included worsening traffic jams, longer queues, delays on public transports, power outages, worsening pollutions, rising congestion and crime levels, etc. In addition, the air qualities and environmental pollutions in many major cities globally are getting to such poor levels which have become hazardous for the health of their populations. These reinforce the essential needs for the major cities in the world to prioritise their efforts to accelerate their clean renewable energy transformation and to achieve the large reductions in GHG emissions to meet their Paris Agreement commitments (Imperial College's Digital Economy Lab, Digital City Exchange, 2019).

There has been widespread recognition internationally that the commitments made by national governments under the Paris Climate Agreement would be very difficult to achieve without concerted action by major cities globally. Many mayors of leading cities around the world have shown strong commitment to tackle climate change and pollution. They have also shown good willingness to collaborate internationally to improve their cities and achieve the strict climate goals. A good example is the new C40 Cities network. This is a global network of the mayors of 40 world's megacities. They have agreed to work together to address the key climate change challenges to cities globally and to meet their Paris Agreement commitments. The C40 City group has published its analysis report titled "Deadline 2020," on the potential emissions-reduction pathways that their cities would need to achieve as part of their contribution to keeping the global average temperature rise within the safe limits of below 1.5°C as advocated in the IPCC 1.5 Report (C40, 2020 City Report, 2018).

Climate experts globally have predicted that whilst the technologies and expertise may exist to limit the potential temperature increase to 1.5°C globally, there are likely to be significant challenges plus high resistance from some governments and corporations. With major cities already stretched to meet multiple competing priorities, the city leaders must determine the critical policies and actions which they will need to take to improve their worsening environment and emission trajectories. They will have to work proactively with their stakeholders and communities to build and invest in the appropriate new smart low-carbon infrastructures. City leaders have to enact suitable municipal policies and incentives to make significant progress towards achieving their green city targets. City leaders will also need to prioritise appropriate climate actions around key initiatives that would catalyse systemic changes. Their key priority actions should include greenification, decarbonisation, building energy efficiencies, waste recycling, energy management improvements, etc. These key areas will be described in more detail in the sections below with relevant examples (Mckinsey, Climate actions in cities to 2030, 2018).

Greenification will be very important for future smart low-carbon city designs and developments. Sustainability experts have predicted that future smart cities would need to transform quickly to become green carbon-neutral cities. The future green carbon neutral cities will need to undertake significant energy transformation by reducing their fossil fuel consumptions and promoting renewable applications. Low-carbon transportation will be an essential part of the future smart cities. These should include electric vehicles, zero-emission vehicles, green public transport, bike-sharing schemes, etc. The future green cities should also include new smart buildings and green skyscrapers where living and office space will be designed together with various green features. These should include solar roofs, urban greenhouses, high-rise vegetable patches, heat pumps, etc. These city greenification improvements should help to reduce greenhouse gas emissions and lower pollution. These should help to improve the city's air quality significantly whilst improving the living standards for the city residents.

Decarbonising the electricity grid and power supplies for cities around the world will also be an important requirement for cities to achieve the new UNIPCC targets. These should include a massive expansion of large-scale renewable power generation and phasing out of fossil fuel power generation. These should help to decarbonise the city electricity grid and power supplies globally. Major cities and their urban residents are normally the key customers for major electric utility and generators globally. This should give them significant leverage to shape and choose the future energy profiles of the electricity that are being generated for their consumption within their metropolitan areas. A good urban example is that some leading utility companies in the UK have already been offering their customers the choice of buying 100% green electricity, generated totally from renewable sources, when they set up their electricity supply contracts to their residential home.

Experts have advised that capturing these city greenification opportunities will not be easy. Municipal city administrations will have to work closely together with various key stakeholders to achieve these goals. Utility companies and regulators will need to play their roles in ensuring that the optimal mix of renewable energy applications should be applied at the city level. In addition, the application of new advanced components, such as energy storage and smart grids, should be encouraged so as to achieve the required electricity grid flexibility and reliability. City leaders and municipal governments will also have essential roles to set clear new decarbonisation and emission goals and targets. These would be key for aggregating energy demands for renewables plus promoting energy efficiency. In addition, municipal city governments should shift more of the future urban energy consumptions into electricity especially in the transportation plus the heating and cooling sectors in their cities. Through focused acceleration, and close collaboration between utilities and regulators, city experts have forecasted that major cities globally should be able to achieve an optimal grid mix of 50–70% of clean renewable electricity. The renewable sources should include solar and wind, together with other zero-emission clean energy generation sources such as hydropower. These future clean renewable energy transformations in cities could help to capture 35–45% of the total emission reductions required by 2030. In addition, the predicted future cost reductions in renewable energy generation should help to maintain electricity costs to as low as $40–80 per megawatt hour for smart cities (IRENA, 2018).

A major area of improvement in smart cities is to improve and optimise the energy efficiency of buildings in the cities. Experts have estimated that for buildings around the world, heating and cooling have accounted for 35–60% of their total energy demands. These heating and cooling energy requirements have also produced nearly 40% of the greenhouse gas emissions from buildings.

Looking ahead, reducing energy uses and emissions from buildings will not be easy. These will require significantly more focused effort than most cities have currently been taking. The improvements should include raising building standards for new construction, retrofitting building envelopes, upgrading HVAC and water-heating technology, implementing lighting, appliance and automation improvements, etc. To realise good progress in these various areas will require city leaders and urban planners to work closely with building owners, both residential and commercial, plus real-estate developers and building occupants. Combined actions by all parties should help to reduce building energy costs as well as providing more resilient, comfortable spaces to live, work and play for future smart city residents through to 2050 and beyond.

Another major area for future smart city improvements will be in the field of transportation and enabling the next generation of smart mobility in cities globally. City leaders have access to a wide range of mobility and transportation options. These include public–private transportation mix, bike-sharing schemes plus hybrid and electric vehicles, etc. City administrations and urban planners should apply appropriate urban mobility and land-use planning to transform the transportation systems around their cities. The key to reducing emissions through various transportation modes will be to ensure that all residents will have access to a variety of attractive, affordable low-carbon mobility options. Public transit-oriented transport developments can help to promote smart densification through better land-use planning. These should also help to lay the foundation for more multi-modal transportation systems and reduced carbon emissions in the long term. Urban initiatives to encourage walking and cycling around cites can help to improve city life and transportation. Targeted enhancement of mass transit, such as the introduction of bus rapid transit (BRT) in main urban arteries, should help to reduce traffic jams plus lower GHG emissions. In addition, cities can accelerate emission reductions by enabling the uptake of the next-generation clean vehicles, including electric vehicles and new energy cars, via appropriate licensing and registration incentives. New autonomous digital technologies can also be used to optimise freight transport and delivery in cities. Experts have forecasted that suitable focused acceleration in appropriate urban transport action areas should contribute to urban emission reductions of 20–45% of the 2030 targets. These emission reductions will be dependent on various factors, including urban income levels and population density. These improvements can also help to promote sustainable city economic developments and GDP growths, by reducing congestion and improving city efficiencies. In addition, these should help to improve the quality of life for residents by alleviating local air pollution and improving equitable access to mobility options in cities.

Future smart cities will also need to tackle waste recycling and emissions in resource-effective ways. Urban planners should adopt a prioritised approach involving the "highest and best use" approach. It would involve first reducing waste upstream and re-purposing as many useful finished recycled products as possible. There should be increased recycling, composting and recovering waste materials for useful purposes. Cities will also need to manage waste disposals to minimise emissions of the remaining organic waste materials. Methane emissions from waste landfill site could potentially have very high impacts on the near-term global warming as methane is a strong GHG. Reducing wastes should help to reduce GHG emissions and improve energy efficiencies. Innovative models for waste management can help cities rethink their need for traditional waste collection and disposal infrastructures.

Some forward-looking cities are already going further and planning their transition to a full "circular economy" model. This will involve shifting resource consumption from linear flows to continuous reuse and recycling. Waste experts have estimated that waste-management improvements could help to achieve up to 10% of the emission reductions needed by 2030. These improvements will also provide additional benefits including improved local resource resilience, waste reductions and improved energy efficiencies.

One innovative urban circular economy development is the integrative use of urban waste recycling and incineration system together with new urban district heating systems. A good example is that the utility company EON in the UK has developed and implemented new district heating systems, which are powered by the urban waste recycling and incineration stations in London, for some new residential developments in Greenwich in London (*Guardian*, London District Heating Systems, 2017).

Asia's smart city developments and challenges

In Asia, the combination of high economic growth rates and rising urbanisation together with the fast-growing urban populations has brought serious environmental challenges to their major cities. Asia is already home to over half, about 53%, of the world's urban population. This is followed by Europe with 14%. Hence, there are particular pressing needs to harness businesses, citizens and policy makers to improve urban planning and the design of future green smart low-carbon cities in Asia.

As more people are moving into Asia's cities to live, work and play, the number of motor vehicles, motorcycles, bikes and trucks have also risen significantly in the cities. These have caused heavy traffic jams and gridlocks in many cities globally. In addition, the running and idling car engines, during traffic jams, would be generating more GHG emissions and causing heavy air pollutions in some of the world's most congested and polluted metropolises.

At the last World City summit, held in 2016 in Singapore, many city mayors and urban leaders have identified transport planning and management as one of the biggest challenges facing cities. Various serious city challenges have also been covered in many future energy scenarios published by energy experts. A good example is the Shell Sky Scenario which covered potential future transport improvement options for key Asian cities. These scenarios have shown that changing and improving the modes of transportation for people and goods in cities could be one of the crucial steps for many cities around the world to meet the goals of the Paris Agreement (World City summit, Innovative Cities of Opportunity, 2016).

Asian cities have many opportunities to be innovative and bold with improving their transportation systems and models. Building new compact low-carbon cities that will efficiently integrate the public and private modes of transport together with key technology innovations will be very important. Looking ahead, electrification is likely to be a very important area for transport improvements and innovations in the smart cities in Asia and globally. The use of electric vehicles has been rising globally but there are still many hurdles, including customer preference, battery life, travel ranges, etc. (Shell, Shell Sky Scenario, 2018).

A good country example is that China has been leading the world in promoting electric vehicles. In Beijing, despite the government cutting EV subsidies by as much as 40% in 2017, the sales of electric vehicles have still been increasing. These have been largely driven by consumer preferences and demands. These rising electrification trends have shown the importance of customer preferences as an important driver for electric car sales. Currently, electric vehicles have made up only 0.3% of China's total vehicle fleets. As China's economy continues to grow, its cities should continue develop fast with high urbanisation rates. These are mainly driven by the continued high migrations from rural to urban districts in China. Currently, over half of China's population is still living in the rural areas. Looking to the future, experts have forecasted that many more in the rural areas will be migrating to nearby cities to seek employment and better lives. Transport experts have also forecasted that the number of electric vehicles in China would likely to continue to rise further. Looking ahead, it is likely that over 25% of China's passenger vehicle kilometres would be driven by electric vehicles in 2040. By 2050, it is expected that half of the cities in the world may be following China's suit with rising numbers of electric vehicles being driven on their city roads (Shell, Shell Sky Scenario, 2018).

In addition, the development and use of hydrogen in future smart green cities are likely to be very important for future green transportation developments in Asia and globally. Hydrogen vehicles do not produce carbon emissions and will be important for future green smart cities to achieve their Paris Agreement commitments. A good example is that Japan has been a leader in hydrogen applications for smart cities. Japan has already released in 2017 a blueprint towards a possible "hydrogen society" by 2040. Cars running on hydrogen do not produce carbon emissions from the tail-pipe. Buses powered by hydrogen fuel-cells have already been running in Tokyo. The Japanese government is planning to use the Tokyo Olympics and Paralympics in 2020 to showcase hydrogen technology in their Olympic athletes' villages. Today, out of Japan's 70 million vehicles, only 2,200 are fuel-cell cars. Looking ahead, the Japanese government is aiming to increase the number to 40,000 by 2021. It is also planning to increase the number of hydrogen-filling stations in Japan from 91 to 160 in the same period (Japan, Blueprint hydrogen society by 2040, 2017).

Looking ahead to 2070, different cities across the world will need to improve their designs and performances, including their transport systems. These will be essential to achieve their net-zero carbon emission targets in line with the latest UN IPCC recommendations and to meet their Paris Agreement commitments. Looking ahead, transportation experts have predicted that over half of the world's total vehicle and freight kilometres could be driven by new electricity or hydrogen vehicles in the green smart cities in Asia and globally in future (Toyota, Sustainability Environment report, 2018).

Smart cities' digital and big data developments

Looking ahead, future green smart cities will have to apply advanced big data systems plus new internet of things (IOT) techniques and digital IT systems to improve their various city operational performances. An important area of digital IT application will be in traffic management systems, as many cities will need to make their traffic systems smarter so as to improve traffic management and reduce traffic jams. A good example will be to use a network of advanced sensors around the smart city which will then provide a host of data about how the city is performing. This will allow different city systems to be linked up and optimised so that they can ultimately all work more efficiently together with advanced digital big data analysis systems.

Many technology companies, including Siemens, IBM, Intel and Cisco, have been working on smart city IT applications plus investigating how best to hook up smart cities into smart networks. A good business example is that IBM currently has 2,000 digital projects ongoing in various cities around the world. Good examples included crime prevention analytic systems in Portland, Oregon and advanced water databases in California. It has also been working on smarter public transport management systems in Zhenjiang in China.

An exciting smart city big data development is that in Rio de Janeiro in Brazil, IBM has built an advanced city operation centre. This has been described as the new digital "nerve centre" of the city. It was built initially to help to deal with the floods that had regularly threatened the city. Further developments have enabled the centre to effectively co-ordinates some 30 different government agencies.

The centre has also generated special mobile apps for the citizens, which will help to keep them updated on potential accidents, traffic black-spots and other essential city updates.

Another good example of smart city big data development is the new City Pulse System. The US Silicon Valley firm Screampoint has developed a new City Pulse System which is a new form of city performance digital dashboard. The new big data system with many smart sensors will take various key digital inputs or pulses of the city from various key data sources or sensors. These would include energy usage, waste management, number of jobs available, etc. Kansas in the USA has already installed one of these new City Pulse Systems. Amsterdam and Barcelona are also considering installing one of these new City Pulse Systems.

Smart cities can also use big data to predict crime and improve security for their residents. A good example is that the security firm AGT has been working with cities around the world to create an overall digital picture of how safe a city is at any given time. These new security systems will use city-wide data and predictive algorithms to generate security updates for residents and communities on the latest city crime and security situations. Then police and communities can use these new systems to help to prevent crime and improve security around the smart city.

Crowd sourcing has also becoming very important consideration for the design of future smart cities. Leading researchers, including those at Columbia University Committee on Global Thought, have advocated that it would be important for city leaders and urban planners to recognise that the behaviour of a future smart city will be driven by the behaviour of its citizens. It is also very important to realise that advanced IT systems will be playing increasingly important roles in the lives of its citizens. Hence, it should be important for various corporates working on smart city designs to undertake adequate consultations with citizens, community groups, stakeholders, city councils, etc. In addition, urban data-collecting schemes and surveys will require the consent of various citizens and stakeholders to make these meaningful (Columbia, Committee on Global Thought, 2019).

A good example is the new IBM water project in Dubuque, Iowa, USA. The company has offered various households in the city access to digital information about their water consumptions. The majority of citizens then quickly changed their habits and saved more water when they were given access to their water use data. Interestingly, the citizens who were also given access to their neighbour's water use information were found to be twice as likely to make changes to save water.

Many leading smart city researchers, including the MIT Sense-able Cities Lab, have highlighted that the powers and opinions of the crowd and communities in future cities would be crucial for the development of smart cities of the future. Experts have predicted that there might be some conflicts of interests in future between what big corporations may want to sell to cities and what the citizens would actually need. Experts have generally forecasted that the power of the crowd and what they want will become more important as cities get smarter. A good example of citizen consultation and crowd sourcing is the Honolulu crowd-sourcing scheme. The city has undertaken survey and collated data from citizen where all the defibrillators should be located in different buildings around the city. This has helped to optimise the defibrillator locations so that these should offer the best immediate help to patients if someone has suffered a heart attack in the city (MIT, Senseable Cities Lab, 2019).

Climate flooding risks and future sponge city developments

Climate change and global warming have led to rising sea levels globally. Looking ahead, climate scientists have predicted that sea levels globally will rise more rapidly in the next 100 years with the melting of the polar ice caps induced by global warming. Ocean scientists globally have estimated that the sea levels could potentially rise by a further 1–4 feet, or 30–100 cm. These high sea level rises could bring serious flooding risks to many major coastal cities globally. There will also be widespread flooding of many small Pacific island states, such as Vanatu.

Hence, many coastal and low-lying cities around the world will have to start to prepare for these rising flooding risks. These cities will have to invest heavily to install the appropriate flood defences, such as seawalls plus catchment ponds, so as to handle and control these expected serious flooding events.

City planning experts have proposed that major cities in future should combat these floods by transforming themselves into "green sponge cities". The general idea is that a modern sponge city can better utilise its wetlands and wet areas, such as marsh, swamps or shallow ponds as well as green spaces and floodplains, to absorb large amounts of water before the flood water would flood and submerge the streets in the city. City planning experts predicted that if cities could reconsider the power of their wetlands and other natural infrastructure, then it would be possible for new sponge city designs to help modern cities to protect themselves better from the growing risks of urban floods caused by climate change and global warming. Good city flooding examples include many cities in Thailand that have suffered flooding regularly during monsoon season. In 2011, Bangkok suffered serious major flooding and it was estimated to have costed damages of some USD41 billion.

In recent years, high economic growths and rising migrations from rural areas have led to rapid population growths in many Thai cities like Udon Thani. The rising urban migration and growths in urban population have contributed to serious changes in urban land use in the city. These urban changes had exacerbated the flooding risks by increasing the area covered in concrete, asphalt and other impervious surfaces. These new expanded impervious surfaces would prevent rainwater seeping into the ground. All these would reduce water runoff leading to excessive water build-ups, which resulted in more frequent flooding in the cities.

A good example is Udon Thani which is one of the major cities in the northeast region of Isan in Thailand. It has been particularly negatively impacted by rising population and flooding incidents. During the Thai monsoon season every year, the city's drainage systems have been seriously overwhelmed. These have resulted in large areas of the city being flooded and inundated. Many homes and buildings were flooded plus many roads became impassable. In addition, there were serious health risks generated by raw sewage mixing with flood waters. All these have led to serious hazards to the city residents plus generated serious damages with high financial penalties.

As Udon Thani has been growing rapidly, the city leaders have to find suitable solutions urgently to alleviate the increased flood risks. So the Udon Thani municipal city government has decided to adopt plans to transform its city into a "green sponge" city. These transformations should help the city to better mitigate flooding by using "natural infrastructure," including wetlands, trees and parks. The Udon Thani Green Infrastructure Master Plan proposed combining natural and built infrastructure systems for the Udon Thani city regions. Landscape architects, engineers and scientists worked together to test the feasibility of natural infrastructure to soak up excess water so as to minimise flooding incidents. They used a hydrological model, in combination with advanced city design and engineering tools. They managed to design a natural infrastructure network which would link up various green areas across the city. Their computer simulation work shows that these wetlands and green areas would help to buffer water flows. These should then help to reduce flooding by slowing water flows during storms with increased infiltration. In essence, these would act like sponges to soak up water in the city to minimise the risk of a serious flood in the city. As part of its new plans, Udon Thani has been working to protect the existing wetlands, but also to restore lost and create new wetlands, along with other natural infrastructure. These will all contribute to the overall aim of protecting the city from future flooding. In addition, these will help to provide additional benefits for the citizens, such as more green and recreational spaces in the city. There are plans for a new park on a canal in Udon Thani which will create a new wetland in the city. This will help to slow the speed of water during storms plus increase infiltration during both dry and monsoon seasons (Cgiar, Fighting Floods by Sponge Cities, 2018).

The new green sponge city concepts have shown that careful city planning using wetlands and other natural infrastructure to create a new green sponge city is important. These should help to create greener, healthier and less flood-prone cities for the future.

These new sponge city concepts are now being adopted by more leading cities in Asia and around the world. Research in Asia by the International Water Management Institute (IWMI) has also highlighted the value of urban wetlands in India both for the urban poor and for flood minimisation. A good example is that the wetlands within the city of Hyderabad in India have supported the growing of rice, vegetables and cattle fodder that have been sold in the city markets. These have been a major contribution to the livelihoods of many subsistence farmers in the cities plus helping to reduce flooding risks in the city. Similarly in India's northeast, the wetlands of Kolkata have not only helped to reduce flooding in the city, but also helped to support 32,000 residents who are fishing for a living. In addition, these have helped to treat the city's rising sewage outfalls.

Both cities have also been working to control the haphazard urban sprawl that has caused degradation and minimise the loss of their valuable wetlands. In Kolkata, the loss was particularly serious at up to 50% between 2000 and 2012. These have posed serious threats to the poorest residents who have also been most dependent on the benefits that the wetlands would provide. These wetland degradations in Kolkata have also seriously increased the flooding risks in the city.

The Sri Lankan government has also recognised the vital benefits of urban wetlands and sponge city. It is working hard to conserve and enhance its wetland potentials, including flooding mitigations. Colombo is aiming to be one of the first official "Wetland Cities" with the new sponge city concept, which is accredited by the Ramsar Convention. City planners have forecasted that these new sponge city transformations will not only improve flood protection, but also help to create more competitive and liveable international cities in future.

The UN has also just announced its plans to develop new floating cities as an innovative approach for future urban design to combat climate change and global warming. The UN-Habitat team has just announced its new partnership with the Massachusetts Institute of Technology Center for Ocean Engineering, The Explorers Club and the floating cities non-profit group Oceanix to jointly develop designs for new floating cities. They have just started work and have forecasted that their new designs should benefit existing cities in their fight against climate change and global warming (UN, Floating City to fight Climate Change, 2019).

Smart low-carbon green city economic benefits

There have been many questions on what are the potential economic benefits and payoffs for green smart low-carbon city developments. Many stakeholders have questioned what are the major economic benefits to cities and urban residents from the push by many cities in their transformation to become smart low-carbon green cities. We shall analyse the transformations undertaken by some of the leading cities around the world and discuss various major benefits below.

A good smart city benefits' case study example is Copenhagen in Denmark. The impetus for Copenhagen's climate plan and drive for carbon neutrality started when Copenhagen hosted the COP15 global climate conference in 2009. The Copenhagen city leaders believed that they should walk the walk and talk the talk, plus set an example for other cities. There have been lots of obstacles and challenges plus setbacks during their transformation journey. Copenhagen is now well on its way of becoming carbon neutral by 2025.

Copenhagen has been undertaking extensive clean energy transformation, by reducing its fossil fuel consumption and promoting clean renewable energy applications, as part of their transformation plans. These have helped to create new jobs, new economic activities and new businesses in the city. The city government of Copenhagen has been moving rapidly towards meeting the goals of its 2025 Climate Plan to become the world's first carbon-neutral city by 2025. It has been working hard to reduce and offset carbon emissions with extensive clean energy transformations. Copenhagen city officials have reported that the same policies that have protect the city's environment have also helped to improve sustainable economic developments and global competitiveness in the Denmark capital city. By focusing on reducing carbon emissions and becoming more sustainable, the city is helping to enhance their citizens' health, well-being and comfort, plus also improving their economies and employment (Berger, Copenhagen: Economic Payoffs, 2017).

Economists have estimated that each time Copenhagen spends \$1 on its climate plan, it would help to generate \$85 in private investment elsewhere in the city. Economic studies have shown that the Copenhagen climate plans and actions would be generating an economic surplus of almost \$1 billion over its lifetime which is a very significant economic benefit. In addition, there are significant additional intangible benefits which include improving living standards, better environment, improved air qualities, etc.

In line with the Copenhagen 2025 Climate Plan, the city government is aiming to reduce Copenhagen's carbon emissions by 37% with new energy policies and targets. After that, the city will purchase additional carbon offsets via the Carbon Emission Trading Schemes CETS so as to achieve the remaining 63% of carbon reductions that would be required to become carbon neutral. It is recognised that although the purchased carbon offsets will, in principle, result in zero-net carbon emissions, the local effects of residual carbon emissions would still be felt.

Copenhagen has succeeded in reducing its carbon emissions by more than 40% since 1990. This is despite the fact that its population have grown by over 50% in the equivalent period. The city is now home to nearly 600,000 people, with greater Copenhagen comprising two million people. As the city's population increased between 2005 and 2014, its economy also grew by 18%. In contrast, its per capita CO_2 production fell by 31%. These reductions have been achieved mainly due to the city's massive climate protection efforts. The city has managed to hold onto its various climate change improvements and gains. The residents of Copenhagen have become the Danes that are producing proportionately less carbon than other Danes elsewhere in Denmark. With 40% of Denmark's population living in greater Copenhagen, the city is only emitting 30% or a per capita emission of 2.5 tons per person, of the whole nation's carbon emissions.

These notable accomplishments in carbon emission reductions have been achieved by various hard works. Copenhagen has been transforming its private and public transport systems. It has been encouraging its residents to use low-carbon transport. This has led to about 45% of all road trips now being made by bicycle. Over 75% of the cyclists have also been riding their cycles all year-round despite the cold winters. The city has put in place a good bike-sharing system with dedicated bike lanes plus cycle routes where cyclists could travel safely at designated speeds.

The city government has also increased the proportion of its cars running on electricity, biofuels or hydrogen to 64%. The city has established the goal of having all city vehicles converted to run on clean renewable energy by 2025. It has also been implementing carbon-neutral bus service to replace its existing bus fleet which have been running on diesel.

Copenhagen has also been improving its energy efficiencies with major investments. Energy-efficient district heating systems have been used to heat approximately 98% of the city. All the heating in the city is planned to be done by energy-efficient district heating systems by 2025. Architects have predicted that there would be no chimneys on the roofs of house in Copenhagen as there would be no individual heating in the houses or flats in Copenhagen in future.

The improvements in energy efficiency in Copenhagen have resulted in significant savings to consumers and businesses in the city. The adoption of innovative energy efficiency technologies has helped to bring new green products and technologies to the market. The energy efficiency improvements have also helped to lower production costs which have made the city's economy more competitive.

Copenhagen city government has also developed specific new investment strategy for its low-carbon transformations. To reduce the emissions from its district heating systems, Copenhagen has been producing heat from recycled municipal wastes. It is building a biomass-fuelled power plant named BIO4 at Amagerværket to replace a 600-MW coal power plant. The new waste to power plant is scheduled to be ready by 2020. The new electricity generation plant has been designed to reduce CO_2 emissions by a big 1.2 million tons per year.

Copenhagen's clean energy transformation and smart city transition have demonstrated that these can help to reduce GHG emissions plus generating significant economic benefits. Copenhagen city leaders have said that it has not been expensive for Copenhagen to go green. In addition, it has helped to generate better environment and created new low-carbon employment for the city residents. City officials have reported that going green has been very good for the local economy and has helped to create more new local jobs for the residents. It has also helped to create a more vibrant city which is more liveable for its residents. These are key components for a world-class competitive smart low-carbon city which is a good role model for other major cities globally.

Smart city, clean energy and smart grid developments

Major cities around the world have been transforming their energy mix by reducing their use of fossil fuels and promoting clean renewable energy applications, including solar, wind, hydro, bioenergy and geothermal. These fossil to clean energy transformations should help these cities to better meet their rising energy requirements as well as reducing pollutions and CO_2 emissions. Some leading cities have also committed to move to 100% clean energy in future as part of their Climate Action Plan. A good example is Copenhagen in Denmark which has committed to become carbon neutral by 2030, which we have discussed earlier in the smart city benefits' case study, in this chapter.

Many major cities in the developed countries and emerging economies have been actively supporting their fossil to clean energy transformations. These transformations have largely been driven by local economic needs and the political commitments of the local and national governments. The clean energy transitions should help them to capitalise on their available local natural resources plus maximise the use of available clean renewable energies whilst minimising the import of expensive fossil fuels, such as crude or natural gas.

Decarbonising the electricity power generation and electricity supply grid of major cities around the world is an important requirement for these cities to achieve their clean energy transformation and achieve the UNIPCC targets. Power generators, utility suppliers, regulators and grid companies have to work together to ensure that the overall mix of clean energy should be appropriately balanced together with reliable supply security to all the customers in their cities. In addition, critical components such as energy storage and smart grids should be in place to ensure grid reliability and efficiency.

A good example is that in the UK the electricity and energy systems in the major cities have been changing to maximise economic benefits for businesses and households. Over a quarter of the UK's electricity is now being generated by renewables, including wind, solar and waste. New energy storage technologies are being applied. The costs for future advanced energy storage systems have started to decline significantly with technological innovations and cost reduction measures.

In 2017, UK Government Ministry BEIS and Ofgem have put forward new plans to upgrade the UK smart grid and clean renewable energy systems so that consumers in its major cities will have more control over their energy uses using innovative new technologies. The UK government has also launched its £246 million Faraday Challenge to boost technological innovation and developments of new battery and energy storage technologies. These should help to develop a smarter, more flexible energy system with new smart green battery and energy storage technologies (UK BEIS, Smart City & Grid Report, 2017).

There has also been good international co-operation on new smart materials and clean battery research and innovations. A good example is that the UK and China have been cooperating on new battery and new material research works particularly on graphene. Graphene is seen by many researchers as one of the world's thinnest, strongest and most conductive material. Scientists have been forecasting that graphene could revolutionise aircraft and car designs, plus create new battery and new material applications. Graphene was first isolated from graphite mineral by Andre Geim and Kostya Novoselov at the University of Manchester in 2004. They were awarded the Nobel Prize for Physics in 2010. China has included graphene as one of the strategically important new material in its 13th Five-Year Plan (2016–2020). A new five-year UK-China research programme between China's Beijing Institute of Aeronautical Materials (BIAM) and the National Graphene Institute (NGI) at the University of Manchester, UK has been established. The research co-operation agreement was signed during a special visit by PRC President Xi Jinping to the NGI at Manchester during his state visit to the UK. The key objectives of the joint research are to develop new graphene-based polymers which can be used in a variety of applications, including new battery, new aircraft plus high-speed trains and vehicles. It is expected that the new graphene material will contribute to light weighing of new auto vehicles, i.e. making them lighter in weight and thereby improving their fuel efficiencies. In addition, the material will improve robustness and performance. In particular, the researchers will be focusing on developing new graphene-based composites with enhanced mechanical and conducting properties, together with improved electrical and thermal conductivities. These new materials will be very important for new applications in new smart grids, new EV charging stations, and new battery and new energy storage system designs.

China's smart city and clean energy development case study

The People's Republic of China (PRC) economy has been growing fast in the last few decades. These high economic growths have also generated some serious problems including pollution, climate change and environmental damages. China has been changing its economic growth model and its policy focuses on its latest 13th Five-Year National Plan. In the past, China has primarily focused on economic growths and GDP rises. However now, China is more focused on climate change and green economy plus green developments. This is a big policy shift and has major implications both nationally and globally. A good example is that the PRC Central and local government officials have now to perform well on environmental protection and climate change, as well as on economic developments.

China's future development strategy is closely linked with climate change, environmental improvements and green developments. The Chinese government has elevated climate change and sustainable economic developments to be key national strategies in their 13th Five-Year Plan. The Chinese government has also started to implement its new national environmental concept of "ecological civilisation." There is a famous motto by Chairman Xi Jinping who has said: "The Green Mountains and Green Rivers are as valuable as Mountains of Gold and Rivers of Silk." In China, it is common to describe healthy rivers and water in shades of green.

The PRC government's National Energy Agency (NEA) has also announced that China is planning to invest 2.5 trillion yuan or over USD360 billion into China's renewable energy sector. It has also announced that China, which is now the world's largest energy market, will continue to shift away from coal power generation towards cleaner fuels and renewable power generation.

The PRC government's National Development & Reform Commission (NDRC) has also predicted that these clean renewable energy and low-carbon economy investments in China will help to create more than 13 million new jobs in China. It has also forecasted that the total installed renewable power generation capacities in China, compromising of wind, hydro, solar and nuclear power together, should be contributing to about half of the new electricity generation capacities in China by 2020–2030.

The NDRC has also announced that the solar power sector in China will be receiving some one trillion yuan or over USD140 billion of new investment. Looking ahead, China is planning to increase its solar power capacity by five times. This is estimated to be equivalent to adding about 1,000 new major solar power plants across China. In addition, new investments of some 700 billion yuan or USD100 billion are planned to go into new wind farms across China. New investments of another 500 billion yuan or over USD70 billion are planned to go into new hydropower stations across China. New investments by China into new tidal and geothermal power generations are also being planned.

There is also growing international co-operation in renewable and clean energy by leading international clean renewable energy companies with leading Chinese energy companies. A good example is that the Asian Development Bank (ADB) has recently signed a loan agreement to provide a loan facility of $250 million to a new Icelandic-Chinese Joint Venture. The joint venture partners are Arctic Green Energy Corporation (AGE) and Sinopec Green Energy Geothermal Company Limited (SGE). They will both be working together to expand geothermal district heating systems in China. These will replace coal-based district heating systems which have been one of the major causes of air pollution in the PRC, particularly in the Beijing-Tianjin-Hebei region. The funding from the ADB will enable AGE and SGE to significantly expand their operations to support the smart cities in the PRC to improve their environment plus reduce pollution, whilst providing much needed clean district heating to key smart cities in the PRC.

AGE is based in Iceland and is a leading global developer and operator of renewables, including geothermal technology and energy efficiency projects. SGE was established in 2006 and is the world's largest geothermal district heating company in terms of service area. The new joint venture between AGE and Sinopec Star of the Sinopec Group should provide good synergies in both advanced technology transfer and new market developments plus support smart city developments in the PRC and globally.

There are also important smart city transformation plans and developments being implemented for key economic regions in the PRC. China has some of the largest cities in the world. Good examples include Beijing with an urban population of 25 million and Shanghai with an urban population of 34 million. These have made them two of the largest cities in China and amongst some of the largest cities globally. The urban population in China is currently representing 57% of the total population of 1.38 billion. Looking ahead to 2020–2025, it is expected that rising urban migration should increase the urban population in China to about 60% by 2020–2025. It is estimated that around 250 million Chinese farmers and peasants will be moving from rural regions to urban cities as part of their move to become seasonal migrant workers in the big cities and to seek employments.

Putting this PRC rural urban migration into the global perspective, the Global Commission on the Economy and Climate has forecasted in its recent report that more than two billion extra people are expected to be moving into different cities globally in the coming decades (Global Commission on the Economy and Climate Report, 2018).

China is also in a period of transition with new urban smart cities being planned and implemented. A good example is Xiongan which is a new state-level special economic area in the Baoding area of Hebei, China. It is situated about 100 km southwest of Beijing and active urban developments are ongoing. Xiongan is part of the new green low-carbon smart city development master plan for the Greater Beijing region in China. Xiongan represents a fundamental change in China's national strategy and its long-term city planning strategy. It will share some functions with the capital but it will also take over some tasks from Beijing. A lot of non-core capital and municipal government functions and administrations in Beijing will be moved out to Xiongan. A good example is that Peking University has planned to invest and move some of their research functions from Beijing to Xiongan. The main functions of Xiongan will be to serve as the new development hub for the Beijing-Tianjin-Hebei economic triangle. The implementation of this new smart city project will include significant green sustainable developments. A good example is that the central government of the PRC has forbidden some polluting industries from entering the new area. In addition, some real estate development projects have been stopped until the detailed planning and reviews are finalised and approved by relevant government agencies. Xiongan will also include new smart city designs with advanced modern technologies including smart highways, subways, green buildings and green transportation (Xinhua, Xiongan New Area in Hebei, Beijing, 2017).

There are also ongoing good international exchanges and co-operations between some key Chinese city mayors with other international city mayors plus urban designers. A good example is that the British Town and Country Planning Association (TCPA) experts have been discussing with China city mayors and urban designers about new low-carbon smart city designs. They have been exchanging views and learnings on various new potential city and urban designs with low-carbon buildings and smart public transport systems. These international exchanges and co-operations should help China's major cities in their smart city transformations plus ease their severe traffic jams and improve air qualities. The clean energy transformations in the key Chinese smart cities should also help to reduce pollution and carbon emissions (Wang, Sino-British Summit Paper, 2017).

The PRC government has been supporting electric vehicle and new energy car developments and deployment in various cities of the country. The PRC government has extended its China New Energy Vehicle Program to 2020.

In June 2012, the PRC government first issued its New Energy Car Program to support the domestic electric car and new energy vehicle industries. Its programme had set a sales target of 500,000 new energy vehicles by 2015 which would then rise to five million by 2020. In September 2013, the PRC government introduced a New Energy Car Subsidy Scheme which provided a maximum subsidy of USD9,800 towards the purchase of a new electric passenger vehicle in China, and up to USD81,600 for a new electric bus in China.

The PRC government's support for New Energy Vehicles should help to create a new world-class new energy and electric car industry in China that would help to create new jobs and exports. A good example is that the Chinese new energy and electric car company, BYD Auto, has overtaken both Mitsubishi Motors and Tesla Motors to become the world's second largest plug-in electric passenger car manufacturer, after Renault-Nissan. In addition, these new electric cars should help to reduce China's fossil oil consumptions and lower the fossil imports. New electric cars will also help to reduce air pollution and GHG emissions in China.

China currently already has the world's largest fleet of light-duty plug-in electric vehicles. China has also overtaken both the USA and Europe in the cumulative sales of electric vehicles. In 2015, China was the world's largest plug-in electric car market, with a record annual sales of more than 207,000 plug-in electric passenger cars which represented over 34% of global sales. China has also become the world's largest electric bus market with over 173,000 plug-in electric buses. Looking ahead, China is expected to account for more than 50% of the global electric bus market by 2025. These rising number of electric vehicles in China should reduce GHG emissions in various cities and help to meet China's Paris Agreement commitments.

9 Renewable finance and investment management

国以民为本
Guó yǐ mín wéi běn
The foundation of a country is made up by its people.
People are a country's roots.

Executive summary

Globally, there are essential needs to control climate changes and manage climate risks. Climate finance and green renewable investments have been growing in recent years. Economists have estimated that renewable investments have exceeded USD1 trillion. Looking ahead, renewable investments have been forecast to grow at about USD200 billion per annum. These should help to improve sustainability and environments globally. Climate change risks could seriously undermine the financial performances and the bottom lines of leading banks and companies globally. New climate risk financial disclosure and governance requirements are being introduced by various key governments and stock markets globally. These would compel all the leading banks and companies internationally to improve their corporate governance and financial reporting. Details of these will be discussed in more detail in this chapter together with international examples.

Renewable finance and investment management

Globally, the green finance and renewable investment sectors have been fast-growing sectors in recent years but probably it is still not fast enough. Global investments in renewable power and clean fuels have been growing strongly in the last decade. These have exceeded USD200 billion per year for the past seven years. A good example is that in 2016 the total new investment in renewable power was over USD260 billion. The green bond market globally has grown to USD155.5 billion. However, this was still only about 2% of all USD6.7 trillion of bonds issued globally in 2017. So there will be much room for further green investment and green bond developments.

Despite these rising investments, the global renewable energy investments are still much lower than, at about one-third, the global fossil energy investments. A good example is that in 2016 over USD530 billion has been invested in various fossil fuel and energy projects globally. This was made up by some USD87 billion lent by the world's 37 top banks for fossil fuel extraction plus some USD437 billion of fossil fuel investments by various oil and gas companies globally. These fossil investments were about two to three times of the clean renewable energy investments.

The current large financing and investment gaps between clean energies and fossil investments have posed major challenges internationally. Looking ahead, these big investment gaps could also help to create significant new investment opportunities. These could lead to bigger future new sustainable green investments as well as growths in many new jobs in green finance and clean technologies globally. However, there are still quite some challenges and hurdles to overcome to fully realise these green finance and renewable investment growth potentials.

Looking ahead, leading climate agencies globally have forecasted that over USD90 trillion of new green investments will be required from now to 2030 to achieve the aspired global new improved sustainable development and climate objectives. These new renewable investments and green finances will have to come from both public and private sources. Economists have generally forecasted that governments will only provide a small amount of public seed investments to kick-start these renewable investment growths. The bulk of the new green finance and renewable investments will have to come from private and corporate sources globally.

A good example is that in the UK the Committee on Climate Change (CCC) has estimated that the total investment required to meet the UK's fifth carbon budget will be some £22 billion per year, which would represent about 1% of the future UK GDP. These would likely involve a public investment of £2.2 billion which is about 0.1% of GDP annually. The remaining investments will have to be funded by the private and corporate sectors in the UK (New Climate Economy Report, 2014).

Many developing economies, particularly China and India, have been growing fast. These developing economies have also huge future potential demands for green finance and new climate investments. These should generate further new international requirements for green finance expertise plus new international trade opportunities.

A good example is that in China the PRC government has announced its new "ecological civilisation" national green transformation programme in its 13th Five-Year National Plan. This would require new renewable investments and green finance of between USD470 billion and USD630 billion, in the period from now to 2030. It is expected that the PRC government will only provide some 15% of green seed public funding. The private and corporate sectors in China will have to generate at least 85% of the required future renewable investments and green financing.

Sustainable renewable investment growth management

Global investments in renewable power and clean fuels have been growing strongly in recent years. These have exceeded investments of USD200 billion per year for the past seven years. In 2016, the total new investment in renewable power and fuels was over USD260 billion. It is also worth noting that for the fifth consecutive year, total investments in new renewable electricity power generation capacities globally have been roughly twice those in fossil fuel electricity power generating capacities internationally (REN, Renewables Global Status Report, 2018).

Global investments in clean renewable energy have been focusing on solar power, followed closely by wind power. Asset finance of utility projects, such as wind farms and solar parks, has dominated global clean energy investments during 2016, with over USD187 billion. In 2017, the new clean investments have continued to be dominated by both solar and wind renewable projects. Each of these class of renewable investments accounted for roughly 47% of total global renewable investments. Solar power investments were over USD113 billion and wind power project investments were over USD112 billion. There have also been significant reductions in clean renewable energy costs with new technological innovations in recent years. These have helped to made renewable generation costs more cost competitive against fossil fuel options.

Internationally, the clean renewable electricity power generation sector has continued to attract far more clean investments than for fossil power or nuclear power generating plants. In 2016, it has been calculated that clean investments of nearly USD250 billion have been committed to construct new renewable power generation plants globally. These investments were about twice of USD134 billion of committed investments in new fossil and nuclear power generating facilities. These included some USD114 billion of investment in new fossil fuel-fired generating capacities and USD30 billion in new nuclear power capacities. Overall, clean renewable power generation has been accounting for over 63% of total new power generating capacity investments in 2016 globally.

Globally, renewable energy investments in developing and emerging economies have overtaken those in developed countries for the first time in 2015. In 2016, clean investments in developed countries retook their lead over developing countries. These were mainly due to new clean renewable energy policy drives introduced by various developed countries, as part of their Paris Agreement commitments. The clean investment trends in renewable energy globally have been varying widely by regions. Clean investments have generally increased in Europe and Australia whilst investments in India were stable. However, clean investments have declined in China, the USA, the Middle East, Africa, Asia-Oceania (except Australia) and Latin America.

China has been leading the global clean renewable energy investments with about one-third, around 32%, of global investments. Europe was second with 25% of global investments, the United States was third with 19% and Asia-Oceania was fourth with 11%. The Americas, Brazil and the Middle East and Africa region each accounted for 3% of the global clean renewable energy investments.

Globally, the top ten countries in clean investments included three emerging economies and seven developed countries. The top five countries included China, the United States, the United Kingdom, Japan and Germany. The next five countries included India, Brazil, Australia, Belgium and France.

However, there have also been significant rises in renewable investments in some specific individual countries globally. A good example is Singapore which increased its renewable investments by 14-fold to USD700 million. Vietnam also increased its renewable investments by over 140%, to USD700 million. Indonesia also increased its renewable investments by just below 85%, to USD500 million. Mongolia has increased its renewable investments to USD200 million in 2016 from having no renewable energy investment in 2015. Thailand has increased its renewable investments by 4% to USD1.4 billion. These new renewable investments have made Thailand the third largest country in renewable investments in the Asian region, after China and India.

Renewable finance and investment source management

The growing global clean renewable energy investments and green finances have been provided by a variety of green financial instruments. Debt financing has been making up the majority of clean investments going into many new utility-scale renewable energy projects. These included non-recourse loans, bonds or leasing for different renewable projects. At the corporate level, there have been various debt borrowings by different utility or project developers. Commercial banks have generally provided most of the project-level debt financing for renewable energy projects globally.

In addition to commercial banks and bond issues, other major sources of debt for renewable power assets have been borrowings directly from different national and multilateral development banks globally. Development banks have been providing major financing to renewable projects globally. Good international examples included Germany's KfW which provided USD39 billion for environmental and climate financings. These included USD8 billion for renewable energy and USD23.5 billion for energy efficiency. The Asian Development Bank (ADB) had also provided USD3.7 billion for climate finance investments to support new clean renewable investments in developing member countries (REN, Renewables Global Status Report, 2018).

Green bonds have been an important asset class for clean energy investors around the world. These included various qualifying debt securities issued by development banks, central and local governments, commercial banks, public sector agencies and corporations, asset-backed securities, green mortgage-backed securities, project bonds, etc. In 2016, the green bonds issuance globally almost doubled to USD95 billion. These included the first sovereign green bond which was issued by Poland. Amongst the G7 countries, France has issued the highest number of green bonds, with USD33.7 billion of labelled green bonds which were tracked by the Climate Bonds Initiative since 2009. China has also increased its green bond issuance to USD27.1 billion and overtook the USA with

USD15.5 billion. Germany was at fourth place globally with USD13.6 billion of green bonds issued. The United Kingdom (UK) has been the world leader in structuring, underwriting and listing of international green bonds. However, there is more to do in terms of domestic pound sterling green bond issuance.

Institutional investors such as insurance companies and pension funds have tended to be more risk-averse investors in renewables. They have been more interested in more predictable cash flows of renewable projects that have already been in operation. In Europe, direct investments by institutional investors in clean renewable energy totalled USD2.8 billion in 2016. This represented a big growth, about ten times, of initial renewable investments of USD0.3 billion in 2010.

Electric utilities have continued to be an important source of on-balance-sheet financing and project-level equity financing for renewable projects. A good example is that nine of the largest European utilities have invested a total of USD11.5 billion in new clean renewable energy projects in 2015.

Renewable finance and investment challenges

The growth of green finance and new climate investments has been varying greatly between different countries globally. Despite the overall growth of the green finance sector globally and increasing deployment of low-carbon technologies, the equity finance and transactions for clean technology companies have recorded falls in recent years.

A good example is that the equity finance transactions for cleantech companies have been falling in the UK in recent years. The annual total values of renewable deals in the UK have halved over the last four years. This contrasted markedly with the overall venture capital market megatrend, where investments have increased by more than 50% in the UK between 2014 and 2016 (UK GFT, Green Finance Report, 2017).

The key reason for these disparities was that there have been few green financiers and funders who have been willing to take the significant early-stage risks in cleantech and climate start-ups. This has led to many pioneering low-carbon technology start-ups struggling to attract the initial investment capital required for them to grow and to scale up to the commercialisation stage. There are several serious concerning factors weighing down on the sector and holding back its ability to grow. A major concern has been that there has been low appetite to invest in start-ups with long lead times to commercial development. In many instances, these long lead times have been unavoidable due to long R&D periods. Normally, cleantech start-ups will require longer timescales, and in many cases more upfront capital, to scale up to commercialisation compared to digital technology companies. An example is that the first-investment-to-exit journey time for a renewable hardware start-up could take more than ten years. These long timescales have meant that early equity investment rounds have been typically unattractive and unsuitable for many closed-end financially motivated funds. These funds would typically have a ten-year duration which is common in the UK and other financial hubs.

By contrast, the growths in green venture capital (VC) funds have been stronger. These new green VC funds have been primarily driven by longer-term strategic motivations of their financial backers and ethnical investors. They have also been facing some issues. One critical issue was that the knowledge spill-over market failures have reduced commercial competitiveness. New low-carbon start-ups have to struggle hard to acquire the necessary new skills, knowledge and technology which could help these start-ups to deliver the returns necessary to justify venture equity investments. There has also been serious competition from fast followers who have benefited from spill-over knowledge generated by the innovators and pioneers. A good example of green VC growth is that a lot of green finance and climate investments in Europe and the EU have been generated by different corporate venture capital (CVC) setups by ethnical investors or impact investment funds (EU, Framework for State aid, 2014).

The longer time frames required for cleantech and renewable developments have caused serious concerns and challenges for investors. The vulnerability to knowledge spill-over has also been high thereby increasing the risk and reducing appetite for investment. The start-stop nature of some government grant funding for early-stage R&D could increase the risk of the technology incubation stage and lengthen the prototype development process. As these cleantech companies mature, the absence of a liquid secondary market has disincentivised VCs looking to move their capital into the next suitable opportunity. Private equity or institutional investors have also significantly different time horizons to venture capitalists. These differences have made it more difficult for VCs to exit and monetise their green investments. The situation has also been further compounded by the need for patient capital in new physical technology investments. These have then in turn lengthened and complicated the buy-out due diligence process.

There have also been some specific risks which are particularly acute for some countries. A good example is the UK with its Brexit. If and when the UK completes Brexit and leaves the EU, then it would no longer have access to the European Investment Fund (EIF). This might create a substantial gap in limited partner (LP) funding. Historically, the EIF has been a cornerstone investor in various UK VC funds. The EIF has invested over £500 million across the UK, of which £100 million has been in cleantech. It would be important for the UK to ensure that there would be sufficient new sources of green finance funding to replace those from the EIF, if and when it completes Brexit. It is of paramount importance to ensure the health of the venture capital (VC) ecosystem in the UK. Whilst there is a strong case for government funding support, it must be delivered in a way that would offer clarity and reassurance throughout the process (UK GFI Report, 2017).

These financing challenges and headwinds are likely to seriously affect the growth and development of some countries into low-carbon economies and cleantech hubs. A key reason is that the private sector response alone, with all these issues, would be very unlikely to generate sufficient investments for some countries to become world-class centres for cleantech venture capital. A lack of funders willing to take early-stage risks has knock-on effects for later-stage VC and growth capital investors. The lack of seed funding and Series A funding from institutional investors would lead to high failure rates for early-stage businesses and therefore a smaller pipeline of later stage deals. Hence, different governments should seriously consider these serious challenges so they can develop suitable policy supports and financial incentives to support cleantech developments at different stages of their value chains.

One potential policy support option is for governments to consider setting up a Green Investment Accelerator (GIA) for early-stage green climate technology grant funding. There have been similar accelerators which have worked well for the health, life sciences and infrastructure system sectors. Governments should consider new incubators with comparable mechanisms to focus on supporting early-stage cleantech and climate technology developments. These GIA should have multi-year, multi-call schemes to provide fast-track grants for early-stage cleantech start-ups. These companies could receive new VC funding from suitable pre-qualified institutions with a good green VC track record. These would provide financial support to small businesses at all stages of their development. These should then help to develop a thriving ecosystem, with coordinated government and investor support. These schemes would also need multi-year commitments, with regular calls for applications announced well in advance. These could be complemented by public funding bodies such as Research Councils or Research Institutes, which have clean growths and clean renewable energy development objectives in their core programmes.

A good example is that the UK has already set up a successful Innovate UK Investment Accelerator pilot in health, life sciences and infrastructure systems. The UK has been considering setting up a comparable mechanism to support early-stage cleantech and climate technology start-ups. This could be complemented by funding from the Research Councils UK which has clean growth objectives in the core programmes.

Another interesting support option is that governments should consider establishing a dedicated public–private green venture capital fund. Governments should set up a new green VC fund to leverage their public seed grants and to raise further capital from the private sector. The new green VC fund should focus on backing early-stage cleantech companies and SMEs in their initial growths and expansions. These would also encourage more green capital to flow into the early-stage green investment market. These should then help to support more and larger green finance and investment deals.

Governments should also consider alternative delivery options which could include Co-Investment Fund (CIF). These will be new equity funds matching up to 50% of deal-by-deal investments in start-ups by the private sector on a co-investment basis. The CIF could select a number of experienced private sector institutions to be its accredited partners. These should help to bring various co-investment opportunities to the CIF to assess. Management and governance of the new CIF should be performed by government innovation agencies, together with key investment partners and funders.

A good example is that the UK government is considering setting up a special new VC fund to leverage the public seed grant of £20 million announced in the UK's Clean Growth Strategy. This should help to further raise capital from the private sector and eventually deploy up to £100 million of new capital to support the growth of cleantech companies in the UK. The new UK green VC fund would focus on backing early-stage UK SMEs less than five years old with revenues of less than £1 million. These should encourage more green capital injections into the early-stage market which should then support more and larger deals. The UK is also considering establishing a new Co-Investment Fund (CIF). Management of the CIF would either be performed within the UK BEIS Ministry Energy Innovation team or be outsourced to the British Business Bank (BBB) (UK GFI Report, 2017).

Another potentially interesting policy support option is to consider increasing commercial opportunities for businesses through the use of public procurement processes. In addition to supporting early-stage technology investments, governments should consider how other sources of public finance from public entities and government procurement agencies could help to support delivery of their clean growth strategies through investments in selected products or services. The investment prospects of early-stage companies would be enhanced if they have credible customers or even better have a sound order book.

Annually, government agencies globally have been spending tens of billions of dollars on the public procurement of private sector goods and services. These could present significant opportunities for innovative private sector cleantech companies to scale up through supplying specialist cleantech services to the public sector. The public sector should also take a strategic approach to its energy purchasing, such as considering the new opportunities presented by new cleantech companies. This would help to demonstrate lower-cost, clean energy services which could be scaled up to provide services to the wider economy.

A good example is that the UK has been considering increasing commercial opportunities for renewable and cleantech businesses through the use of public procurement processes. The UK public sector is unique in having some large energy-using sites close to one another. The UK Cabinet Office could provide central purchasing support. The UK public sector offices could then consider using some of their sites as a pathfinder to demonstrate the benefits of innovative cleantech products and services. The UK Green Finance Taskforce has recommended encouraging public sector procurement to lead the UK market in clean alternatives through mechanisms such as the Small Business Research Initiative (SBRI) and using climate impact as one of the key factors in public procurement decisions (UK GFI Report, 2017).

Renewable company climate risk financial reporting management

Globally, there have been many rising concerns from various governments and regulators about the impacts of various serious climate risks on leading companies globally plus how well prepared they are able to handle these. Many stock markets globally have implemented "Environment, Social and Governance (ESG)" reporting requirements on their listed companies. Good examples of actions by leading stock market regulators included the Hong Kong Stock Exchange and the Philippine Security Exchange Commission. Both the Hong Kong Stock Exchange and the Philippine Security Exchange Commission have stipulated new ESG reporting requirements for their listed companies. However, financial experts have advised that in addition to ESG reporting there should be climate risk reporting as these could poise serious environmental and reputational impacts that could seriously affect the sustainability of various businesses plus their future financial performances and results.

In the G20 Finance Ministers meeting in 2015, it was generally agreed that the first step towards better management of climate change and climate risks by business would be to improve the accurate measurement and reporting of these important areas. Hence, Mark Carney, the International Financial Stability Board (FSB) Chair, was asked to create the G20 Task Force on Climate-Related Financial Disclosures (TCFD) in December 2015. The G20 TCFD was chaired by Michael Bloomberg and composed of 32 industry leaders across the world. They have undertaken extensive engagements, surveys and reviews with over 30 countries across the world in developing their recommendations and report over a two-year period.

In the April 2017 meeting of the G20 Finance Ministers and Central Bank Governors, they generally accepted the TCFD recommendations and supported their voluntary adoption by companies and banks globally. As it is a private sector report, the G20 Ministers did not have to approve the report. However, it is worth noting that the April 2017 meeting of the G20 Finance Ministers and Central Bank Governors generally accepted the TCFD recommendations and supported their voluntary adoption by companies and banks globally. Looking ahead, it is likely that some key countries will be leaning towards introducing new regulations in future to enforce the TCFD recommendations. Some other countries might prefer softer approaches such as recommended guidances for voluntary adoption. Looking ahead, it is generally believed that these new TCFD recommendations will become important new international requirements, which leading companies and banks globally will have to meet and comply with in future. Otherwise, they could face serious challenges and even lawsuits from the regulators, media, investors, shareholders and stakeholders.

In June 2017, the G20s Financial Stability Board's "Task Force on Climate-Related Financial Disclosures" (TCFD) published its final report and recommendations which contained detailed recommendations on voluntary climate-related financial disclosures. The Task Force on Climate-Related Financial Disclosures (TCFD) Report recommended that leading banks and companies should make their future climate disclosures in line with a new framework underpinned by seven key principles. Their recommendations sought to balance the global need to raise the bar for existing climate financial disclosure standards, together with the desire to achieve widespread adoption by leading banks and companies globally. They have provided new guidelines on how leading banks and companies globally should use their mainstream, and publicly available, financial reporting instruments to report on their climate change risks and opportunities which they would face in the short, medium and long term. In general, the TCFD recommendations represented very carefully considered, open and transparent new approaches for climate-related financial disclosures by leading banks and companies. The TCFD team has also identified some key industrial sectors globally that could suffer higher climate risk internationally. These sectors included the energy, transportation, construction, agriculture, food and forestry sectors (G20, TCFD Report, 2017).

Recognising that these new approaches would evolve over time, the Task Force has developed a set of seven key principles to underpin the new disclosures that companies should prepare. The TCFD Report recommended leading companies and banks globally to report on four key corporate areas covering climate governance, climate strategy, climate risks and management targets.

On climate governance, it has been recommended that the boards of leading banks and companies should disclose details of their new governance processes and systems for assessing and managing climate change-related risks and opportunities. These should include the governance systems via which the boards would be overseeing climate governance plus the associated governance processes. These should include how frequently would the board be informed on progress and how they would review these with their top management. In addition, the boards should disclose how they would be assessing the actual governance outcomes against major business plans or risks. In addition, the boards should define what would be the top management's roles and accountabilities in addressing these climate-related risks and opportunities.

On climate strategy, the company boards and senior management would be required to report on various climate strategies and scenarios that they have considered. These should include what would be the actual and potential impacts of climate changes on the business and performances of leading banks and companies. They should also consider climate impacts on their business organisation, strategy and financial planning.

On climate risks, the senior management of leading banks and companies should give details on their climate risk assessments and risk management systems. These should include how do they will actually evaluate, identify, assess and manage climate risks plus opportunities. In addition, they should disclose their risk management systems and action plans, which they have put in place to mitigate the serious climate risks and their potential impacts on their businesses.

On climate metrics and targets, the board and senior management should give details of the appropriate climate metrics, KPIs and targets that have been established for their management and businesses to achieve. These new metrics and targets should ensure that management would be undertaking its tasks in assessing and managing climate change risks and opportunities effectively.

It is important for international banks and companies globally to recognise that climate change impacts and climate risks on their businesses could also be heavily influenced by new government policies and changes in the law. A good example is the changes in the new energy policies for fossil fuel and renewable energies that are being introduced by various key countries globally as part of their Paris Agreement commitments. There are also ever rising risks of litigation by regulators, stakeholders and shareholders globally.

In the face of all these intense international, government and shareholder pressures, leading banks and companies globally have to take these new requirements on climate-related financial disclosures very seriously. The corporate boards and top management have to put in place the necessary new systems and processes to compile with the new disclosure and reporting requirements. They will need to try their best to prepare the required corporate disclosure reports on their climate strategies and climate risks. Otherwise, they may be opening themselves to serious challenges and even lawsuits from the regulators, investors, shareholders and media.

China's renewable finance and investment management case study

Renewable finance and green investments have been growing fast in China. It is estimated that the new "ecological civilisation" transformations of China which are included in their 13th Five-Year Plan would require new green finance and investments of between USD474 billion and USD633 billion in the period 2015–2030. Experts have forecasted that the central government of the PRC would only provide some 15% government seed green investments. At least 85% of the planned green finance and investments for China would then have to come from the private sector. Green finance and green bonds have been growing steadily in China. The concepts of ESG (environmental, social and corporate governance), TCFD and impact investment are also being increasingly accepted and supported by the PRC government, regulators, financial institutions and listed companies. The key developments and outlooks in these areas will be discussed in more detail below with business examples.

PRC commercial banks have been active in green finance in China especially through their green credit business. In 2018, the total balance of green credits in China has exceeded RMB9 trillion or USD1.3 trillion. Looking ahead, it is expected that China's growth trends in green finance will continue for the foreseeable future. The total balance of green credit in China is expected to surpass RMB10 trillion or USD1.5 trillion by the end of 2019. Furthermore, there are important policy discussions on whether the risk weighting of green assets can be or should be reduced. These are being closely watched by commercial banks as any breakthroughs in this area would be a strong incentive for green credit business growths.

The green bond market in China has been growing well. In 2018, China's green bond market issued more than 120 labelled green bonds worth around RMB220 billion or USD32.6 billion. China's green bond market has so far still remained a small share of the overall China's bond market. There are challenges on motivating issuers and investors plus market scale up challenges in China. Looking ahead, it is expected that an increasing number of green asset-backed securities and infrastructure green bonds would be issued in 2019–2020. In addition, there will be further regulations of the green bond market in China. The China Green Bond Standard Committee was established in December 2018 under the guidance of the People's Bank of China (PBOC), the CSRC and other financial regulators. The committee has been chaired by the National Association of Financial Market Institutional Investors (NAFMII). This committee is China's first self-regulatory and coordination mechanism for green bonds. It is expected to propose, in the near future, the harmonisation of green bond standards and market access of green bond verifiers. The second edition of the Green Bond Endorsed Project Catalogue, which has been discussed for a long time, is planned to be released later in 2019/2020. The requirements for qualifications, technical standards and self-regulation of verifiers which have been set out in the Guidelines for the Assessment and Certification of Green Bonds (Interim) will also be implemented in stages in 2019. These further regulating of China's green bond market should improve its transparency and raise market confidence (Guo, SynTao, Responsible Investment, 2019).

Green finance and investments have also been growing at the local government and provincial levels in China. Local government and provincial administrative regions had been releasing various green finance policies, which covered green bonds, green credit, green equities, green insurance, green development funds, environmental finance, etc. In 2018, the number of green finance policies implemented in the provincial, prefectural and municipal administrative region levels had increased by over 68%. The number of local policies which had clear quantitative criteria for financial incentives has also increased and had accounted for over 13% of all policies. Looking ahead, it is expected that more local governments would be adopting green finance and more local green finance policies. In 2019, it is anticipated that local governments will continue to issue more new policies to support the development of green finance and renewable investments. These should include new municipal policies, facilitative measures, substantive financial incentives, regulated standards, quantifying assessments, etc. These should help to deepen green finance and renewable investment developments, especially at the green finance pilot zones in leading provinces.

Green finance and sustainable renewable investments have also been important parts of the large China's Belt and Road Initiative (BRI). These have attracted considerable investments to date and are expected to rise in future. Since the launch of the Belt and Road Initiative, the international community has been closely following the environmental and social implications of various Belt and Road investments. In November 2018, the Green Finance Committee (GFC) of the China Society for Finance and Banking and the UK City of London jointly released the Green Investment Principles for the Belt & Road Initiative. It advocated the incorporation of sustainability principles in asset classes, financial products, project implementation, management of participating agencies and other management processes. These principles have been endorsed by many large financial institutions and enterprises in China and globally. It is anticipated that these green investment principles will play important roles in making various BRI investments more sustainable and environmental friendly. Chinese and international financial institutions will be closely following these principles. These should encourage better management of the environmental and sustainability risks of the Belt and Road investments in China and globally.

In context to international green finance co-operations, China has been continuously enhancing possible international co-operations on green finance and sustainable investments with leading financial regulators and institutions globally. China has carried out bilateral and multilateral co-operation and pilot programmes with the UK, France, Germany, Luxembourg and other countries. These covered green finance fields such as financial regulation, green bonds, information, disclosure, etc. A good example is the UK-China pilot on G20 Taskforce on Climate-Related Finance Disclosures (TCFD). Looking ahead, the trend of international co-operation will continue in the foreseeable future with active participations by leading financial institutions in China and overseas.

In relation to FinTech, there are rising fintech applications in green financing and renewable investments. In July 2018, the G20 Sustainable Finance Study Group discussed fintech's potential in promoting sustainable financial developments in its 2018 Sustainable Finance Synthesis Report. Potential fintech applications included providing more abundant, accurate and effective data through cheaper and faster means; reducing search cost, improving the pricing of ESG risks and opportunity cost; optimising the measurement, recording and verification of sustainability indicators; offering sustainable financing in a more creative and inclusive way; etc. With the strong growth of internet and IT companies in China, there is also strong growth of fintech technologies in China. Looking ahead, it is anticipated that fintech companies will increasingly apply new fintech technology to support the growth of green inclusive financing and ethnical impact investments, especially in how to combine it with poverty reductions in China (G20 Sustainable Finance Synthesis Report, 2018).

In context to ESG, China is expected to issue its official ESG reporting guidelines soon. China is likely to, in line with the general deployment of the Guidelines for Establishing a Green Financial System, make it mandatory for all their listed companies to disclose their environmental information by 2020. In September 2018, the China Securities Regulatory Commission (CSRC) has, in its revised Corporate Governance Code for Listed Companies, established an environmental, social and corporate governance (ESG) information disclosure framework for listed companies. In October 2018, the Shanghai Stock Exchange (SSE) has supported the World Federation of Exchanges (WFE) in developing the Principles for Sustainable Exchanges, which recommended leading stock exchanges globally to issue ESG disclosure guidance. Looking ahead, it is likely that China will issue the ESG reporting guidelines for the A-share market in 2019. This will in turn push the Chinese listed companies to improve and upgrade their Corporate Social Responsibility (CSR) Reports into new ESG reports with significant improvements in material and quantitative reporting of environment, social and governance aspects (Guo, SynTao, 2019).

In context to TCFD, China has been cooperating well with the UK City of London Green Finance Team on important TCFD pilots. The UK-China Climate and Environmental Information Disclosure Pilot project which involved ten China financial institutions together with the UK City of London Green Finance Team was started in 2018. The pilot project has been progressing well and would be entering its second stage in 2019. This should encourage more Chinese financial institutions especially commercial banks to improve their accounting and disclosure of environmental information relating to their asset portfolios. It should also promote the Chinese listed companies to improve the disclosure of their environmental and climate information.

Leading banks in China have also been discussing their draft Principles for Responsible Banking and are expected to endorse these draft principles soon. At the UNEP Finance Initiative (UNEP FI) Global Roundtable and the Sixth China SIF annual conference at the end of 2018, the draft Principles for Responsible Banking was officially released for consultation with both English and Chinese versions. The draft principles provided banks in China with a consistent framework incorporating sustainable development elements in their strategic, investment portfolio plus in transaction levels and in all business areas. Looking ahead, it is anticipated that these new principles will be supported by the Chinese regulators, banking industry associations and leading Chinese banks in the foreseeable future. The Industrial and Commercial Bank of China (ICBC) has been a core working group member and will likely be one of first banks in China to endorse the new Responsible Banking Principles, probably in 2019/2020 (UNEP-FI, Responsible Banking Principles, 2018).

For mutual funds, ESG has been playing important roles in the Chinese mutual fund market. More ESG-themed mutual fund products are expected to be launched in China. At the end of 2018, the Asset Management Association of China (AMAC) released its draft Guidelines for Green Investment. The AMAC had advised that ESG is an important emerging investment strategy in the global asset management industry. ESG is also an important initiative for the investment fund industry in China to implement as part of its aspiration to establish a sustainable, green financial system in China. The AMAC will be facilitating the implementation of the Guidelines across China. In 2018, several Chinese mutual funds have also joined the UN-supported Principles for Responsible Investment (PRI) which would motivate these mutual funds to develop more ESG investment products. Looking ahead, it is anticipated that more Chinese funds will be adopting ESG investment strategies in 2019–2020 and they will be introducing more ESG-themed mutual fund products. The China Securities Index Co. Ltd (CSI) and the MSCI are also expected to launch more ESG-themed indices in 2019–2020. These ESG-themed mutual fund products should enable Chinese investors to have more channels to directly participate in responsible investment and green finance. In addition, the public sale of mutual fund products should improve the education and dissemination of ethnical investment knowledge amongst investors and general public in China.

For insurance funds, ESG has been playing important roles in their investment approaches as long-term asset owners. ESG and responsible investments with long-term values fit in well with the investment approaches of long-term assets owners, such as insurance and pension funds. The Chinese insurance regulator has also been encouraging insurance funds in China to increase the proportion of high-quality listed companies in their portfolios. Looking ahead, it is expected that insurance funds will be paying more attention to their ESG strategies in 2019 plus to minimise their investment risks with secure mid-and long-term stable returns. China Life Asset Management Company Limited and China Ping An, the giant Chinese insurer, have both become signatories to the UN Principles for Responsible Investment (UN PRI) in 2018 and 2019 respectively. Looking ahead, these should encourage more insurance asset management institutions in China to recognise and endorse UN PRI. Insurance companies are likely to issue more ESG green insurance products in future (UN PRI, 2019).

As far as Social Security is concerned, the China National Social Security Fund (NSSF) has said that it will have a closer look at the ESG and TCFD principles. It is anticipated that NSSF will be including the new ESG and TCFD principles when it selects which fund managers to manage its investments in 2019–2020. This should then stimulate more mutual funds and fund managers to adopt ESG and TCFD.

Charities in China are also likely to endorse the new ESG and TCFD principles. The PRC's Ministry of Civil Affairs has promulgated the Interim Measures for the Administration of Investment Activities of Charitable Organizations for Value Preservation and Appreciation in 2018. Charitable organisations in China would be allowed to entrust their assets to professional asset management firms for investment purpose if such investment will not violate their missions or damage their reputation. It is anticipated that charitable organisations will take steps to introduce new responsible investment concepts including ESG and TCFD principles (PRC Ministry of Civil Affairs, 2018).

Chinese PE and VC funds have also started to look into ESG and TCFD integrations. Many PE and VC investment funds have started to systematically incorporate ESG into their investments to minimise risks. The AMAC has stated for the first time, in its draft Guidelines for Green Investment, that private equity funds may reference the green investment concept. The G20 Sustainable Finance Study Group also identified the development of sustainable PE and VC funds as key research areas. Currently, Chinese domestic PE and VC companies, including CITIC Private Equity Funds Management, Hony Capital and Sequoia Capital China, have already made ESG investment trials. Looking ahead, investment strategies in line with ESG principles should enhance the robustness of target companies or projects, whilst reducing risks posed to PE and VC investors. More PE and VC funds are expected to incorporate ESG into the whole process of project screening, due diligence, investment decision-making, post-investment management and even exit strategy.

The rising public interest in environment and climate change plus the rising litigation risks should also promote ESG and TCFD adaptation in China. In 2018, China has introduced a nationwide environmental damage compensation system on a pilot basis. These have helped to lay the groundworks for environmental public interest litigations, which used to be difficult during the early stage of the implementation of the new Environmental Protection Law. In 2018, environmental and resource protection cases had accounted for more than half of 90,000 public interest litigations initiated by prosecutorial authorities all over China. Looking ahead, it is anticipated that in future more environmental public interest litigations cases will be entering judicial proceedings in China. The retrospective effects plus joint and several liabilities of such litigations will be extended to financial institutions, especially some commercial banks which have business linkages with polluting enterprises.

A good litigation example in China is that in 2018 the Green Garden Environmental Friendliness Center brought a lawsuit against Xiangda Agricultural & Animal Husbandry Co. Ltd. for polluting the Hanjiang River. It has also applied to have two commercial banks in China that had provided bank loans to the defendant to be named as co-defendants (China Water Risk, Top 10 Responsible Investment Trends for 2019 In China, China 18 March 2019).

In January 2019, the Supreme People's Procuratorate in China and other nine national agencies issued the Opinions on Enhancing Cooperation and Coordination in the Prosecution of Public-Interest Litigations to Legally Fight against Pollution. This is expected to address many challenges in environmental litigation practices in China. With the improvement of these legal systems in China, various financial institutions, including commercial banks, will be confronted with a greater risk of environmental public interest litigations. Hence, it is very important that companies should urgently consider and adopt the new ESG and TCFD principles. In addition, the corporate legal departments should be better prepared for increased risks of litigation in China in future (PRC Supreme People's Procuratorate, 2019).

10 Renewable digital transformation and cybersecurity management

船到桥头自然直
Chuán Dào Qiáo Tóu Zì Rán Zhí
As the ship reaches the bridge, it has to align with the bridge to berth.
Cross the bridge when we come to it.

Executive summary

Companies in both emerging economies and developed countries are facing serious climate change, digital transformation and cybersecurity risks. These could seriously affect their future business growths and sustainable business profitability. In particular, renewable companies have to develop appropriate digital transformation strategies to improve their performance and efficiency whilst maintaining high cybersecurity. Cybersecurity improvements are key to protect renewable companies against growing cyber attacks and risks of fraud. There should be strong management support for the elimination of legacy systems and organisational reforms to accelerate digital reforms and improve cybersecurity. Different interlinkages between climate change, renewables, digital transformation and cybersecurity will be discussed in this chapter with business examples.

Risks of Renewables, climate change, digital transformations and cybersecurity

Climate change, digital transformation and cybersecurity are serious risks for the future growths and sustainable developments of various countries and renewable companies globally. Climate change, renewables, digital transformation and cybersecurity are all important strategic elements for the sustainable future growths of companies globally, especially for companies in the renewable and clean energy sectors. Renewable companies have to develop appropriate digital transformation strategies to improve performance and efficiency in light of the serious climate change risks. Cybersecurity improvements are key to protect renewable companies against growing cyber attacks and frauds plus climate change risks. There should be strong management support for elimination of legacy systems and organisational reforms to accelerate digital reforms and improve cybersecurity for companies globally.

These serious digital and cybersecurity risks would apply to all international companies, private companies and state-owned companies, especially those operating in the renewable and clean energy sectors. There have been rising cases of cyber attacks on key government installations and various companies globally. Many state-owned companies have suffered serious digital attacks and threats. A good example is the very serious cyber attack on Saudi Aramco which crippled most of its computer systems in Saudi Arabia.

For companies to continue their green growth and renewable developments in a sustainable manner, it is important for them to have good digital transformation strategies with strong cybersecurity systems which would have also taken into account various climate change risks. The corporate boards, managers and shareholders should prioritise management support and focus for climate change, renewables, digital transformation and cybersecurity as part of their top management priorities so as to ensure sustainable business growth and corporate profitability.

Digital transformation, climate change and renewable challenges

Over the past decades, the exponential growth of digital technologies has generated many changes and interesting opportunities for companies globally. It is estimated that nearly five billion people globally are using computer devices daily. However, unfortunately all these digital technologies have not yet been translated into significant productivity gains for many companies and improved their performances. The key hurdles seemed to be that many companies have not been changing their processes to allow the digital technologies to reach its full potential. In addition, their cybersecurity systems have not been robust and strong enough to defend against frequent digital attacks.

It is important to recognise the fact that adopting advanced digital technologies alone would not normally bring about real digital transformations in companies by themselves. Many management teams have been adopting digital transformation with no clear coherent overall strategy plus have not carefully consider the cybersecurity risks and the threats from climate change. Different business divisions in companies have often been allowed to adopt their own pet digital application or analytics tools, with little linkages with other business divisions. All these shortcomings have resulted in companies falling short of their digital transformation goals. The wrong focus was typically put on how applying advanced digital or IT technologies could change the business quickly. Instead, they should be refocusing on how the enterprise should change its business organisation and processes so as to fully embrace the full potentials of digital transformation and innovative technologies in light of the climate change and clean renewable energy transformation implications.

Management globally should recognise that the true digital transformation for companies would require more than just a technology-based approach. Companies would have to reform and improve their management organisations, processes and systems. They should maintain strong focuses on the desired corporate digital transformation management objectives and not just on importing new digital technologies and infrastructures. In addition, they would have to take into account the serious rising climate change risks and increasing fossil to clean renewable energy transformation requirements into their corporate strategy and business planning so that they can develop the appropriate digital and cyber strategies to support renewable growth and sustainable business performances.

The deep digital transformation of companies should start with the appropriate management process reforms and innovative organisation transformations taking into account the requirements of digital transformation, cybersecurity and climate change. One good digital business example is that companies will have to implement the appropriate digital reforms to embrace the new advanced real-time analytics together with predictive decision making involving the Internet of Things (IOT) and Big Data. These advanced digital technologies should help to generate better information and data analysis for different companies. However, companies are not likely to get full benefits unless their management can transform their key business processes plus change the mindset of their staff to act quickly on this new digital information.

One key digital transformation area is in data process and decision making. Traditionally, many of the traditional data processes used by companies have required staff to move data from one corporate database to another. It could take even longer if these data have to cross many functional silos, which is normally the case in most companies. Then they will need to process the data and generate appropriate reports for management to review and to make appropriate decisions. New advanced in-memory computing digital technologies could significantly accelerate these processes and reduce the processing time greatly.

A good digital business example is the High-Speed Analytical Appliance (HANA) digital technology, which uses advanced digital data compression to store data in the random access memory of computers. HANA's performance is 10,000 times faster compared to standard computer disks. These advanced digital technologies should allow companies to analyse their important data in a matter of seconds instead of hours before. These should help company management to have quicker and more accurate pictures of how their businesses are doing which should better support management to make the appropriate decisions quicker, taking into account varying needs of the business, climate change, etc.

These advanced digital technologies should help to significantly improve and accelerate data processing and analysis in companies. These should then support management to have faster agile decision making and take appropriate actions to improve business performances. However no matter how fast the analysis would be, the real benefits could only be realised by having appropriate corporate processes for management reviews and decisions so as to fully realise the benefits of improved insights generated by advanced digital technologies. Corporate management should consider appropriate reorganisations of its back office and front office functions and processes so that they would be able to utilise new digital technologies and systems to produce the improved management information and business reports to aid executive decisions. Management should also eliminate legacy systems and traditional databases so as to reduce the traditional barriers to achieve the full benefits of digital transformation with in-memory analytics. These would usually involve some tough painful organisational reforms plus staff redeployment or redundancy, which some management might be reluctant to make.

Global digital transformation experiences have shown that the ability for companies to modernise their core systems with advanced digital technologies, such as in-memory computing and innovative new digital applications, could be highly beneficial for companies globally. These should help to improve business productivities and efficiencies significantly. However, it is very important that the corporate management should be committed to eliminating traditional legacy systems and processes plus take into considerations the requirements of climate change and the business. These reforms are important in order to integrate new digital reforms and technologies into the overall business architecture. These would help to support digital transformation and deliver the real business improvements to companies globally.

In many companies, there are different serious management and organisational challenges to digital transformation and cybersecurity, such as adherence to pet legacy systems and processes. In many cases, they have also not fully taken into account the climate change and global warming risks. These would impede the ability of companies to enjoy the full benefits of digital transformation and innovative technologies. Management would have to tackle these major hurdles effectively so that they can embrace digital transformation and maximise the value gains.

One of the most serious organisation hurdles is the organisational resistance to changes. Management should recognise that the majority of staff will normally have big concerns about changes and uncertainties which could challenge their roles or reduce their job security. Digital transformation, by its very nature, could change a lot of job roles and could also reduce some job securities. The resistance to changes could manifest itself in a myriad of ways in companies. These could include digital projects taking a long time to develop and implement. They could also be delayed by inadequate expertise and resource availabilities. There could also be different technical, commercial and legal review requirements in companies which could slow down the digital transformation.

One of the most famous digital transformation business resistance and failure case example is Kodak, the photography company. Its corporate research staff had actually invented the new digital camera technology whilst the company was having a very successful photography film manufacturing and processing business. The Kodak internal corporate resistance to the new digital change was very huge. Many of the Kodak management and staff were concerned about the potential threats of the new digital photography to Kodak's legacy film business profits. These concerns resulted in Kodak not developing its new digital technology to maximise its full values. This strategically wrong decision eventually led to the serious declines in the Kodak film business and final demise of the company.

However, there have been some successful business digital transformation cases. One of the most interesting digital transformation business success case example is the successful transformation of Bell Atlantic into Verizon. The Bell management realised that the future of landlines was looking bleak with digital advances in broadbands and mobile technologies. It was able to overcome internal resistances and eliminated legacy systems. These bold transformations enabled Verizon to become a leading digital business in broadband, wireless and cable television industries. These good strategic decisions enabled Bell Atlantic to continue its business successes on a sustainable basis in light of the digital and climate change impacts. Their management succeeded by accepting digital advances and made the difficult organisational decisions required to adapt to the new digital transformation requirements.

Another major risk to digital transformation is the lack of a clear corporate vision for a digital customer journey. Companies would usually only succeed in creating a digital customer value proposition by developing a clear vision of how they would actively consider and meet their customers' changing digital needs. They would also need to set clear objectives and strategies to achieve their digital vision. Then the management would have to be committed to executing its digital transformation strategies, which could take a long period over multiple years.

To develop a clear digital transformation strategy, management would have to take stock of its assets, brand, customer base, intellectual property plus strengths and talents of staff together with the cyber and climate change risks. It must also study its market to really understand its customers' needs and aspirations. It has to understand the emerging technologies, innovations plus shifts in consumer behaviour and technology. Then it should establish the appropriate processes to support the digital transformation and meet the new future customer needs. Its new processes should be aligned to its digital visions in light of the cyber and climate change impacts. It should also try to continuously transform in future to match new learnings and new technology developments.

Ineffective gathering and leveraging of customer and climate change data could represent major risks for successful digital transformations. Many organisations have a myriad of legacy siloed data systems in different business divisions. They also have no effective ways to pull the business data together to generate really meaningful management reports. To overcome these hurdles, companies should first determine their key customer attributes and matrices. Then companies should try to eliminate legacy systems with new systems so they can serve and sell to their customers more effectively. They have also to understand the climate change risks to their business and develop appropriate climate strategies, scenarios and risk mitigation strategies to handle the climate risks.

Inflexible technology legacy portfolios and rigid development processes have been some of the biggest hurdles to successful digital transformation. Many companies have technology development processes involving inflexible cycles such as quarterly release cycles. Companies have to improve these legacy systems with new agile processes and technologies that would support continuous developments and frequent new product releases to meet the fast-changing customer requirements. This is particularly important for companies in the clean renewable energy sector with the fast pace of technological innovations and manufacturing developments.

Renewables, climate change and digital solution developments

There are important new technological and digital innovations being developed which will help with the tough climate change and environmental challenges. These digital improvements have included new emission sensors, satellite earth emission scanning systems, wind power radar systems, blockchain technologies, etc. Details of these will be discussed more below with international examples.

One important area is the application of new advanced digital approaches to improve the measurements of methane emissions globally. Methane is a very potent greenhouse gas (GHG) which has more than 80 times the near-term global warming power of carbon dioxide. Human-made methane emissions have been responsible for a quarter of all the global warming being experienced today. Some of the largest methane emissions have been from the oil and gas industry, as natural gas is mostly methane.

The International Energy Agency (IEA) has estimated that the global oil and gas methane emissions have been about 75 million metric tons per year. These huge methane emissions, if captured, would be enough to generate all of Africa's electricity twice over. The IEA has also estimated that the oil and gas industry should be able to reduce those methane emissions significantly, by up to 75%, by better measurements and controls plus operational improvements.

The new digital methane sensors and advanced digital measurement systems have helped to achieve these tough climate challenges. A good example is the new reliable, low-cost methane sensors which allow remote monitoring with accurate methane emission measurements. These new advanced methane sensors have enabled better measurements of methane emissions globally both from earth and from space.

These improved measures have helped to identify sources of methane emissions so actions can be taken on the responsible companies to ask them to reduce their industrial methane emissions. These have contributed to one of the fastest and effective way to reduce GHG emission and global warming (WEF, New climate change solutions, 2018).

Extensive research led by the Environmental Defense Fund (EDF) from 2012 to 2018 showed serious methane emissions and leakages from the US oil and gas sectors. It launched a big scientific research effort involving more than 140 researchers from 40 institutions, along with four dozen oil and gas companies which provided site access and technical advice. The researchers used a range of advanced digital technologies, including new digital sensors mounted on drones, airplanes and even Google Street View cars. These enabled them to accurately measure methane emissions for each steps of the US oil and gas supply chain. The results showed that the US oil and gas industry has been emitting 13 million metric tons of methane each year. These have been nearly 60% more than the estimates made by the US Environmental Protection Agency. It was also shown that these methane emissions could be controlled and reduced, often through simple maintenance.

These advanced and more accurate methane emission data measurements have been instrumental in convincing both industry leaders and policy makers of the serious methane emission challenges. These important findings have helped to shape new emission regulations in US states such as Colorado, Wyoming, California and Pennsylvania plus national-level policies. These new environmental policies and regulations have helped to reduce methane emissions from oil and gas production on federal and tribal land in the USA (WEF, 2018).

These digital data-driven transparency and improvements have led to leading oil and gas companies setting new stricter methane emission reduction targets and actions. Good examples include BP setting its first quantitative methane emission reduction target plus ExxonMobil has also committing to reduce emissions and flared gas volumes. Shell, Qatar Petroleum and other producers have also committed to reduce methane emissions across their natural gas supply chain.

Looking ahead, environmentalists are also calling for a reduction of 45% in global oil and gas methane emissions by 2025. These reductions would have the same 20-year climate benefit as closing one-third of the world's coal plants.

Further new advanced digital technological developments are being worked on which could help to provide even better methane measurements. These measurements should help to achieve these tough methane emission reductions by 2025. A good example is the development of MethaneSAT. This will be a new satellite mission which is planned for launching in 2021. It has been designed to continuously measure methane and map emissions globally with new improved monitoring and measurements from space. MethaneSAT will enable researchers and companies to measure accurately methane emissions in places where it has been difficult to measure previously. In addition, the MethaneSAT measurements will be open access and available for free to public stakeholders for review. These should help countries, companies and public to spot new emission problems and identify new reduction actions. These should also allowed measurements of emission reduction progress over time. Other advanced space-based methane monitoring tools have also been developed. Good examples included the European Space Agency launching its TROPOMI satellite in 2017. A high-tech private company, called GHGSAT, has already one methane measuring satellite in orbit and another due to launch soon.

Looking ahead, it is looking hopeful that the new methane measurements and digital data from MethaneSAT should help to reach 45% reduction of methane emissions by 2025, and to virtually eliminate the US oil and gas industry's methane emissions by 2050. This is a good example on how the deployment of advanced sensor digital technologies together with advanced digital analysis systems has helped to cut methane GHG emission significantly. These should contribute to significant slowdown of global warming and climate change improvements globally.

Digital technologies have also been applied in the commercial and agricultural sectors to help to reduce climate change impacts. Good examples include retailers and consumer brands having been using digital blockchain technologies to improve accountability and sustainability across their supply chains. New digital sensors have been helping farmers to reduce the amount of chemical and fertilizer usages on their fields. Smart boats with sensors and digital technologies could help fishermen to manage their catch more effectively and help to conserve fish stocks in the sea.

Advanced digital technologies have also shown that the world's oceans have been absorbing more heat and are warming up at an accelerating pace. Ocean scientists, using the latest digital ocean temperature measurement robotic technologies, have shown that there has not been any hiatus in ocean temperature rises globally. The latest ocean temperature measurements have given much more precise estimates of ocean heating and temperature rises. More accurate ocean temperature results have been generated by a new fleet of advanced digital ocean monitoring robots called Argo. These digital robotic fleets have included nearly 4,000 floating robots which have been launched to drift throughout the world's oceans globally. These Agro robots have dived, every few days, to a depth of 2,000 meters to measure the ocean's temperature, pH and salinity, and collect other relevant ocean information. These Argo ocean robot measurements have helped to provide consistent and widespread data on ocean heat content since the mid-2000. The improved ocean measurements have help scientists to have better understanding of climate change on oceans plus to develop mitigation strategies (Princeton, Earth's oceans, 2018).

There have also been exciting new digital system innovations for renewables, especially in wind renewable energy. A good example is the DONG Energy's advanced BEACon radar system, developed by SmartWind Technologies from the USA. Their advanced digital system will provide minute-by-minute three-dimensional data of wind as it flows through a wind farm or stretch of sea. The advanced digital radar can also provide valuable insights to help to inform and optimise the siting, design and operation of future offshore wind projects (CleanTechnica, Wind Power Radar System, 2016).

Digital technology and Internet of Things (IOT) challenges

Digital transformation and the Internet of Things (IOT) are important strategic considerations for leading companies globally in light of global warming and climate changes. We will look at some of the ways in which digital technology today, specifically the IOT and digital transformation, is working to mitigate the climate change risks and to support renewable company growths.

At the current rates of global warming and climate change plus fossil energy consumptions, experts have estimated that we would need more than 1.5 times current earth's capacity to achieve a sustainable future carrying capacity. Climate change and global warming have already caused serious damages to earth's environment and sustainable developments.

We have to find some way to control climate change and undo at least some of the damages that have been done. That's where advanced digital technology and IOT can help. As sustainability takes centre stage, new and emerging technologies are being applied to help to reduce dependence on fossil fuels and non-renewable energy sources plus to reduce pollution and emissions (IOT Agenda, Technology, 2017).

Digital transformation and the Internet Of Things (IOT) are some of the most promising technologies which could be applied. IOT, as a self-communicating and largely self-managing system of interconnected devices, is in many ways the technological embodiment of sustainability. The new digital networks together with new smart sensors should be able to help to collect an incredible amount of information from the real world. If these pieces of information are then analysed with the appropriate new big data systems (BDS) then these could help to provide more accurate management data. In addition, the application of appropriate IOT and BDS analysis could lead to the developments of entirely new operational models and systems which could help to minimise the impacts of climate change and global warming. With IOT, it is not just about the data collected by various IP addressable devices but also about how these data can be instantly communicated up and down in a chain of purpose-specific terminals. These could help to ensure that relevant information would be available at the right places for analysis so that appropriate actions can be taken.

In many ways, IOT should be able to tackle previously hard-to-isolate problems which have resulted from global warming and climate change. These could help to promote renewable energy growth plus support new cleantech developments and circular economy developments in emerging economies globally. A good example of IOT's roles in renewables and circular economy developments includes improved operational insights with advanced digital sensors and big data analysis. These should empower renewable operators to improve their system efficiencies plus manufacturers to better manage their processes to reduce wastes.

IOT technologies can also help to reduce carbon and GHG emissions by improving the management of renewables, transport, traffic and mobility systems. Whilst the numbers of electric cars are increasing, fossil ICE cars are still generating high emissions and pollutions. Experts have estimated that close to 30% of carbon dioxide emissions globally have been caused by cars, with up to 45% of those emissions occurring around intersections managed by traffic lights. IOT technologies can help to improve traffic management in cities and reduce pollutions.

A good traffic example is that city planners have been installing IOT-enabled traffic management systems in smart cities which would respond to real-time conditions instead of preprogrammed timers. With these, traffic lights should be able to detect asymmetric strains on the transportation infrastructure and then adapt intelligently to optimise traffic flow management. A good example is that instead of cars idling at lights for one to three minutes with the old-style timer control when there is no traffic coming in the opposite direction, a new IOT traffic management system can change traffic lights safely according to the numbers of cars that it has detected at an intersection based on actual traffic flows. Experts have estimated that these advanced digital IOT traffic control systems could help to cut the equivalent of 35 million vehicles' carbon emissions over the next five years.

IOT-enabled sensors can also help to improve monitoring of water and air qualities from afar. Normally, water and air quality have to be monitored by collecting and analysing physical specimens. These have often been laborious tasks especially for remote locations. With IOT-enabled sensors, environmental scientists should be able to remotely monitor polluted rivers, contaminated soil and brownfields in remediation, without having to waste time and resources.

With advanced digital IOT technologies, the entire monitoring process could be done remotely. Advanced sensors could collect data about the surrounding environment and push these data to a dedicated IT server. Then researchers can review and analyse the large amount of environmental information with appropriate big data systems. A good example of advanced IOT sensors includes the new advanced air quality monitoring devices which use a laser light in conjunction with sensors to detect particulate emissions in the atmosphere.

Globally, oceans are covering over 70% of the earth's surface. Global warming and climate change have huge impacts on the oceans around the world. Sea temperatures and water qualities are key measurements required to monitor climate impacts. Scientists have been recording sea surface temperature (SST) to better understand the climate change impacts on oceans globally. To measure SST, scientists have deployed temperature sensors on satellites, buoys, ships, ocean reference stations, and through marine telemetry. Advanced digital IOT water quality sensors on suitable buoys or carriers have been launched remotely into oceans or seas so that they can collect valuable water quality data for detailed analysis. Advanced IOT ocean temperature and water sensors included sea surface temperature (SST) measurements by advanced satellite microwave radiometers and infrared (IR) radiometers which are in moored or drifting buoys. Ocean scientists could then apply BDS to analyse the global ocean data collected through the IOT sensors so as to better identify the climate change impacts on oceans globally. Then suitable mitigate actions could be developed and applied accurately at different ocean locations so as to minimise climate change and global warming damages to oceans globally.

Climate change cybersecurity developments

Cybersecurity attacks globally have been becoming more frequent, well organised and unfortunately often successful to date. Companies and their security personnels have also faced many business and climate change challenges which could affect their cybersecurity. These included demands for energy utility services always being online, intensifying regulations, new climate policies, higher mobility and replacement of ageing industrial control systems with "smart" devices. All these could seriously affect many companies' cybersecurity.

Hence, it is very important that management and their cybersecurity experts should develop business-focused cybersecurity strategies which take into account the implications of climate change and renewable transformations. It should be noted that there are no fail-safe ways to secure all computer assets in most companies all the time. An alternative practical cybersecurity strategy may be is to focus on empowering an organisation that can be prepared for and can quickly detect cyber attacks when they occur, helping in dealing with them efficiently and quickly.

One of the most famous case in history of cyber attack on a leading company occurred in 2012 when the world's largest oil and natural gas producer, Saudi Aramco, discovered that a computer virus had infiltrated over 30,000 of its computer workstations. Saudi Aramco had no choice but to isolate all of its computer systems from outside access during the emergency. Whilst the cyber attack did not affect their key oil and gas production operations, many employees were cut off from e-mail and corporate servers for several days. They had to revert to written notes and faxes for business communications. The virus had also erased significant amount of company data, documents and e-mail files on 75% of Aramco's corporate computer systems (New York Times, Cyberattack on Saudi Firm, 2012).

Cyber attacks to date are unfortunately getting more well organised and constantly evolving. Many viruses could disguise themselves within the corporate's IT ecosystem in a way that would be very difficult to be discovered for long periods. The consequences of cyber attacks are often very serious and could lead to massive financial losses. Cyber crimes could also seriously damage the company's brands, undermine customer confidence and damage revenue generation. Cyber attacks on energy utility systems and renewable power systems could often lead to massive power outages, paralyzing communities plus endangering public safety. A recent serious cyber attack example is the globally coordinated WannaCry ransomware attack which infected more than 250,000 computers in over 150 countries globally.

In the global energy sector, technology evolution and innovations have partly contributed to the elevated cyber threat environment. Many industrial and process control systems have been designed to communicate with each other online via TCP and IP protocols. Many smart grids and energy distribution systems have relied on computer monitoring, optimisation and control. The energy transition from fossil fuels to clean renewable energies has also resulted in the growth of decentralised distributed clean renewable power supply and management systems. These systems are more susceptible to cyber attacks and hacking which could result in serious disruptions.

An important consideration in developing a cybersecurity strategy for different companies would be to understand that the cyberspace is being used by cyber criminals as a fast and interconnected tool to attack operations and steal sensitive information. The motivations of different cyber hackers and adversarial groups are often different. They also have their own sophisticated hacking techniques for stealing targeted information and attacking company computer systems.

In addition, companies have to be aware of the high risks of malicious insider cyber attacks. These could include employees, consultants or contractors who have given authorised access to company systems and information. They are in unique positions to use these to inflict harm, including industrial espionage and sabotage. Insiders can often act alone or may be under the influence of external groups. Most companies have considered insider attacks to be one of their highest cybersecurity threats.

Hacktivists globally have also been actively seeking to expose and embarrass leading oil and energy companies. These have included hacktivists protesting on various specific environmental and social causes. They could act alone or in groups to gain unauthorised access to confidential corporate computer files or networks. A good hacking example is the Anonymous group of hackers who have recently attacked top multinational oil and gas companies. They wanted to voice their strong objections to these companies undertaking oil and gas drillings in the Arctic. They were able to access, steal and publish some 1,000 e-mail addresses of major oil and gas company employees.

There are also opportunistic transnational cyber-criminal enterprises that are focusing on stealing confidential company data, customer information, payment data and other sensitive information. They would often steal these cyber data for quick financial gains. Oil and gas energy companies are particularly vulnerable to organised cyber gangs stealing confidential corporate resource secrets plus hijacking their production platforms or technology infrastructures for extortions. Cyber intruders would often focus their attacks to exploit the IT integration in oil and gas exploration, production, refining, and distribution and transmissions. Energy companies, in both fossil and renewable sectors, with advanced integrated digital process control and SCADA systems would be particularly vulnerable to cyber attacks on their corporate networks and internet-facing TCP/IP protocols. Cyber criminals could use sophisticated cyber viruses, such as Stuxnet, Flame, Night Dragon and Shamoon, to infiltrate an energy company's TCP/IP networks and gain access to sensitive process data and control systems. Some advanced hacker viruses could hid themselves and lie in wait for the most opportune time to attack. These viruses could go unnoticed for months which would allow them lots of time to exfiltrate a variety of confidential corporate data and secrets.

Spear phishing attacks on companies are often very sophisticated and damaging. These attacks usually involve creating some form of communication that would appear to the unsuspecting users to be legitimate. They would normally ask the recipient to click on links or supply credentials such as e-mail user names and passwords. Skilled spear phishing criminals would often design their messages to be in line with typical norms and formats of the targeted organisation. A good attack example is that in 2011 the Night Dragon hackers attacked specific leading global energy companies using both social media and spear phishing attacks. These attacks have resulted in exfiltration of many company e-mails and other sensitive corporate documents.

Cybersecurity in various companies is often only as strong as the weakest links in the companies which have often been employees and executives. They are often not adequately trained in countering security threats and in anti-spear phishing techniques. Hence, more cybersecurity trainings in companies will be very valuable.

Increasingly, more cyber attacks are coming from the cloud. IT experts have estimated that over one-third of oil and gas companies globally are using some form of cloud computing. This is likely to be increased higher in future as companies modernise their digital technology infrastructures with more cloud-based computing. However, this will also increase their susceptibility to hackers and cyber attacks.

Integrated energy and utility companies are particularly susceptible to cyber attacks as they are required to provide utility services to public. These systems are often required to be always online and available with high reliabilities. The utility supplies and electricity infrastructures are also the key linchpin of most nation's critical utility infrastructures.

Energy companies have to develop more secure operating environments and cyber incident-response plans for their various inter-connected technology assets so as to mitigate the potential risks of cyber attacks. It is important that company's cyber-incident response plan should involve frequent testing of its response procedures involving simulated attacks. These should be similar to the major crisis and disaster recovery plan exercises which are already being undertaken regularly in many energy and utility companies plus leading corporations, in emerging economies and developed countries globally.

More stringent regulations are being introduced by many countries as cyber threats intensified. A good example is that in the USA energy companies have to provide more disclosures of non-privacy–related breaches under the new Securities and Exchange Commission guidance requirements. The new SEC guidance has also stipulated that if an organisation failed to gain an accurate understanding of cyber risks then these could expose them to significant regulatory and litigation challenges.

The energy sector's ageing computing systems and infrastructure could become serious cyber risks. Many energy companies have to modernise their outdated technology infrastructures and improve their back office integration. Many cyber attacks are targeting the valuable intellectual property (IP) of energy companies. These could include the confidential locations and sizes of their oil and gas reserves plus details of new potential resource and new technology innovations. The increasing integration of oil- and gas-producing fields with their head office would normally require complex computer systems which will increase their susceptibility to cyber attacks. In addition, some energy companies have outsourced these computing systems in order to reduce costs. Outsourcing could cut operational costs, but it could also introduce new cybersecurity risks.

With the escalation of cyber threats and attacks, it is very important that companies have to safeguard their operation networks, data transmission systems and data application systems. Recent security surveys have found that fewer than half of the leading energy companies have formal programs to monitor for and respond to advanced persistent threats (APTs) which are the most dangerous long-term cyber risks.

Many companies have appointed chief information security officers (CISOs) to develop business-focused security plans and controls for the company's network, data, users and customer systems. There is often no fail-safe method to ensure absolute 100% cybersecurity in any of the companies. The CISO should take actions to create a realistic security program which would enable the company to prepare for and quickly detect cyber attacks plus safeguard its most valuable data and operations. In addition, the overall corporate executive leadership team must be committed to cybersecurity as a business imperative. Energy companies embedding cybersecurity into their strategic plans in their businesses are usually better able to handle cybersecurity risks and protect themselves against potential cyber attacks. Moreover, these companies would also be better able to explain their cybersecurity strategy to relevant government regulatory bodies, shareholders, employees, stakeholders, etc.

Effective cybersecurity would also require a culture shift in the company. All the management and employees should understand the importance of cybersecurity and their roles in protecting it. Cybersecurity should also not be viewed as a technology-focused cost centre in companies but an essential part of their business operations. Leading companies in emerging economies and globally are leveraging their cybersecurity models as part of their corporate competitive edge.

Public–private partnership (PPP) in cybersecurity is becoming more important with increased government focus on corporate cybersecurity. Leading companies are increasingly working with relevant government agencies on promoting new cybersecurity initiatives, in both emerging economies and developed countries globally.

In summary, leading companies with successful cybersecurity strategies will normally focus on three key areas. First, companies should prioritise corporate resources to protect those areas which are most valuable. Secondly, they should proactively implement cybersecurity practices that would protect their key businesses. Thirdly, companies should actively engage with policy makers and government regulators to form effective public–private partnerships on cybersecurity initiatives.

Renewables, climate change and cybersecurity strategies

Climate change and the fossil to renewable energy transformations are having serious impacts on critical digital infrastructures and IT networks plus their cybersecurity. There are also several parallels between climate-related threats on the world with cybersecurity. In good advanced digital systems, the computer servers, routers, firewalls or other digital systems are sitting at the outermost edge, or perimeter, of a protected computer network. These cyber devices should form a boundary between the vulnerable internal resources and outside networks. In many cases, hackers would often attempt to breach these digital devices' sitting on the perimeter of advanced digital IT systems. A good example is that strong cyber attacks at the web application layer could bypass the digital perimeter security systems which would normally include system network firewalls plus IT server, router security systems, etc. These cyber attacks could then bypass the traditional, basic one-dimensional and perimeter-focused cybersecurity strategies being applied by many companies.

These cybersecurity situations are similar to various serious climate change and global warming threats to various cities and countries, which could be multifaceted and multidirectional. By drawing connections between how climate change creates threats to critical computer infrastructure and how hackers threaten cybersecurity plus companies' data, we could provide more insight into the effective prevention and detection of cyber attacks plus generate appropriate responses to cybersecurity and climate change threats. These could help to develop new approaches to address the multidirectional attacks on cybersecurity systems and the climate-related multi-channel threats to critical infrastructure around the world (Techtarget, Climate change threats, 2018).

A common cybersecurity problem would involve illegal cyber attack actions attempting to overload computer systems by putting much more data onto a digital buffer than it could normally handle. A computer buffer has normally a small amount of memory that would be used to temporarily hold data awaiting to be processed. When this buffer is inundated with data, it could result in a computer failure condition normally referred to as buffer overflow. These could pose serious security threats because writing data outside the buffer or allocated memory could corrupt IT data, cause computer program crashes or allow the execution of malicious code created by a hacker. The Open Web Application Security Project has recommended that the top cybersecurity strategies to avoid buffer overflow would include fully patching web and application servers plus following bug reports on applications that support the code being used. When a computer system gets overloaded with so much externally generated requests, which have been generated by hackers or attack groups, to a point where it would cause problems in its ability to provide its specific service, it becomes a computer denial-of-service (DoS) attack. These denial-of-service attacks are typically accomplished by flooding the targeted digital IT computer systems with numerous superfluous requests which would overload the digital IT systems so as to prevent them performing some or all of other legitimate requests for computer services. When a computer system is overwhelmed with an influx of various packets, generated by hackers, that occupy the maximum number of connections, the target IT system's resources would be depleted and its connection bandwidths would be weakened.

An analogous climate change situation would be the rising frequency of climate-induced heavy rainfalls which could then lead to heavy storm water surges and floodings. These extreme storm water surges and flooding incidents have often caused major disruptions in cities, resulting in serious property damages.

Floodings in cities caused by excessive storm water and rainfalls are analogous to computer systems that have been over-inundated with excessive data generated by hackers. Drainage and sewer systems would experience something similar to DoS attacks when confronted with the heavy floodings caused by climate-induced extreme heavy rainfall incidents.

Both computer systems and sewers would suffer; even if the service of the system is not fully denied to legitimate users, there will be a slowing or "degradation of service." These would result in compromised or corrupted access, lower efficiency and poorer performance of the flooded systems.

Cybersecurity strategies to prevent DoS attacks would typically involve the use of a combination of digital detection and IT response tools that would block web traffics that have been identified as illegitimate. However, these advanced cyber tools must also be configured to allow normal legitimate IT traffics to go through. This might be difficult as hackers would often use advanced attack systems to confuse these detection tools.

Similarly in city climate change protection systems, they should use flood detection and water response tools that would identify and block sewage traffic from mixing with storm water traffics, so as to prevent combined sewer overflows (CSOs). These could help to reduce the occurrence of wide spread floods. These advanced systems should benefit cities and communities which have frequent flooding problems caused by excessful climate-induced storm water.

It is interesting to note that similar approaches could be used in cybersecurity for the identification and diversion of illegitimate traffic as in climate change for detection of storm surges and flooding. The approaches for detection and handling of legitimate traffics in cybersecurity have many similarities to handling of storm water and sewages to segregate water flows to reduce flooding in cities. These are good examples of a useful environmental application of a commonly used DoS cybersecurity strategy.

So in summary, buffer overflow is probably the best-known form of software vulnerability in cybersecurity. As discussed, a buffer overflow condition could occur when external programs used by hackers attempt to put more data in a buffer than it could handle. It would then lead to corrupted data, program crashes or extreme cyber attacks allowing the execution of malicious codes from hackers which could lead to serious cyber damages.

Similarly, climate-induced extreme heavy rainfall incidents could lead to storm water surges and floodings when the combined sewer overflows (CSOs) involve the mixing of excess inputs that compromise the system at large. A CSO is caused by storm water surges that enter sewer systems, mix with sewage and overflow into rivers and cities. These would compromise the integrity of the drainage systems in cities and pose serious flood risks with threats on water quality, sanitation and infrastructure. These serious consequences of climate-induced floodings would mirror a denial-of-service cybersecurity attack which will lead to serious impairment of services.

New approaches to prevent overflows to both computer and sewer systems could be approached in similar ways. Advanced digital cybersecurity denial-of-service prevention tools could consist of front-end detection hardware placed in the network before traffic reaches the servers. It could be used on networks in conjunction with IT routers and switches. These front-end cybersecurity detection hardware devices would analyse data packets as they enter the system, and then identify them as priority, regular or dangerous.

Similar advanced digital detection systems could be developed and used in city sewage systems to detect and segregate storm water drainages and sewer flows. These could involve smart intelligent channels or sump basins that would help to manage climate-induced storm water run-offs while diverting other traffics like sewage and polluted outflows.

Both approaches would adopt analogous approaches to remediate and mitigate against similar situations like the DoS cybersecurity attacks. These new approaches would involve apply new in-depth, multilayered defence strategy incorporating three different phases which comprise readiness, reaction and resolution. For both cybersecurity and climate change mitigations, the application of advanced digital detection and preventative technologies should help to pre-emptively detect possible surges and attacks. It would help to better position IT systems and cities on improved handling of these overflows and eliminating the excessive inputs/attacks. These would help digital systems and cities to recover quicker from attacks and restoring faculties to effectively perform their intended functions.

Renewables, climate change, digital cybersecurity way forwards

Digital transformation and cybersecurity are both important strategic elements for sustainable future growth of many companies globally in light of climate change and the renewable transformations. Companies have to develop appropriate digital transformation strategies to improve performance and efficiency whilst taking account of the climate change impacts.

Cybersecurity improvements are key to protecting companies against growing cyber attacks and risks of fraud. There should be strong management support for elimination of legacy systems which are often energy inefficient and not in line with new climate change requirements. Management should also implement organisational reforms to accelerate digital transformations and improve cybersecurity for companies in both emerging economies and developed countries globally.

Successful digital transformations would involve companies having to make major changes to corporate systems, workflows, business rules, organisations and roles. Management has to develop clear digital visions and digital transformation strategies as part of its overall corporate strategy and priorities.

Corporate management should be fully committed to executing these strategies and eliminating legacy systems. These may involve painful organisational reforms and role changes for many staff. However, companies which have successfully embrace digital transformations should have real competitive edges over their peers particularly in light of the serious climate change impacts. In addition, these should help to improve corporate efficiency, transparency and governance. These will support companies being better able to cope with climate change and the renewable transformation requirements. These should help companies to better achieve sustainable performances with continuous developments and growths.

A good international business digital transformation example is Netflix which has successfully shifted from DVDs to online streaming as part of its digital transformation strategies. This shifting has enabled it to improve its business performances and global growths. Other good retail business examples include eBay and Alibaba which have created the world's biggest retail channels without buying any inventory as part of digital commerce strategies.

Cybersecurity is an important management priority for successful companies especially those in the energy sector which are also most likely to be affected by global warming and climate change. Companies with successful cybersecurity strategies should prioritise corporate resources to protect areas which are most valuable. They should also proactively implement cybersecurity practices that would protect their business against attacks.

In addition, companies in emerging economies and developed countries globally should actively engage with relevant government policy makers and regulators to form effective public–private partnerships (PPP) on digital transformation and cybersecurity plus climate change and fossil to renewable transformations. It would enable good sharing of best practices and knowledges plus promote digital transformation and cybersecurity improvements.

11 International companies' renewable strategy management

入乡随俗
rù xiāng suí sú
When you enter a village, then you should follow its customs.
When in Rome, do as the Romans do.

Executive summary

International companies are recognising that many emerging economies and developed countries globally have enacted new energy policies to promote their fossil to clean renewable energy transformation whilst reducing their fossil fuel consumptions so as to meet their Paris Agreement commitments. This has led many leading energy companies, including gas and oil companies, to adopt new corporate strategies to reduce their GHG emissions and to make new investments into renewables. Experts have reported that the new renewable energy investments by leading oil and gas companies globally have already grown by over USD3 billion over the last five years. Looking ahead, these are expected to grow further in the foreseeable future. The clean renewable energy growths in various leading oil and gas energy companies, including state-owned enterprises and multinational companies, will be discussed in more detail in this chapter with international business examples.

Renewable corporate strategy transformations and risks

Leading companies globally, in both emerging economies and developed countries, have to take account of the rising climate change and global warming impacts on their future business performances, as the values at stake could be enormous. The World Bank has estimated that the combined revenues of global businesses could rise to more than $190 trillion within a decade but there are many risks, especially climate risks. It is important for company boards and managements, for both public and private companies, to developed suitable new climate change strategies with good clean renewable energy investment strategies (Mckinsey, Competing in a world of sectors without borders, 2016).

Leading companies, in both emerging economies and developed countries globally, should ensure that they would compile with the growing new climate regulatory, environmental and clean renewable energy requirements. Companies should also take into consideration various key market and consumer drivers for climate change and sustainability improvements. Managements have to reduce GHG emissions and improve environmental performance of their production sites. They also have to improve their corporate strategies to take account of the rising climate change risks and clean renewable energy requirements. Organisations have to recognise and anticipate climate-related risks plus important drivers such as changing government policies, clean energy regulatory requirements, product-preference shifts and price volatility.

Experts have showed that there are, in broad terms, six different kinds of key climate risks which may affect leading companies globally. These climate risks would include value-chain risks and external-stakeholder risks plus stakeholder risks which we shall discuss more below with international business examples (Mckinsey, How companies can adapt to climate change, 2015).

Value-chain physical risks are normally related to the damages that could be inflicted by extreme weather incidents, on infrastructure and other corporate assets, such as factories and supply-chain operations. Climate change has led to increased frequency and intensity of extreme weather events, such as wildfires, floods, hurricanes, typhoons, etc. The frequency and severity of these climate-induced extreme weather disasters have increased markedly since the 1970s. These could negatively affect company performance and cause serious damages.

A good business damage example is Cargill, which is one of the world's largest food and agricultural companies. In 2012, Cargill had to post its worst quarterly earnings in two decades. This was caused largely by the serious US droughts, which were induced by climate change. These extreme droughts have led to food crop failures and poor agricultural yields. These have then led to serious reduction in the corporate revenues for Cargill, which resulted in it having to post its worst quarterly earnings.

Another interesting business example is Western Digital Technologies, which is a major supplier of hard disk drives. In 2011, it had posted a sharp decline in corporate revenues, after serious climate-induced flooding in Thailand. These floodings have severely affected most of its manufacturing plants in Thailand, which affected their production and global supplies. Their loss of production also meant a global slump in hard disk supply worldwide, which had severe reverberations for the company plus many other computer manufacturers. It is good to note that Thailand, after experiencing these serious floods, has been implementing the new low-carbon sponge city designs in many of its major cities so as to better protect them from the rising flooding risks induced by climate change.

Companies have to take steps to prepare for severe climate-induced events which are likely to occur more frequently in years and decades to come with the rise of climate change and global warming. Companies should consider a range of possible scenarios together with potential mitigation actions.

Digital tools for climate forecasting can help to estimate high-level risk probabilities by region, such as for flood, drought or sea-level rises, and for long-term changes in such factors as temperature, humidity or rainfall patterns. Advances in digital technologies and big data systems have helped to improve the accuracy of climate forecasting and weather modelling with super computers.

Climate change can bring serious price risks that can negatively affect companies. These serious price risks could include increased price volatility of raw materials, feedstock supplies to companies, etc. A good example is that climate change has resulted in extreme weather incidents which could lead to widespread droughts. These could then lead to unexpected high price rises of water supplies to many companies in emerging economies and developed countries globally.

New energy policies and climate-related regulations could also drive up the cost of fossil fuel supplies as countries promote the switch from fossil fuels to renewable clean energy. High-tech and renewable energy industries could also face unexpected price risks in their competition for resources globally. A good example is the rising competition for rare earth materials, which are being used in the production of advanced battery systems, computer hard drives, televisions, wind turbines, solar photovoltaic systems, and electric vehicles. China is currently the world's leader in the production and supply of rare earth material.

Rising global warming has also resulted in unstable weather which has forced companies to cope with increased risks of production, energy, transport and supply chain disruptions. Many leading companies have been taking proactive steps to manage these potential serious risks so as to minimise business disruptions and interruptions to their supply chains.

A good business example is that Ikea has been undertaking clean energy transition away from fossil fuels to clean renewable energy supplies at many of their stores, in both emerging economies and developed countries globally. Looking ahead, Ikea is planning to become largely self-sufficient with regard to electricity power supply based on clean renewable power generation integrated with advanced digital distributed power management systems. It would give Ikea better control of what prices it would have to pay for power and energy supplies, together with improved power security. It would enable Ikea to be better able to insulate itself against global and regional energy price spikes, plus protect against unplanned power disruptions. In addition, Ikea has established a new partnership with NESTE. This partnership is exploring new commercial production of bio-naphtha and bioplastic from waste oil recovery in Europe. Ikea is planning to apply these new bioplastics in its packaging and furniture products globally so as to reduce consumption of plastic chemical materials. More details of the Ikea Neste pilot are given in Chapter 6 on bioenergy in this book.

Another good example is that the German car manufacturer Volkswagen (VW) is also undertaking clean energy transition away from fossil fuels to clean renewable energy for its car manufacturing operations. VW has implemented various hedging strategies against the possibility of rising fossil fuel prices and has invested €1 billion in renewable energy projects. It has plans to power its various car manufacturing sites globally mainly through its on-site renewable power productions, integrated with advanced distributed power control systems.

Looking ahead, it is expected that increasingly leading manufacturing companies globally will want to go "off-grid" and become self-sufficient in power generation, for both strategic and economic reasons. Like Volkswagen and Ikea, it is expected that increasingly leading companies will undertake clean energy transitions. They plan to reduce the use of fossil fuels and increase clean renewable energy applications for their manufacturing operations. To generate their own clean renewable power reliably, they would need to employ advanced distributed power digital technologies and power storage systems, with their renewable power generation, including solar, wind or biomass. They would also need to ensure that they have good cyber security for their new digital power systems so that these will have high reliability and not be affected by hackers which could cause severe disruptions.

Climate change can also induce serious product risks which could seriously affect company performances. Product risks could include core products becoming unpopular or even unsellable due to various reasons. These could cause companies to lose market shares or in severe cases to go under entirely. A good example is that climate change could promote the development of alternative cooling technologies with environmental friendly refrigerants. These would then have major impacts on conventional air-conditioning systems with chemical refrigerants, which have high global warming impacts.

On the positive side, new greener products have been emerging in a number of industries to cope with global warming implications. The construction and infrastructure sectors have been developing new products and services that cater for cleaner low-carbon smart cities. These included new energy-efficient buildings, electric-vehicle charging infrastructure, renewable integration, smart metering, smart grids, congestion-fee systems, plus high-performance green building materials and technologies. These have created new business opportunities for some traditional construction companies.

A good international business example is Saint-Gobain, the construction and packaging giant. It has recognised the important implications that climate change will have on its construction and packaging businesses. It has taken these climate risks into consideration when developing its new sustainable corporate strategies. It has incorporated the development of new sustainable housing technologies at the core of its new green product development strategy.

Climate change and global warming can also lead to higher operational risks and uncertainties. A good example is that many ski resorts in Europe and the USA had suffered significantly less snow falls, due to abnormally high winter temperatures induced by global warming. Many of these ski resort operators had to apply artificial snow generation so as to ensure that their ski runs have sufficient snow cover for the skiers to enjoy.

New climate-related regulations in many countries have also resulted in the introduction of additional carbon tax or new higher carbon emission costs in some countries. These have increased the coal and fossil fuel power generation costs significantly. A good example is that carbon taxes have raised the price of coal power generation in many markets above that of clean renewable energy on a full life cycle basis. These would also lead to additional ripple effects on the associated coal mining industries, coal mining-equipment manufacturers and related coal supply industries with reduced demands, which have led to unemployment in some sectors.

Many utility companies have also been changing their traditional power supply business models in many markets globally so as to participate in the fossil fuel to clean renewable energy transitions. A good example is that advances in digital distributed power technologies with renewable power generations have resulted in more decentralised power generation together with advanced distributed power management systems being applied in many countries. These could help to provide electricity power to one billion people in more remote communities globally who previously have no access to electricity or power. However, these new systems must also have good cyber security protections built into the digital management system so as to ensure good power supply reliability plus guard against hackers or terrorists which could cause severe disruptions.

In the important business-to-consumer (B2C) sector, fast-changing retail and consumer preferences are making inroads as consumers have become more willing to pay for greener products. A good business example is the fast-growing organic food and green grocery sectors which have seen double-digit growths for the past decade in many countries globally driving by new customer preferences. Consumers are now able to find plentiful supply of organic food in many supermarkets globally.

Companies will need to be actively monitoring these emerging megatrends so as to revise their corporate strategies accordingly. One way is to adopt a "design to sustainability" approach, in which new products are designed to minimise waste and to be designed for breaking down for reuse or recycling. Another is to redefine corporate strategy so as to align business interests with climate-change mitigation and adaptation. A good business example is that Siemens has developed a new dedicated "environmental portfolio" of new carbon-efficient products as part of its new corporate climate change and product strategies.

Climate change has also raised external-stakeholder monitoring and risks for companies globally. Whilst these risks could vary widely between and within industries, companies with carbon-intensive activities should proactively manage these potential risks. A good example is that more than 4,000 corporates have proactively decided to report their carbon exposure on a transparent basis to the Carbon Disclosure Project (CDP). Many leading oil and gas majors have also been applying new internal carbon pricings on their evaluation of new fossil projects, so as to better guide some of their strategic investment decisions globally.

Around the world, many governments have been introducing new climate change and clean energy policies which could affect the business prospects of many leading corporates. A good example is that China has launched its new national carbon emission trading programme, following trial carbon emission trading programmes in seven regions. The new carbon emission trading system will initially cover the power sector in China. It is expected that many power companies in China will have to improve their operations and accelerate their fossil to renewable transitions, so as to reduce their GHG emissions.

Another good clean energy example is that most US states have also introduced new renewable portfolio standard (RPS) which will require a certain proportion of the state's electricity to be produced from renewable sources. In Africa, Ethiopia has also developed a new climate master plan to actively develop its low-carbon economy so as to become a middle-income emerging economy country, through low-carbon economy growths with its climate resilient green economy strategy.

It is important to recognise the potential political uncertainty of new climate change policies, at both the national and international level, deriving from new election results. A good example is the significant change in the US approach to climate change and the Paris Agreement following the election of the US President Donald Trump. Companies globally have to actively monitor and manage these potential political and regulation changes and the associated risks. They should be active in understanding the changing political and policy landscapes in the countries that they operate in. In some cases, leading corporates have to undertake active government lobbying, so that they can help to shape future regulations and policy options. Companies must also develop new climate change strategy so as to put the company in a position to react quickly and effectively to possible new regulations and policy changes. These should also work with external stakeholders, such as regulators and industry groups, to proactively share their perspectives and provide inputs into future policy formulations.

Climate change has also increased reputation risks for companies and governments globally. These could be either direct or indirect risks. Direct reputation risks could stem from a company-specific action which could influence the corporate reputation. Indirect reputation risk could come in the form of public perception of the whole industrial sector. In the climate change context, negative reputation risks could lead to declines in business performance and profitability. A poor corporate reputation in climate change could also damage company sales. In the worse scenarios, it could lead to consumer boycotts or local community protests against the company. It could also damage investor relationships and corporate image. In some worse cases, it has led to ethnical impact investor and shareholder actions against the company board and management. A good example is the recent shareholder challenges to the Commonwealth Bank of Australia on its poor climate risk management on its housing investments.

There are also growing global ethnical investor concerns on climate change. Investors are asking companies for disclosure on their carbon emissions and footprints. In some cases, investors have started to lodge serious concerns about potential "stranded" assets in the fossil fuel to clean renewable energy transformation. These might include fossil fuel assets which are becoming unusable or unprofitable due to climate-policy regulation or physical climate change. A good example of stranded assets includes old coal-fired power stations which would have to be phased out in future to reduce environmental pollution and minimise GHG emissions.

Globally, there are growing numbers of customers who believe that sustainability and environmental friendliness should be essential elements of the companies from which they would want to buy products from. Non-governmental organisations (NGOs) are getting more influential and are actively measuring and comparing corporate performances in the climate change area. University graduates are also hesitant to apply to companies with poor climate change performances.

A good corporate challenge example is the recent serious challenges by ethnical investors and shareholders to the ExxonMobil management. They have severely challenged the company management on their climate strategies as they do not believe that the management has developed adequate climate risk management approaches. These challenges have led to sustained declines in the ExxonMobil share prices and serious reputational damages globally.

In response to the climate change and renewable transformation implications, many companies have taken active steps to improve their climate change strategies and reputation. A good example is Unilever, the Anglo Dutch conglomerate. Unilever has led the FTSE CDP Carbon Strategy risk and performance index and has improved its carbon efficiency by 40% since 1995. It stated that corporate environmental improvement goals are to reduce the carbon and water footprints of its various products to half of their 2010 levels by 2020. Another good retail example is Kohl, which has won recognitions for its efforts to improve the environmental impacts of its operations and to reduce GHG emissions significantly.

In the digital IT sector, IBM has also won positive feedbacks for its good actions on climate change. These included setting up new rigorous greenhouse gas emission standards for its computer suppliers and value chains. IBM has won a 2013 Climate Leadership Award from the US Environmental Protection Agency for supply-chain leadership. It was also recognised in 2014 for its greenhouse gas management.

It is encouraging to see that many good leading corporates understand the importance of climate change and renewable transformation. They have been actively managing these and improving their environmental performances. Many other companies have to do more to improve their climate change and renewable transformation strategies. Otherwise, they could be exposed to serious risks and negative impacts, including product, operational, pricing, reputational, etc.

Clean renewable corporate investment strategy analysis

Global investments in clean renewable energy by international companies and corporations have risen strongly in recent year. These investments have taken place via different investment models and various channels for different companies. It has been estimated that the global investments in clean renewable energy have exceed USD1 trillion in the last decade. The annual investments in clean energy have also exceeded USD200 billion for the past seven years. A good example is that in 2016 the total new investment in renewable power and fuels was over USD260 billion in both emerging economies and developed countries (IRENA, Investments in Renewables Analysis, 2018).

Looking ahead, experts have predicted that the global clean renewable energy investments are expected to continue their strong upward trends. A good example is that the Chinese government has announced major renewable investment plans, as part of its 13th Five-Year National Plan, to spend USD360 billion on clean renewable energy projects through to 2020/2025. These clean energy investments should reinforce China's position as the world's leader in clean renewable energy investments (UNEP, Renewable Investment Global Trends Report, 2019).

Globally, most of the clean energy and renewable electricity investments have continued to be dominated by electricity power generation plants owned by big utilities or large investors. The scale of various clean energy power plants, including solar PV, wind power and CSP, has continued to increase with new technical innovations. Some of the key clean renewable power generation equipment have also continued to grow with technological advances and innovations. A good example is wind turbines which have continued to increase in size with new material advances and new technological innovations (REN, Renewables Global Status Report, 2018).

The leading utility companies in China, Denmark, Germany, India, Sweden and the United States have continued to invest in large-scale renewable energy projects, especially in solar PV and wind power. Interestingly, these leading utility companies have also started to, in some cases, invest in renewable energy technology companies as part of their innovation and technology drives.

International analysis has highlighted that some leading oil and gas companies which have traditionally been working in the fossil fuel sectors, such as oil, gas and coal, have also started to move aggressively into the clean energy and renewable energy sectors. Many leading energy companies have developed new clean renewable energy investment strategies and made major announcements globally. A good example is Shell which has announced its new clean renewable energy investment strategy, especially in the growing areas of new electric vehicle charging and offshore wind developments.

Globally, many major international corporations and institutions have also been making large commitments to purchase clean renewable electricity from different sources, including from emerging economies. Many leading businesses around the world have also joined the RE100 alliance. This is a global initiative of businesses which have committed to achieving a target of 100% renewable electricity in future. New RE100 corporate members have included major companies in China and India, as well as international heavy industrial corporates (RE100, Report and Briefings, 2019).

Many leading companies globally have been making major purchases of clean renewable energy as part of their new energy and power supply strategies. The bulk of these clean power purchases have been in renewables, such as wind energy and solar PV. Most of the international corporates have been procuring their renewable electricity through renewable energy certificates (RECs). Many major corporates have also increasingly entered into new power purchase agreements (PPAs) or applied new direct clean power ownership models.

An increasing number of large corporations have negotiated and committed to new power purchase agreements (PPAs) of unprecedented large sizes. Many of these PPAs have been contracts undertaken directly with renewable energy generator companies rather than with utility companies. A good example is that the overall volume of PPAs in 2016 has rose to 4.3 GW which was the second highest amount on record globally.

There have also been some interesting clean renewable energy community project investments in recent year. These involved investments by a growing number of local communities in new renewable projects in some countries. A good example is that Canada has seen its first community wind farm starting operation recently. Another good example is that Chile has been implementing a new dedicated policy for clean community energy projects since late 2015. Chile has now registered 12 new communities to receive investment funds for new community clean renewable energy projects.

However, the growths in community energy projects in some other countries have been declining. These included parts of Europe, Germany, the United Kingdom and Japan. A lot of these declines were caused by new clean energy policies shifting away from FITs towards competitive tendering. A good example is that in the United Kingdom over 40 community energy projects have stalled after new policy changes that have reduced tax benefits and FIT rates. Another good example is that in Japan renewable policy amendments that have removed priority access for renewable energies have meant that many community power projects would no longer be able to connect to Japan's national electricity grids.

International companies' renewable strategy management

Leading international corporates in emerging economies and developed countries around the world have worked on developing their corporate renewable strategies plus energy transformations, in light of the serious climate change threats. Looking ahead, it is expected that a rising number of leading manufacturing companies globally will be accelerating their energy transformation from fossil fuel into clean renewable power supplies. These companies have set new corporate targets to become self-sufficient in power generation, for both strategic and economic reasons.

Good international business examples included Volkswagen and Ikea. Ikea has said publicly that its long-term corporate direction is for all Ikea Group buildings to be supplied with 100% renewable energy. In addition, Ikea is aiming to improve the Ikea Group's overall energy efficiency performance globally by 25%, compared with its 2005 performances. Amongst other energy-savings initiatives, Ikea will be using energy-savings light bulbs in its stores, where possible, plus it will have the lights on only when warehouses are open. Ikea has also pledged to install extra insulation to save on energy for heating and cooling in its stores and warehouses. Ikea has also said that it is going to make sure that all Ikea Group stores, warehouses, distribution centres, factories and offices will be heated and cooled using renewable fuels such as wind, water, solar power, biofuels and geothermal energy in future (Ikea, Goes Renewables, Sweden, 2019).

Volkswagen (VW), the international auto manufacturer, had its corporate reputation severely damaged by its roles in enabling its diesel models to cheat laboratory emission tests in the USA and the EU in 2015. It has developed new corporate improvement strategies and is now aiming to become a leading provider of sustainable mobility for emerging economies and developed countries globally. VW has founded a new subsidiary called Elli Group GmbH, based in Berlin. The new unit will develop green auto products and services, relating to clean renewable energy and electric vehicle (EV) charging for its new EV products. VW has said that as one of the world's largest automakers, it will going to force the pace of the urgently needed global transport and energy transitions to emission-neutral e-mobility. The new VW business unit is expected to contribute a renewables-based smart charging solution for electric cars. VW believed that it will be entering a strategically relevant and exciting business area that would offer considerable opportunities for strengthening ties with existing customers as well as accessing entirely new customer groups in the emerging economies and developed countries globally (PV Magazine, Volkswagen green energy supplier, 2019).

Looking ahead, it is expected that increasingly international companies will undertake energy transition away from fossil fuels into renewable energy. These have been driven by new government energy policy drives and requirements to reduce GHG emissions plus drives by companies to improve their environmental performances. These companies have, in order to secure their own clean power reliably, applied renewable power generation integrated with advanced distributed power storage and digital distributed power management technologies. They are applying advanced digital systems to manage their new renewable power supplies efficiently and reliably. At the same time, they must also improve their cyber security to guard against hacker or terrorist attacks to these systems, which could result in severe supply disruptions.

We shall discuss two good international digital company business case examples covering Google and Telefónica, in more detail below. Both have accelerated their clean energy and digital transformations to support the sustainable development of their key global businesses in light of the rising climate change threats.

Google has been active in pursuing its new corporate pledge of transforming its power supplies to 100% renewable energy. It has actively ramped up its acquisition of green power supplies from both emerging economies and developed countries. Google has said that its clean renewable energy transformations are currently on course to have all its data centres globally to be powered by renewable energy sources in future. It has pledged to purchase enough wind and solar power to support its global operations. Google has said that reaching its 100% renewable energy goal will be a multi-year effort. It will also be improving its datacentre energy savings and efficiency. Google engineers have undertaken digital and technical improvements on its data centres in many countries across the world. They have made these data centres to be 50% more energy efficient than the industrial average. Google has also applied advanced digital technologies, including the use of machine learning and artificial intelligence, in its datacentres. These have helped Google to improve its energy robustness and energy efficiency plus meet the rising climate challenges (Computer Weekly, Google datacentres, 2016).

Google has, in its drive to ensure that it will have sufficient renewable energy power supplies for its office as well as its fleet of datacentres, been buying directly additional wind- and solar-generated renewable electricity for its operations. It has been buying clean renewable power from projects funded by its own purchases globally. Electricity costs have been one of the largest components of Google's operating expenses. A long-term stable supply of renewable power at pre-agreed costs will therefore help Google to provide good power security and protection against energy disruptions plus price swings. To date, Google's purchasing commitments have resulted in infrastructure investments of more than USD3.5 billion globally, with around two-thirds of the investments in the USA. Google has estimated that these new renewable projects should generate tens of millions of dollars per year in revenues to local renewable plant owners, plus tens of millions more to local and national governments in tax revenues.

Telecom companies have also been accelerating their renewable digital transformation in light of climate change pressures. A good example is Telefónica, the international telecom company. Telefónica is the operator behind UK's O_2 mobile network. It has been actively pushing its energy transitions to renewable energy supplies as part of its corporate strategy to handle climate change risks. Telefónica has said that it is planning to speed up its commitments in fighting climate change and to achieve its Paris Agreement commitments. It is striving to source 50% of its electricity from renewable energy sources by 2020 and 100% by 2030. Its businesses have already been operating with an internal corporate renewable energy business plan. As of June 2017, 44% of its electricity consumption has come from renewable energy sources. This is equivalent to the total average power consumption by over 203,000 homes (Computer Weekly, Telefónica, 2017).

Telefónica had also claimed it is already on 100% renewable power supply in Germany and the UK, plus 79% in Spain. It is planning to keep 1.5 million tons of carbon dioxide (CO_2) emission from entering the atmosphere over the next 12.5 years. At its Madrid HQ, solar panels have already been generating more than 3 GWh per year. Telefónica has also now joined the RE100 alliance, which is a worldwide collaborative alliance for businesses which have committed to achieving the 100% clean renewable energy goal in future.

Telefónica believed that its new corporate renewable energy plans have helped it to improve competitiveness, reduce operational costs and make sustainable business growths which are compatible with their corporate sustainability strategy. Its new corporate goal is to have the best digital network with excellent connectivity in technological terms, but also one that it is the most efficient and clean in the sector in terms of energy and carbon. Its renewable energy plan has four action areas which differ slightly depending on the local market regulations where it operates. These included acquisition of renewable energy with a guarantee of origin, long-term purchase power agreements (PPAs), shorter bilateral agreements and self-production.

In Latin America, Telefónica will be relying heavily on PPAs for clean renewable energy supplies to its operations in various Latin American emerging economies. In Mexico, it already has a power purchase agreement which will see two solar photovoltaic power plants coming online in the near future to supply 50% of its in-country electricity consumption for the next 15 years. It is hoping to sign similar PPA deals in Argentina, Chile and Colombia. Meanwhile, in Brazil, it is acquiring renewable energy through bilateral agreements and hopes to save €15m per annum. In Uruguay, it is installing 16 small solar plants in rural areas to generate 600 MWh of energy each year. In Colombia, it recently invested USD1.4 million in new solar photovoltaic generation to replace old equipment which has relied on diesel fuel. Its fossil to clean renewable energy shift has helped to eliminate CO_2 GHG emissions of over 470 tons per annum.

State-owned enterprises' renewable strategy management

SOEs in the emerging economies and developed countries have been growing and expanding rapidly to become world-class companies in their countries and globally. It is conservatively estimated that SOEs internationally have been contributing more than 10% of the combined sales of the world's largest businesses listed in the Forbes Global 2000. The proportion of SOEs, amongst the Fortune Global 500 companies, has also grown from 10% in 2005 to over 25% now. The combined SOE corporate sales revenues are currently accounting for more than 6% of the global GDP and are larger than the GDP of some key developed economies, such as Germany or France. SOEs globally have to deal with rising threats from climate change, digital transformation and cyber security. They have to develop appropriate strategies and mitigation actions to ensure their sustainable business growths and successful operations.

Experts have found that state-owned enterprises (SOEs) have been major players in both fossil energy and electricity power sectors. SOEs have major investments in fossil sectors, including oil, gas and coal. The OECD has reported that the total SOE investments could amount to over USD300 billion in the G20. SOEs are also major players in fossil fuel markets and have been estimated to own roughly 60% of coal mines and coal power plants globally. Experts have also reported that electricity power generation companies owned by state enterprises are currently owning more fossil fuel-based generation capacities than those owned by privately owned electricity generating companies. As a result, SOEs have been major producers of GHGs and are currently accounting for a substantial quantity of greenhouse gas (GHG) emissions in emerging economies and globally. Experts have estimated that the combined GHG emissions of the top 50 energy-related SOEs in the world would rank third in a list of country-level GHG emissions, just after China and the United States (OECD, SOE transition away from coal and coal-fired power, 2018).

At the same time, SOEs have continued to invest heavily in fossil resources and technologies. Experts have estimated that SOEs are currently responsible for two-thirds of planned power investments globally, of which more than half are in fossil fuel-based technologies. The International Energy Agency (IEA) has found that, between 2012 and 2017, the share of global energy investment driven by SOEs increased to 42%, with public sector investors found to be "more resilient" to changes in the markets for oil, gas and thermal power (IEA, WEO, 2018).

Many state-owned enterprises (SOEs) in emerging economies and developed countries around the world are beginning to appreciate the serious climate change challenges and the fossil to renewable transformation requirements. Many SOEs have transformed their corporate strategies and have started to invest in renewable and clean energy projects. New pieces of research on state-owned enterprises in the fossil to renewable low-carbon transition showed that SOEs have major influences on renewable investments in emerging economies and globally. State ownership in some of the SOEs, in the electricity power sector, has encouraged these SOEs to invest more in new renewable capacities with new clean energy policies. It is encouraging to note that recent pieces of research have shown that SOEs in the OECD and G20 countries have, between 2000 and 2014, increased the share of renewables in their electricity capacity portfolios from 9% to 23% (OECD, Investment in Low Carbon Infrastructure, 2018).

Looking ahead, the International Renewable Energy Agency (IRENA) has estimated that all renewable electricity technologies, with ongoing technology innovations, should become cost competitive with, or even undercut, fossil fuels as early as 2020. This will mean that this should further promote the shift of fossil power to clean renewable power generation (IRENA, 2018).

In addition to the cost competitiveness of renewables, the fall in production and use of coal will be driven by climate change improvements and new environmental policies linked to air pollution improvements. The IEA has estimated that to keep the global temperature increase well below 2°C, coal-fired power plant emissions must be reduced by more than half globally by 2030 (IEA, 2018).

These global megatrends should help to drive more SOEs to improve their climate performances by reducing GHG emissions and invest more in renewables to continue to support the fossil to renewable transitions. A good SOE example is Vattenfall of Sweden. Vattenfall is fully owned by the Government of Sweden and has invested in power generation facilities globally. It has power generation assets in Finland, Denmark, Germany, Poland and the Baltic countries, amongst others. In 2010, Vattenfall's board and top management adopted new sustainability targets and strategies for the SOEs. These included reducing their carbon dioxide GHG emissions by more than 30% by 2020. As part of the efforts by the SOE to meet these new targets, Vattenfall's management decided in 2014 to divest off its lignite coal mines and associated coal-fired power plants in eastern Germany. Vattenfall's investments for 2018 and 2019 have been focused on renewables including wind power and solar plus decentralised digital power solutions, advanced energy storage and e-mobility (Vattenfall, Road to Fossil Freedom, 2019).

Multinational oil and gas energy companies' renewable strategy transformation

Experts have predicted that an increasing number of multinational fossil oil and gas companies will be investing in the renewable sector, as the potential for wind and solar energy grows globally and the costs of renewable decline with technological innovations. Many of the leading multinational oil and gas companies have also recognised the importance to compile with the new clean energy and emission policies introduced by various governments in emerging economies and developed countries globally, as part of their efforts to meet their Paris Agreement commitments. Many oil and gas companies have developed new corporate strategies which have included expansions into clean energy and reductions in GHG emissions.

Many multinational oil and gas companies have created new clean renewable energy business divisions to invest in renewables and to promote their clean renewable energy transformations. The oil and gas industry has already seen some of the sector's largest companies, including Shell, Total, BP etc., announcing that they are making big investments in renewable and clean energy projects. Recent analysis showed that Big Oil's cumulative investments in renewable acquisitions over the past five years have reached over USD3 billion, most of which have been into solar renewables (CBC Business, Big Oil, 2018).

The rising renewable investments by oil and gas companies globally have been driven by a number of key factors, including climate change, fossil to renewable transformation, GHG emission reductions and technology innovations. In addition, the renewable generation costs have reduced significantly with technological innovations and cost reduction measures. Good examples included cost reductions of 50–70%in solar and wind renewable power generation in recent years with various technological innovations and cost reduction measures (IRENA, 2018).

Looking ahead, experts are predicting more renewable growths with rising investments. These are driven by renewables becoming cost competitive against fossil generation options, with government subsidies no longer required in future. A good industrial example is that as renewable generation costs have come down significantly recently, the power generation price required to justify an investment in solar or wind power generation should be cheaper than that of a natural gas co-generation plant in emerging economies and developed countries.

Looking ahead, energy experts have predicted that natural gas will continue to be an important fossil transitionary fuel for some time globally. Many emerging economies and developed countries have promoted gas power generation and domestic consumptions as part of their new energy policies to reduce coal consumptions and to improve environmental pollution. There are also important complementary roles for natural gas with renewable applications. A good example is that wind and solar renewable power generation are currently not yet able to supply power continuously around the clock, 24/7. The integration of natural gas with solar or wind renewable power generation can be a win-win partnership in terms of providing reliable power supplies on a continuous basis.

A lot of new investment capital has been coming into the renewable sector from different sources. These included investments from energy companies, pension funds and life insurance companies plus sovereign wealth funds, etc. A good example is Norway's $1 trillion government-owned sovereign investment fund. Norway's sovereign wealth fund has announced its new strategic objectives to combat climate change whilst creating value and being good stewards of the national funds. The Norway investment fund managers have said, in early 2019, that it would be divesting off 134 companies which have been developing fossil oil and gas businesses. These included oil and gas companies such as UK-based Tullow Oil, Premier Oil, Soco International, Ophir Energy and Nostrum Oil & Gas. The fund managers have also said that they will be retaining their investment positions in Royal Dutch Shell and BP because both have adopted new clean energy strategies and established new renewable energy business divisions. The Norway fund managers have also announced that they will be redirecting the funds, which they have earned from their oil and gas investments, and invest them in clean energy projects instead (Forbes Energy, Big Oil Dipping into Green Energy, 2019).

At present, most oil and gas companies are continuing with their investments into their tradition oil and gas pillar business, whilst also making new investments into renewable and clean energy businesses. In 2018, experts have estimated that oil and gas companies globally have spent about 1–1.5% of their investment budgets on renewable energy sectors. These have included wind and solar plus power battery storage and carbon capture. CDP, formerly known as the Carbon Disclosure Project, has reported that Europe's Equinor, Total, Shell and Eni have ranked highest for leading the low-carbon transition whilst China's CNOOC, Russia's Rosneft and US Marathon Oil have lagged further behind. CDP has also reported that since 2016 over 145 deals have been made in alternative energy and carbon capture. A total of USD22 billion has been invested in renewable and alternative energies since 2010 (CDP, 2017).

A good oil and gas business example is Equinor. It has developed new corporate strategies which aim to rebrand the oil and gas company into a broad energy company. As part of its new clean energy strategic shifts, it is planning to invest 15–20% of its future capital expenditures in renewable and new energy solutions by 2030.

There are also growing pressures from ethnical impact investors globally on many multinational companies, including oil and gas companies. Financial experts have estimated that some $26 trillion globally is being invested in line with the environmental, social and corporate governance (ESG) criteria. In the USA alone, investments of about $6–7 trillion are being invested in line with the ESG principles. Climate Action 100+ has also reported that multinational companies focusing on the triple ESG bottom lines, including economics, environment and social, have been outperforming other broader market indices globally. Investment experts have also reported that well-managed renewable infrastructure investments have been bringing steady, stable returns, making them attractive investments globally.

Many major multinational oil and gas companies have also come under intensive scrutiny from ethnical investors, climate activists, stakeholders, etc. These have been asking companies to become more transparent about how they manage their climate risks and reduce their CO_2 emissions. These have driven many of the oil and gas companies to develop new climate and renewable investment strategies. In addition, these have driven some oil and gas companies, including Chevron, ExxonMobil Corp. and Occidental Petroleum, to join the Oil and Gas Climate Initiative, which is developing new clean energy and carbon capture solutions. Some other leading oil and gas companies, including BP, Shell, Statoil and Total, have also been reviewing carbon emission trading system and carbon tax applications plus discussing these with relevant governments globally.

We shall examine further below two leading oil and gas companies on their new renewable corporate strategies and renewable investments together with international business examples.

Shell renewable strategy case study

Royal Dutch Shell is taking the clean energy transition seriously. The latest Shell global energy scenarios have predicted strong future growths in renewables, clean energy, green transportation and smart cities. It showed that there are good international growth opportunities in renewables, clean power, wind, biofuel, EV charging and e-mobility, in both emerging economies and developed countries. Their analysis has shown that the share of electricity in final energy consumption is currently around 22%. Looking ahead to 2070, they have predicted that global electricity consumption will be more than twice, to over 50%. These include growths in many end-user energy consumptions as electrification expands into transportation, home heating and cooking, and industrial sectors. These green growths will be driven by global decarbonisation efforts to address climate change and to shift to a net-zero energy system globally (Shell, Sky Scenario, 2018).

As part of Shell's new corporate strategy, a new integrated gas and new energy division has been established. One of its key business objectives is to develop Shell's renewable business and investments to become one of the largest clean power companies in the world by the early 2030s. It is planning to create a new global clean energy business that is more holistic than businesses of other companies. It hopes to offer its customers the opportunity to buy all their energy requirements from the company, covering both fossil fuel and renewable energies. It believes that this will be a unique competitive edge as many other power providers cannot make these links and customer propositions (GTM, Shell New Energies, 2019).

A good clean power business example is that Shell has renamed its UK-based energy supplier First Utility as Shell Energy Retail, under the broader Shell Energy brand. It has started serving all of its British residential customers with 100% renewable electricity. Shell's renewable energy offerings are being certified by the Renewable Energy Guarantees of Origin. It will certify that for every unit of electricity that Shell Energy supplies to its customers, a unit of renewable electricity will be supplied into the grid by renewable power generators in the UK. Shell Energy Retail will also be rolling out a range of smart home technology offers throughout the year, starting with the free Nest smart thermostats for UK customers who sign up for a three-year, fixed-price contract and discounts on home EV charging. Shell is also enhancing customer's loyalty by connecting the Shell Energy electricity customers to Shell's existing loyalty system for its fuel network. It will enable its renewable customers to get a discount when they fill up their cars with fossil fuel products at any Shell fuel retail stations in the UK (GTM, Shell New Energies, 2019).

Shell also plans to become a major regional clean electric power player in the USA in future. It is planning to invest in various deregulated US states where it would be possible for international power companies to compete. A good example is that Shell has invested in 2018 in the US retail power supplier Inspire Energy, which already offers clean energy plans in deregulated US states. In 2018, Shell also purchased Texas-based MP2 which has been expanding its power offerings to corporate and industrial customers. Shell New Energies has also purchased a major stake in US solar developer, Silicon Ranch.

Shell is currently investing $1–2 billion per year on renewable and new energy solutions, out of a total investment programme of more than $25 billion. Good examples of recent clean energy investments included the acquisition of the German home energy storage firm Sonnen and the purchase of the Dutch electric vehicle EV charging provider NewMotion. Shell has also invested in two Singapore-based solar firms, Sunseap Group and Cleantech Solar, which have been building solar farms for corporate customers across South and Southeast Asia (GTM, 2019).

In line with global ethnical impact investor developments, rising numbers of Shell's international investors and shareholders have been asking the Shell management to demonstrate that its investments are a force for good in the world. In response, the Shell management has been trying to show these investors that their investments can do good, whilst also delivering good returns. A good new energy business example is Sonnen, the new Shell Germany clean energy subsidiary. Sonnen has been selling new home-based clean energy optimisation solutions built around a battery system, together with advanced digital software systems connecting and optimising various aspects of energy application in the home. As their customers are purchasing the new energy products for their home applications, Sonnen's balance sheet is effectively zero, whilst maintaining a growing and profitable business on a sustainable basis.

Shell's experience in the fossil fuel industry could actually be an asset in the clean energy sector. Shell's business records have shown that the company has historically been able to find ways to be successful in establishing new difficult and competitive businesses. In addition, many of their technical and commercial competences and expertise in the oil and gas sector can be applied in the new renewable and clean energy sectors. A good example is that Shell's global oil fuel retail network experience can be applied in its new EV charging retail venture which aims to establish new EV charging stations and retail networks in the USA, Europe and Asia.

In other renewable energy sectors, Shell is also actively developing onshore and offshore wind projects in North America, Europe and Asia. In context to biofuel, Shell has established a USD12 billion joint venture with Cosan, Raizen, which is focusing primarily on Brazilian sugarcane and first-generation ethanol.

British Petroleum renewable strategy case study

BP's energy scenario forecasts have shown that renewable energy is the fastest growing segment of the global energy industry with over 7.5% growth each year between 2011 and 2030. BP has announced that it is planning to invest significantly in the renewable sector in future. BP's alternative energy division has strategised to focus its renewable energy portfolio on various renewables, especially biofuels and wind energy. This is mainly because BP has forecasted that by 2030 renewable energy from these sources is likely to meet around 6% of total global energy demands (BP, Global Energy Scenarios, 2018).

In context to biofuels, BP has invested in sugar cane ethanol mills in Brazil for bioethanol manufacturing. BP has also been producing biofuel from its biofuels joint venture, Vivergo Fuels, in the UK. As far as wind renewables are concerned, BP has been developing onshore and offshore wind farms in various locations. A good example is that BP has been developing wind farms in different US states, including Kansas, Pennsylvania and Hawaii.

Bibliography

ABC News, South Australia Biogas Human Waste Pilot Plant, Australia, April 2019.

ACS America Chemical Society, Selective Electrochemical Reduction of Carbon Dioxide Using Cu Based Metal Organic Framework for CO_2 Capture, USA, 2018.

Africa Dev Forum, Electricity Access in Sub Saharan Africa, World Bank, USA, 2019.

Albright & Calderia, Reversal of Ocean Acidification Enhances Net Coral Reef Calcification February 2016, Nature, USA, 2016.

Amadeo K, Carbon Tax, Its Purpose, and How It Works, USA, June 2019.

APEC, Life Cycle Assessment of Photovoltaic Systems in the APEC Region Report, Singapore, April 2019.

Asia Development Bank, ADB Signs Landmark Project with Icelandic, Chinese Venture to Promote Zero-Emissions Heating, ADB, Manila, 2018.

Asian Development Bank, Green Cities, ADB, Manila, 2012.

Assessment Agency (EU EDGAR), Emission Database for Global Atmospheric Research, EU Belgium, 2011.

Bank of England, Quarterly Bulletin: The Bank of England's Response to Climate Change, UK Q2, 2017.

BBC, How Will Our Future Cities Look? BBC London, UK, 17 February 2013.

BBC Environment, Carbon Bubble Could Cost Global Economy Trillions, UK, June 2018.

BBC News, Stephen Hawking's Warnings: What He Predicted for the Future, UK, 15 March 2018.

BBC News, Climate Change Impacts Women More than Men, UK, 8 March 2018.

Bloomberg, A Decade of Renewable Energy Investment Led by Solar, USA, 6 September 2019.

Bloomberg, NEF Bullard: Tech Investments Are Powering Up Clean Energy, USA, October 2018.

Bloomberg, Tesla Finishes First Solar Roofs, USA, August 2017.

Bloomberg, All Forecasts Signal Accelerating Demand for Electric Cars, USA, July 2017.

Bloomberg, India's Blue Sky Pledge Gives Power to Country's Green Bonds, by Anindya Upadhyay, USA, 24 July 2017.

Bloomberg, Beijing to Shut All Major Power Plants to Cut Pollution, USA, 2015.

Bloomberg, China Boosts Solar Target for 2015 as It Fights Pollution, USA, 2015.

BNEF (Bloomberg New Energy Finance), Battery Power's Latest Plunge in Costs Threatens Coal, Gas, USA, 26 March 2019.

BNEF, Electric Vehicle EV Battery Pack Cost Forecasts, USA, 2018.

BNEF, The Future of China's Power Sector. From Centralised and Coal Powered to Distributed and Renewable? USA, 14 October 2013.

BNPP AM, Revised Coal Investment Policy, Paris, France, 2019.

BNPP AM, Sustainability Roadmap to Deliver Paris-Aligned Investment Portfolio by 2025, Paris, France, 2019.

Boao Forum for Asia, 2015 Forum Speeches & Proceedings, BFA, Hainan, PRC, 2015.

Boao Forum for Asia, 2014 Forum Speeches & Proceedings, BFA, Hainan, PRC, 2014.

BP, Global Energy Scenarios, London, 2018.

BP, Carbon Neutral Management Plans, London, 2017.

C40 City & Arup, Deadline-2020 City Report, UK, 2018.

Canada Ecofiscal Commission Report on Carbon Pricing, Canada, April 2018.

Canada Govt Agriculture and Agri-Food Dept, Holos Climate Change Agriculture Model, Canada, 2018.

Canada Govt Agriculture and Agri-Food Dept, Climate Change and Agriculture Impacts, Canada, 2018.

Carbon Brief Food & Farming, Rise in Insect Pests under Climate Change to Hit Crop Yields, UK, 2018.

Carbon Tracker UK, Carbon Majors Report, UK, 2017.

CBC Business, As Renewable Energy Grows, so Does Interest from Big Oil, USA, 10 May 2018.

CDP, The Annual Carbon Majors Report for 2017, UK, 2017.

CDP, Global City Report, UK, 2016.

Center for Global Development, Why Forests Why Now Report, USA, 2015.

CGIAR, Fighting Floods by Sponge Cities, Udon Thani Thailand, Thailand, 2018.

Chartered Management Institute, 'Winning Ideas – Top 5 Management Articles of the Year', London, UK, February 2016.

Chevron, Chevron Produces Renewable Alternative Energy with Geothermal Energy, USA, 2010.

China Carbon Forum, China Carbon Pricing Survey, Beijing, PRC, 2017.

China Dialogue, Expert Roundtable: Is China Still on Track to Reach Its Paris Targets?, PRC, June 2018.

China Dialogue, Five Things to Know about the China National Carbon Market, PRC, December 2017.

China National Bureau of Statistics, Statistical Communiqué of the People's Republic of China on the 2014 National Economic and Social Development, PRC, 2015.

China Water Risk, Top 10 Responsible Investment Trends for 2019 in China, PRC, 18 March 2019.

Christian Aid, Counting the Costs – A Year of Climate Breakdown, UK, December 2018.

CIFOR Center for International Forestry Research, Forests and Climate Change, Indonesia, 2019.

City of London Corporation, Total Tax Contribution of UK Financial Services, UK, 2017.

CleanTechnica, World's First Advanced Offshore Wind Power Radar System Now Operational, USA, 2016.

ClientEarth, Review of UK Companies' Climate Disclosures, UK, 2016.

Climate Action Tracker, China, US and EU Post-2020 Plans Reduce Projected Warming, USA, 2013.

Climate Central, John Upton, "China, India Becoming Climate Leaders as West Falters", Canada, April 2017.

Climate Policy Info Hub, The Global Rise of Emissions Trading, EU, 2018.

Columbia University, Committee on Global Thought, USA, 2019.

Comiso & Hall, Climate Trends in Arctic as Observed from Space, WIREs Climate Change, USA, 2014.

Computer Weekly, Telefónica Increases Use of Renewable Energy to Fight Climate Change, USA, 2017.

Computer Weekly, Google to Hit 100% Renewable Energy Target for Datacentres in 2017, USA, 2016.

Craig Idso, CO_2, Global Warming & Coral Reefs: Prospects for the Future, USA, 2009.

CSO Energy Acuity, Global Renewables Top Ten Companies, UK, 2019.

Cuéllar-Franca & Azapagic, Carbon Capture Storage Utilisation Technology Review, USA, 2015.

Daily Mail, WHO, Air Pollution Big Killer than Smoking, UK, March 2019.

Dominic Barton, China Half a Billion Middle Class Consumers, by Global MD of Mckinsey & Co, The Diplomat, USA, 30 May 2013.

Drax Power Station Announcement, Drax Closer to Coal-Free Future with Fourth Biomass Unit Conversion, UK, August 2018.

DuPont, Sustainable Energy for a Growing China, May 2013, USA, 2013.

Dutch Marine Energy Centre, FORESEA Funding Ocean Renewable Energy through Strategic DW, Nile Dam Project: Talks Stall between Egypt and Ethiopia, Germany, 2019.

Economist Intelligence Unit, The Cost of Inaction: Recognising the Value at Risk from Climate Change, UK, 2015.

EEA European Environmental Agency, Agriculture and Climate Change, EU Brussels, 2018.

EIA, Explosion of HFC-23 Super Greenhouse Gases Is Expected, USA, 2015.

Elsner, JB, Kossin, JP, & Jagger, TH, The Increasing Intensity of the Strongest Tropical Cyclones, *Nature* 455, no 7209, USA, 2008.

Energy Foundation, Statement on China's Launch of the National Emissions Trading System, USA, December 2017.

Energy Narrative, Is 2¢ a kWh Solar Power Real? By Jed Bailey, USA, 15 February 2018.

Energy Research Institute, China 2050 High Renewable Energy Penetration Scenario and Roadmap Study, USA, 2015.

Environmental Defence Fund, Five Reasons to Be Optimistic about China's New Carbon Market, USA, December 2017.

EU, Clean Energy for All Europeans, EU Brussels, 2018.

EU, An EU Strategy on Heating and Cooling, EU Brussels, 2016.

EU, New Renewable Energy Directive to 2030, EU Brussels, November 2016.EU, Framework for State Aid for Research and Development and Innovation, Brussels, 2014.EU Commission, Causes of Climate Change, EU Brussels, 2019.

EU Environment Agency EEA, Renewable Energy in Europe Report, EU Brussels, 2017.

EU ESCO Committee of China Energy Conversation Association. "Notice on the Disposal of Hydrofluorocarbon", European Commission, Joint Research Centre (JRC)/ Netherlands Environmental, EU Brussels, July 2015.

European Action Project, Netherlands, 2019.

European Commission EU, CCS Directive, EU Brussels, 2012.

Fenby, Jonathan, "Will China Dominate the 21st Century?" London, UK, 2014.

Financial Post Canada, Ottawa to Return 90% of Money It Collects from Carbon Tax to the Canadians Who Pay It, Canada, 2018.

Fine and Tchernov, Coral Reef Impacts by Low Ocean PH, USA, 2006.

Fisher, R, Ury, W, & Patton, B, Getting to Yes: Negotiating Agreement Without Giving In. Penguin Books, New York, USA, 1991.

Forbes Energy, Big Oil Is Feeling the Heat and Dipping into Green Energy, USA, April 2019.

French National Centre for Scientific Research CNRS, Climate-Driven Range Shifts of the King Penguin in a Fragmented Ecosystem, France, 2017.

G20 Sustainable Finance Study Group, Sustainable Finance Synthesis Report, UK, 2018.

G20 TCFD, Task Force on Climate-Related Financial Disclosures (TCFD) Report, USA, July 2017.

Ghent University, The Breakthroughs of CCS/CCU, Netherlands, 2017.

Global CCS Institute, Global CCS Report, UK, 2015.

Global CCS Institute, Yanchang-Petroleum-Report-1-Capturing-CO_2-Coal-Chemical-Process, UK, 2015.

Global Commission on the Economy and Climate. Global Annual Report, USA, 2017.

Global News Canada, Worried about the Climate and Carbon Taxes, Canada, 2018.

GPCA and McKinsey Report, "Thoughts for a New Age in Middle East Petrochemicals", Released at 10th GPCA Forum, Dubai, UAE, November 2015.

Green, F & Stern, N, China's "New Normal": Structural Change, Better Growth and Peak Emissions, LSE Grantham Research Institute on Climate Change and the Environment, London, UK, 2015.

Greenwich Council London, UK, New E-Car Club for Low Emission Neighbourhood, UK, 2019.

Guardian, Fossil Fuels Produce Less than Half of UK Electricity for First Time, UK, June 2019.

Guardian, London District Heating – London Energy Customers Locked into District Heating Systems, London, UK, 2017.

Guo Peiyuan, SynTao, The Concept of Responsible Investment Is Increasingly Recognized and Accepted by Chinese Financial Institutions, Beijing, PRC, March 2019.

Harford T, Can Solar Power Shakeup the Energy Market, BBC, UK, 11 September 2019.

Harvard Business School, "Should You Make the First Offer?", USA, July 2004.

Hong Kong Stock Exchange, Report on the Analysis of Environmental, Social and Governance (ESG) Practice Disclosure, Hong Kong, 18 May 2018.

Huidian Research, Indepth Research and Forecast of China Ethylene Industry for 2013–2017, Beijing, PRC, 2013.

Hunter, Estimating Sea Level Extremes under Conditions of Uncertain Sea Level Rises, *Climate Change* 99, no 3–4, USA, 2010.

ICIS, Global Annual Base Oil Conference, London, UK, February 2018.

IEA, Global Energy and CO_2 Status Report of 2018, Paris, France, March 2019.

IEA, World Energy Outlooks WEO 2018, Paris, France, 2018.

IEA, WEO Special Air Pollution Report, Paris, France, 2017.

IEA (International Energy Authority), World Energy Outlook IEA WEO Report, Paris, France, 2017.

IEA, IEA Bioenergy Task Report 39, The Potential of Biofuels in China, Paris, France, 2016.

IEA, World Energy Outlook 2015. International Energy Agency, Paris, France, 2015.

IEA, World CO_2 Emissions from Fuel Combustion: Database Documentation. International Energy Agency, Paris, France, 2015.

IEA, Energy Balances. International Energy Agency, Paris, France, 2014.

IEA, Energy Technology Perspectives. International Energy Agency, Paris, France, 2014.

IEA, World Energy Outlook 2014. International Energy Agency, Paris, France, 2014.

IEA, Report & Roadmap for Energy Conservation & GHG Emission Reductions by Catalytic Processes, IEA Paris, France, 2013.

IEA, World Oil Market Report 2012, IEA Paris, France, 2012.

IEA, Energy Technology Perspectives. International Energy Agency, Paris, France, 2010.

IEEFA, ExxonMobil Empty Climate Risk Report & Shareholders wants Transparency, USA, April 2018.

IHA, Hydropower Sustainability Assessment Protocol Presentation, India, 2015.

IHA, SEforALL and IHA to Partner on New Hydropower Preparation Facility Model, Germany, 17 November 2017.

Ikea, Ikea Goes Renewables, Sweden, 2019.

IMF, "Fiscal Implications of Climate Change" International Monetary Fund, Fiscal Affairs Department, USA, March 2008.

IMF, World Economic Outlook Database. International Monetary Fund. Washington, DC, USA, 2015.

Imperial College Digital Economy Lab, Digital City Exchange, London, UK, 2019.

Imperial College London, BECCS Deployment Report, London, UK, 2018.

Imperial College London, Bioenergy with Carbon Capture and Storage BECCS Paper, UK, 2018.

Imperial College London, Climate Change and Environmental Pollutions Have Serious Impacts on Heart and Lung Health, by Maxine Myers, Joy Tennant, Mr Martin Sayers, UK, 12 March 2018.

Imperial College London, Climate Risks and Investment Impacts, Charles Donovan Director at the Centre for Climate Finance and Investment, Imperial College London Business School, UK, 2018.

Imperial College London & ICROA, Unlocking the Hidden Value of Carbon Offsetting, UK, 2014.

Independent, UK Met Scientists Warn CO_2 Levels Expected to Rise Rapidly in 2019, UK, March 2019.

INSEAD, Artificial Intelligence AI Holistic Approach to the Humans+Machines Loop, France, 2019.

International Carbon Action Partnership (ICAP), Lessons Learnt from Chinese Pilot ETSs Cap Setting and Allowance Allocation, UK, 2014.

International Zero Emission Vehicle ZEV Alliance, Zero Emissions Target Announcements, USA, 2015.

IOT Agenda, Using Technology to Save Nature, USA, 2017.

IPCC UN, Special Report CCS SRCCS, UN, USA, 2005.

IRENA, Investments in Renewables Analysis, Abu Dhabi, 2018.

IRENA, Biofuels for Aviation, Abu Dhabi, 2017.

Japan Government, Blueprint Towards a Possible Hydrogen Society by 2040, Tokyo, 2017.

John Berger, Copenhagen Striving to Be Carbon Neutral: The Economic Payoffs?, UK, July 2017.

King Abdullah Petroleum Studies & Research Centre, KAPSARC 2014 Discussion Paper on Lowering Saudi Arabia's Fuel Consumption & Energy System Costs without Increasing End Consumer Prices, KAPSARC Riyadh, Saudi Arabia, March 2014.

KPMG, Investment in PR China Report, UK, April 2012.

LanzaTech, Biological Conversion of Carbon to Products through Gas Fermentation, New Zealand, 2019.

Lord David Howell Column in Japan Times, "Oil and Money, A Combo that Faces a Cloudy Future", Japan, October 2018.

Lord Nicholas Stern, Chair, Grantham Research Institute, London School of Economics and Political Science Speech, Post COP24 Forum "Where Do We Go from Here?" LSE London, December 2018.

LSE Grantham Institute, Post COP24 Forum, London, December 2018.

Lu, SM, A Global Review of Enhanced Geothermal System (EGS), Elsevier, Netherlands, 2018.

Marine Energy.biz, Third MaRINET2 Call Provides €1.2M Testing Boost for Renewables, UK, 2019.

Marine Renewables Canada MRC, State of the Sector Report 2018, Canada, 2018.

McKinsey, Global Energy Perspective, USA, 2019.

Mckinsey, The future of Electricity rate design, USA, 2019.

Mckinsey, Climate Actions in Cities to 2030, USA, 2018.

Mckinsey, Bringing Solar Power to the People, USA, June 2018.

Mckinsey, Smart City Developments and Improvements, USA, March 2018.

Mckinsey, Disruptive Trends that Will Transform the Auto Industry, USA, 2017.

Mckinsey, How Solar Energy Can Finally Create Values, USA, October 2016.

Mckinsey, Competing in a World of Sectors without Borders, USA, 2016.

Mckinsey, How Companies Can Adapt to Climate Change, USA, July 2015.

Mckinsey Quarterly, Battery Technology Charges Ahead, by Russell Hensley, John Newman, and Matt Rogers, USA, March 2018.

Mckinsey Quarterly, Peering into Energy's Crystal Ball, Scott Nyquist, Mckinsey, USA, July 2015.

Mckinsey Quarterly, The Disruptive Power of Solar Power, by David Frankel, Kenneth Ostrowski, and Dickon Pinner, USA, April 2014.

Mike Parr, Diverting Fossil Fuel Investments to Renewables Is Not Enough, Euractiv, Brussels, April 2019.

Mining.com, Scandinavian Biopower to Invest in a Biocoal Plant in Mikkeli Finland, UK, 2016.

MIT, Senseable Cities Lab, USA, 2019.

MIT, Climate Forecasts, USA, 2017.

MIT USA, MIT Climate Action, USA, 2017.

Nagoya University, Evaluating the Contribution of Black Carbon to Climate Change, Japan, 2018.

NASA, Global Climate Change Sea Level Rise Data, USA, 2019.

NASA, What Is Climate Change, USA, May 2014.

NASA Jet Propulsion Lab & CIT, Key Indicator Global Climate Change, USA, August 2014.

National Geographic, The Big Thaw, USA, 2019.

National Research Council, Ecological Impacts of Climate Change, Washington, DC, USA, 2008.

National Resources Defense Council, The Consequences of Global Warming on Glaciers and Sea Levels, USA, August 2014.

Nature, Climate Change, Country Level Social Cost of Carbon, USA, September 2018.

Nature, Albright, Reversal of Ocean Acidification Enhances Net Coral Reef Calcification, USA, 2016.

NCA, USA Fourth National Climate Assessment, USA, 2018.

Nerem, Proceedings of the National Academy of Sciences on Sea Level Rises, USA, 2018.

New York Times, How to Play Well with China on USA President Obama & PRC President Xi Jingping Meetings in June 2013, *New York Times*, New York, USA, 2013.

New York Times, In Cyberattack on Saudi Firm, U.S. Sees Iran Firing Back, USA, 2012.

NOAA, Climate Change Atmospheric Carbon Dioxide, USA, 2018.

NRDC, Global Warming, USA, March 2016.

National Snow & Ice Data Centre NSIDC, Glacier and Climate Change, USA, 2019.

NSIDC National Snow & Ice Data Centre, 2018 Winter Arctic Ice Report, USA, 2018.

Oxford University, Smith School of Enterprise and Evninronment, From the Stockholder to the Stakeholder: How Sustainability Can Drive Financial Outperformance, UK, 2016.

OECD, Investment in Low Carbon Infrastructure, OECD, Paris, France, 2018.

OECD, SOE Transition Away from Coal and Coal Fired Power, OECD, Paris, France, 2018.

OECD, The Greening of Agriculture, Agricultural Innovation and Sustainable Growth, Paper Prepared for the OECD Synthesis Report on Agriculture and Green Growth, Paris, France, November 2010.

OECD, Green Growth Declaration, Paris, France, 2009.

OECD, "Environmentally Related Taxes and Tradable Permit Systems in Practice", OECD, Environment Directorate, Centre for Tax Policy and Administration, Paris, France, June 2008.

OECD MENA Task Force on Energy & Infrastructure, 2013 Report on Renewable Energies in the Middle East and North Africa MENA: Policies to Support Private Investment, with Inputs by Henry Wang and Other OECD MENA Task Force Team Members, OECD, Paris, France, 2013.

OECD & Smith, S, "Environmentally Related Taxes and Tradable Permit Systems in Practice", OECD, Environment Directorate, Centre for Tax Policy and Administration, Paris, France, June 2008.

Offshorewind biz, Shell and CoensHexicon Co. Ltd Agreement for a Floating Offshore Wind Farm in South Korea, UK, June 2019.

OPEC, World Oil Outlooks of 2014, Vienna Austria, 2014.

OPEC, World Oil Outlooks of 2013, Vienna Austria, 2013.

OPEC, IEA IEF Energy Conference 23 March 2015, Riyadh Saudi Arabia, 2015.

People's Republic of China, China's 13th Five Year Plan, Thirteenth Five-Year Guideline, 2016–2020, Beijing, PRC, 2016.

People's Republic of China, "Technology Roadmap for Energy-Saving Vehicles", Beijing, PRC, October, 2016.

People's Republic of China, National Action Plan on Climate Change (2014–2020), Beijing, PRC, 2014.

People's Republic of China, Energy Development Strategy Action Plan (2014–2020), Beijing, PRC, 2014.

People's Republic of China, Second National Communication on Climate Change of The People's Republic of China, November, Beijing, PRC, 2012.

People's Republic of China, China's 12th Five Year Plan, Twelfth Five-Year Guideline, 2011–2015, Beijing, PRC, 2011.

People's Republic of China, China's Pledge to the Copenhagen Accord. Compilation of Information on Nationally Appropriate Mitigation Actions to Be Implemented by Parties Not Included in Annex I to the Convention, Beijing, PRC, 2010.

Petroleum Development Oman PDO, Mirrah Solar Project, Oman 2019.

PRC Government, Catalogue of Investment Projects Approved by Government (2013) 政府核准的投资项目目录 (2013年本), PRC Government, Beijing, PRC, 2013.

PRC Government, The Catalogue of Priority Industries for Foreign Investment in Central and Western China 中西部地区外商投资优势产业目录, PRC Government, Beijing, PRC, 2013.

PRC Ministry of Civil Affairs, Interim Measures for the Administration of Investment Activities of Charitable Organizations for Value Preservation and Appreciation, Beijing, PRC, 2018.

PRC New FDI Measures, Management Measures for Approval and Filing of Foreign Direct Investment (FDI) 外商投资项目核准和备案管理办法, MOFCOM, Beijing, PRC, May 2014.

PRC Supreme People's Procuratorate, Opinions on Enhancing Cooperation and Coordination in the Prosecution of Public-Interest Litigations to Legally Fight against Pollution, Beijing, PRC, January 2019.

Plasteurope, Ikea NESTE Polyolefins from Bio-naphtha Commercial-scale Pilot Plant, Belgium, 2018.

Politico, 5 Takeways from COP24, Paris, USA, December 2018.

Power Engineering International, The Three Ds of Modern Power, USA, May 2017.

Pricewaterhouse Coopers, China M&A 2012 Report, PWC, UK, May 2013.

Princeton University, Earth's Oceans Have Absorbed 60 Percent More Heat than Previously Thought, USA, October 2018.

PV Magazine, Volkswagen Is All Set to Become a Green Energy Supplier, Germany, January 2019.

RE100, Report and Briefings, USA, 2019.

REN21, Renewables 2017 Global Status Report, Paris, France, 2018.

REN21, Renewable Energy Policy Networks for 21st Century, The Renewables 2017 Global Status Report, REN21 Secretariat, Paris, France, 2017.

Reuter, Exxon Asks U.S. Regulator to Block Climate-Change Resolution: Investors, USA, 2019.

Rik van dan Berge & Wang Henry, Report on Clean Coal Technology in China – A Strategy for Netherlands, Twente University, Netherlands, 2009.

Rogers, Greg, "Planning a Successful TCFD Project", Linkedin Blog, USA, November 2018.

Royal Society, Global Responses to Climate Change, London, UK, 2014.

Royal Society, Climate Change Global Warming, London, UK, 2008.

Sabine Christopher, The Oceanic Sink for Anthropogenic CO_2, USA, 2004.

Saudi Arabia, Vision 2030 National Plan, Riyadh, 2016.

SCMP, China's National Carbon Trading Rollout Expected to Have Major Impact on Key Industries, Hong Kong, April 2017.

SCOR, Report of the Ocean Acidification Group, Vienna Austria, 2009.

Seatrade Maritime News, IMO 2020 Sulphur Regulation, UK, 2018.

Seymour & Busch, Centre for Global Development, "Why Forests? Why Now?", Washington, DC, USA, 2016.

Shell International, Shell Sky Scenario, London, UK, 2018.

Slovenia Times, China's Path to a Green Economy, Slovenia, July 2017.

Stephen Hawking, BBC Environment News, Climate Change Tipping Point, UK, 2018.

Sustainable Energy for All, Progress toward Sustainable Energy 2015, UK, June 2015.

Techtarget, How Climate Change Threats Can Inform Cybersecurity Strategies, USA, 2018.

TheCityUK, Key Facts about the UK as an International Financial Centre, UK, 2017.

The Global Commission on the Economy and Climate, The 2018 New Climate Economy Report NCE, USA, 2018.

The Global Commission on the Economy and Climate, "The New Climate Economy Report: Better Growth Better Climate", USA 2014.

The National, China Largest Net Importer of Crude Oil Report 6 Mar 2013, USA, 2013.

The World Meteorological Organisation WMO, State of the Climate Report, USA, November 2018.

Toyota, Sustainability Environment Report 2018, Japan, 2018.

UCL Efthymiopoulos Ioannis PhD Thesis, Recovery of Lipids from Spent Coffee Grounds for Use, UCL, London, UK, 2018.

UK Government BEIS, Smart City & Grid Developments Report, UK, July 2017.

UK Green Finance Team GFI, Green Finance Initiative Report, London, UK, 2017.

UK House of Commons Environmental Audit Committee, Green Finance Inquiry Oral Evidence Published Records, London, UK, 20 February 2018.

UK House of Lords, Electric Car & Battery Storage New Program Review, UK, July 2017.

UK Met Office, Climate Summaries 2018, London, UK, January 2019.

UK Met Office, Climate Projects 2018, UKCP18, London, UK, 2018.

UK Met Office, Warming: A Guide to Climate Change, UK, 2011.

UK Parliament, The Energy and Climate Change Committee, UK CCS Competition, UK, 2016.

UN, United Nations Fact Sheet on Climate Change on Africa, USA, 2018.

UN, COP22 Marrakech Roadmap for Action, Marrakech, Morocco, 2016.

UN, Sustainable Development Goals SDG, NYC, USA, 2015.

UN, Greening the Economy with Agriculture Report, USA, 2012.

UN Brundtland Commission Report, Our Common Future, WCED UN, USA, 1987.

UN Environment, Emission Gap Report, UN, USA, 2017.

UN Environment, Global Emissions Gap Report, USA, 2017.

UN Environment Program, The Global Trends in Renewable Energy Investment Report, US, 2019.

UN Habitat & MIT, Floating City to Fight Climate Change, USA, 2019.

UN Intergovernmental Panel IPCC, Report on Climate Change, USA, 2017.

UNEP, Renewable Investment Global Trends Report of 2019, UN, NYC, 2019.

UNEP, District Energy in Cities Unlocking the Potential of Energy Efficiency and Renewables, USA, 2018.

UNEP Finance Initiative (UNEP FI), Global Roundtable on the Draft Principles for Responsible Banking, USA, 2018.

UNFCCC, Biennial Assessment and Overview of Climate, NYC, USA, 2016.

UNFCCC, United Nations Framework Convention on Climate Change, Paris Climate Agreement, Signed in UN, NYC, USA, April 2016.

UNFCCC, Distributed Renewable Power Generation and Integration, USA, 2015.

UNFCCC Kyoto Protocol Targets for the First Commitment Period, USA, 2012.

UNIPCC, IPCC Special Report on the Impacts of Global Warming, UN, USA, 2018.

UNIPCC, Evaluation of Climate Models, USA, 2013.

UNIPCC, Special Report on Renewable Energy Sources and Climate Change Mitigation, USA, 2012.

UNIPCC, Fourth Assessment Report on Climate Change, UN, USA, 2007.

UNIPCC, Summary for Policymakers in Climate Change, Cambridge University Press, USA, 2007.

UN PRI, PRI Welcome Asset Owner Signatory in China, UN, USA, 4 September 2019.

USA Office of the Deputy Assistant Secretary of the Army (Research & Technology), Emerging Science and Tech Trends for 2017–2047, USA, November 2017.

USA Oak Ridge National Lab, Boden, TA, Marland, G and Andres, RJ, "Global, Regional, and National Fossil-Fuel CO_2 Emissions", Carbon Dioxide Information Analysis Center, US Department of Energy, Oak Ridge, TN, USA, 2013.

US EPA, Global Greenhouse Gas Emission Data, USA, 2019.

US EPA, Overview of Greenhouse Gases in Greenhouse Gas (GHG) Emissions, USA, 2018.

US EPA, Climate Change Science, Causes of Climate Change, USA, 2016.

US EPA, Global Mitigation of Non-CO_2 Greenhouse Gases, Washington, DC, USA, 2012.

US National Hurricane Centre, Tropical Hurricane Report, USA, 2018.

US PNAS Proceedings of the US National Academy of Sciences, Climate-Change–Driven Accelerated Sea-Level Rises, USA, 2018.

Vattenfall, Our Road to Fossil Freedom, Sweden, 2019.

Wang, Henry, Routledge book "Climate Change & Clean Energy Management", Routledge, Oxford, UK, November 2019.

Wang, Henry, Hong Kong Rotary Club of Tai Po Speech, "Climate Change and Clean Energy Management", Hong Kong, November 2019.

Wang, Henry, Oil and Money Conference Geopolitic Panel Speech, London, UK, 9 October 2019.

Wang, Henry, Management Association Philippines CEO Conference Speech on Business Sustainability, Impacts and Future, Manila, 10 September 2019.

Wang, Henry, Asia Investment & Banking Conference AIBC Sustainable Finance Panel Speech, Hong Kong, 29 August 2019.

Wang, Henry, HKUST Business School Skolkovo EMBA Lectures, Doing Business in China and Business Dealings in Asia, Hong Kong, 10 July 2019.

Wang, Henry, Hong Kong Green Council Climate Forum "Global & Hong Kong Climate & Decarbonisation Challenges", Hong Kong, 9 May 2019.

Wang, Henry, UK House of Lords Westminister Energy Group Windsor Summit "China Climate & Energy Challenges", Windsor Castle, UK, 2 March 2019.

Wang, Henry, HK City University Colloquium "China & Hong Kong Climate & Decarbonisation Challenges", Hong Kong, 21 February 2019.

Wang, Henry, HKUST Post COP24 Forum "Hong Kong Climate & Decarbonisation Challenges", Hong Kong, 21 January 2019.

Wang, Henry, UK House of Lords Energy Panel Paper "China Fossil & Renewables Energy Transformations", London, UK, 5 December 2018.

Wang, Henry, FT Asia Climate Finance Summit "Renewables Growth, Challenges and Opportunities", Hong Kong, 21 November 2018.

Wang, Henry, India Institute of Director Global Convention London Paper "Climate Change & Green Finance Governance Growths", London, UK, 25 October 2018.

Wang, Henry, London School of Economics Negotiation Society Lecture, "Business Negotiations in China", LSE London, UK, 17 October 2018.

Wang, Henry, Hong Kong Dragon Foundation Youth Leaders Speech, "International & China Business Negotiations", Hong Kong City University, Hong Kong, 25 August 2018.

Wang, Henry, India Institute of Director Global Convention Proceedings Paper "Climate Change & Climate Finance TCFD Reporting", Mumbai, India, July 2018.

Wang, Henry, University College London HK Alumni Association Speech, "Business Negotiations", Hong Kong, June 2018.

Wang, Henry, HK Rotary Peninsula Club Speech, "Climate Change & Climate Action Plan HK", Hong Kong, May 2018.

Wang, Henry, HK Rotary Taipo Club Speech, "International & China Business Negotiations", Hong Kong Kwoloon Cricket Club, Hong Kong, 14 May 2018.

Wang, Henry, ICIS Global Base Oil Conference Speech, "China Belt & Road Initiative Growths", London, UK, January 2018.

Wang, Henry, Sino-British Summit Paper, China NDRC Renewables and Smart City Plans, UK, 2017.

Wang, Henry, Imperial College Business School MSc. Climate Finance Lecture "Climate Change & Green Finance Growths", London, UK, 24 October 2017.

Wang, Henry, Liechtenstein International Economic Forum Speech, "China Economic Growths", Liechtenstein, June 2017.

Wang, Henry, Hong Kong Science Tech Association Speech, "Energy, Environment and Climate Change Innovations", Hong Kong, 21 April 2017.

Wang, Henry, Hong Kong University Speech, "Energy, Environment and Climate Change Action Plans", HKU, Hong Kong, 9 April 2017.

Wang, Henry, Chinese University of Hong Kong, "Energy, Environment and Climate Change", Hong Kong, March 2017.

Wang, Henry, Imperial College London, "Energy and Environment Growth Strategies" London, UK, February 2017.

Wang, Henry, Kings College London, "International Energy and Environment Growth Strategies", London, UK, January 2017.

Wang, Henry, Energy Markets in Emerging Economies: Strategies for Growth, Routledge, Abingdon and New York, UK, 2016.

Wang, Henry, China Academy of Science Dalin Institute, "Energy Growth Strategies", Dalin, PRC, November 2016.

Wang, Henry, EU Chamber of Commerce China Energy Panel, "Energy Markets in Emerging Economies", Beijing, PRC, August 2016.

Wang, Henry, Transparency International SOE Integrity Forum Paper "Global SOE Management and Governance Improvements", Berlin, Germany, June 2016.

Wang, Henry, OECD Integrity Forum Paper, "Global and MENA SOE Governance and Integrity", Paris, France, April 2016.

Wang, Henry, UK Chartered Management Institute Top Five Management Paper of Year 2015 titled "China Business Negotiation Strategy", CMI London, UK, February 2016.

Wang, Henry, Singapore Energy Week Asia Downstream Conference Keynote Speech and Presentation on "Global Supply Chain Management, Risk Minimisation, Resource and Cost Optimisation Strategies", Singapore, 28 October 2015.

Wang, Henry, ICIS 9th Asia Base Oil & Lubricant Conference keynote speech on "China Demand Growth & Sustainable Growth Strategies", Singapore, 10 June 2015.

Wang Henry, OPEC IEA IEF Energy Conference & IEF KAPSARC Energy Roundtable 23–24 March 2015 discussion inputs, IEF Riyadh, Saudi Arabia, March 2015.

Wang, Henry, UK Chartered Management Institute Management Paper of Year 2014 Submission Titled "Business Negotiation Strategy & Planning in China", CMI London, UK, 2014.

Wang, Henry, UK CBI White Paper on "Business Energy and Climate Change Priorities for the 2015–2020 UK Parliament Consultation Inputs", UK CBI, London, UK, August 2014.

Wang, Henry, OECD BIAC China Task Force Presentation to OECD China Reflection Group & OECD Ambassadors Consultation Inputs, OECD BIAC, Paris, France, 23 & 24 June 2014.

Wang, Henry, Japan Ministry Economic Trade Industry METI Presentation on Saudi Arabia Downstream Industrial Cluster Development Program, SABIC, Riyadh, Saudi Arabia, June 2014.

Wang, Henry, KAPSARC Paper on Energy Productivity Aligning Global Agenda Peer Review Comments, KAPSARC HQ, Riyadh, Saudi Arabia, April 2014.

Wang, Henry, Presentation on Sustainable Petrochemical & Chemicals Outlooks to 2nd IEA Unconventional Gas Forum on 26 March 2014, Calgary, Canada, March 2014.

Wang, Henry, King Abdullah Petroleum Studies & Research Centre KAPSARC First International Seminar on China Keynote Speech & Presentation on "Sustainable Growth Scenarios & Strategies", KAPSARC HQ, Riyadh, Saudi Arabia, March 2014.

Wang, Henry, Presentation on Sustainable Petrochemical & Chemicals Outlooks to OECD Energy & Environmental Committee Meetings, OECD, Paris, France, 26 February 2014.

Wang, Henry, Fourth International Energy Forum & International Energy Authority & OPEC Symposium on Energy Outlooks speech on "Petrochemicals & Chemicals Growth Outlooks & Strategic Developments", IEF HQ, Riyadh, Saudi Arabia, 22 January 2014.

Wang, Henry, International Energy Agency World Energy Outlook (IEA WEO) Peer Review Panel Global Energy & Petrochemical Investment Cost Reviews Commentaries to the IEA WEO Team, IEA HQ, Paris, France, January 2014.

Wang, Henry, Successful Business Dealings and Management with China Oil, Gas and Chemical Giants, Routledge Studies in the Modern World Economy, Routledge, Abingdon, UK and New York, USA, 2013.

Wang, Henry, International Energy Agency IEA Energy Efficiency EE Manual Review Commentary to OECD BIAC and IEA EE Team in August 2013, IEA, Paris, France, 2013.

Wang, Henry, Presentation to China Ministry of Commerce & China National Oil Companies Delegation Visit to Saudi Arabia in May 2013, SABIC, Riyadh, Saudi Arabia, 2013.

Wang, Henry, International Energy Agency World Energy Outlook Peer Review Panel – Global Energy Competitiveness Inputs to the IEA WEO Team in April 2013, IEA, Paris, France, 2013.

Wang, Henry, IEA, OPEC and IEF International Energy Conference Presentation at IEF HQ, Riyadh, Saudi Arabia, January 2013.

Wang, Henry, China Market Developments & Marketing Lecture in April 2012 to EMBA Class at University of Colorado Denver Business School, Denver, USA, 2012.

Wang, Henry, International Energy & Renewables Strategic Co-Development Lecture in April 2012 at University of Colorado Denver Business School, Denver, USA, 2012.

Wang, Henry, Global & Middle East Petrochemical Growth & Developments at University of Colorado Energy Conference, Boulder, Colorado, USA, 2012.

Wang, Henry, India Oil IOC Chairman Petrochemical Conclave Presentation "Opportunities & Challenges in Industries Winning Strategies", IOC, Delhi, India, March 2012.

Wang, Henry, Keynote speech to First International Four Kingdom Carbon International Conference Organised by Saudi Ministry of Petroleum in Saudi Arabia, 2011.

Wang, Henry, Speech & Presentation on Shale Gas Business Growth, Commercialisation & Developments in China, to the First China International Shale Gas Conference on 26–27 October 2010 in Shanghai Organised by IBC Asia, PRC, 2010.

Wang, Henry, Deep-water Drilling Outlook Summit in Singapore in July 2010 Paper on China Upstream Offshore Developments, Singapore, 2010.

Wang, Henry, Asia Pacific Offshore Support Forum in Singapore in April 2010 Paper on China Offshore Support Industry Developments, Singapore, 2010.

Wang, Henry, China International & Beijing State Radio Interview in Beijing on International Earth Day in April 2010 on Green Energy, Renewables, Chemicals, Coal Gasification, Energy Efficiency & Sustainable Developments, China Radio, Beijing, PRC, 2010.

Wang, Henry, China International Radio Interview in Beijing China in April 2010 on World Bank Six Asia Country Energy Report, China Radio, Beijing, PRC, 2010.

Wang, Henry, UK Embassy China in Beijing in 2009 Presentation on China Clean Energy & Sustainable Development by Henry Wang, UK Embassy, Beijing, PRC, 2009.

Wang, Henry, Argus Carbon Report Interview in London UK in October 2009 on China Carbon & Climate Change Trends by Henry Wang with Argus Carbon Editor, Argus, London, UK, 2009.

Wang, Henry, Bloomberg News interview in Singapore in Oct 2009 on China Climate Change Policies Outlooks by Bloomberg Asia Editor, Bloomberg, Singapore, 2009.

Wang, Henry, Carbon Forum Asia in Singapore in Oct 2009 Keynote Speech & Paper on China Climate Change & Sustainable Development Policies, Singapore, 2009.

Wang, Henry, Carbon Forum Asia in Singapore in Oct 2009 Paper on China Carbon Market Management & Outlooks, Singapore, 2009.

Wang, Henry, UK China Chemicals CEO Working Group Forum in Shanghai in Nov 2009, Paper & Presentation on Integrated Energy Management, Clean Energy Technologies & Sustainable Developments in China, UK Embassy, Shanghai, PRC, 2009.

Wang, Henry, China Carbon Forum Government Round Table Keynote Speech on China Clean Energy & Carbon Developments, Remin University, Beijing, PRC, June 2009.

Wang, Henry, China State Council Development Research Council Presentation on Clean Energy & Coal Developments in China & Globally, DRC, Beijing, PRC, November 2008.

Wang, Henry, Remin University and China Carbon Forum Conference in 2008, Speech & Paper on Clean Coal Developments and Copenhagen Negotiations, Remin University, Beijing, PRC, 2008.

Wang, Henry, UCL Distinguished Speaker Lecture on China Advanced Coal Technology & Successful Project Developments at University College, London, UK, 2008.

Wang, Henry, China Netherlands Prime Ministerial Energy Summit at Tsinghua University in Beijing in Nov 2008, Paper on Integrated Energy Management, Clean Energy & Sustainable Development, Tsinghua University, Beijing, PRC, 2008.

Wang, Henry, EU Chamber of Commerce China in Beijing in 2007 Presentation on Clean Energy Developments & Opportunities, EUCCC, Beijing, PRC, 2007.

Wang, Henry, China Daily CEO Climate Change Round Table in Beijing in 2006 interview on Climate Change Outlooks by Henry Wang, *China Daily*, Beijing, PRC, 2006.

Wang, Henry, Energy Seminar for PRC Government Top Officials at Joint Tsinghua Harvard MPA Course presentation & paper on Global Energy Planning, Advanced Technologies & Management to Vice Ministers/Governors, Tsinghua University, Beijing, PRC, 2006.

Wang, Henry, Climate Change & Sustainable Development Seminar for PRC Government Senior Officials Presentation & Paper on International Sustainable Development, Climate Change, Carbon Technologies & Management, Tsinghua University Beijing, PRC, 2006.

Wang, Henry, China Advanced Management Seminar in Beijing China for Top International Executives, Presentations & Papers on China Business Issues, China Energy Planning & China Business Developments, Shell, Beijing, PRC, 2006.

Wang, Henry, UK China Bilateral Energy Strategic Cooperations Paper with UK China Bilateral Energy Work Group, UK Embassy Beijing, PRC, 2005.

Wang, Henry, International Advanced Management Seminar Papers on Global & China Business Issues, Energy Planning in China, Government structures in China & New Business Development in China, New York Bar Association HQ, New York, USA, 2005.

Wang, Henry, China Daily CEO Corporate Social Responsibilities Round Table in Beijing in 2005 Interview on CSR, *China Daily*, Beijing, PRC, 2005.

Wang, Henry, China Global Economic & Leadership Summit, Speech on Energy Economic Developments by Henry Wang with USA Nobel Economists at the Grand Hyatt Hotel in Beijing Organised by China Cajing Economic Publishing Group, Beijing, PRC, 2005.

Wang, Henry, China State Council Development Research Council [DRC] in Beijing in 2005 Presentation on Global & China Energy Scenarios, DRC, Beijing, PRC, 2005.

Wang, Henry, China Ministry of Foreign & Economic Cooperation [MOFCOM] Summit in China in 2005, Speech & Paper on Multinational Co Co-operations & Sustainable Developments in China, MOFCOM, Beijing, PRC, 2005.

Wang, Henry, China Economic Summit at Great Hall of People in Beijing in 2005, Paper on China Energy Outlooks & Scenarios by Henry Wang, China Cajing Economic Magazine, Beijing, PRC, 2005.

Wang, Henry, Netherlands Energy Minister Meeting in Beijing in 2005, Presentation on China Energy Developments, Netherlands Embassy, Beijing, PRC, 2005.

Wang, Henry, Tsinghua University Lecture in Beijing China in 2005, Lecture & Paper on Multinational Cos Operations in China, Tsinghua University, Beijing, PRC, 2005.

Wang, Henry, Board Meeting of a Leading International Chemical Company & a Top Middle East Company Joint Venture in Singapore in 2005, Presentation on China Economic & Energy Outlooks, Singapore, 2005.

Wang, Henry, China Energy & Strategy Seminar for a Leading Asia Government Prime Minister Office PMO & Key Ministries presentations & Papers on China Energy Planning & Developments, Market Access & Cooperation Strategies & Challenges, Shell, Asia, 2005.

Wang, Henry, Wharton Shell Group Business Leadership Program Business Case Paper, Wharton Business School, Pennsylvania, USA, 2004.

Wang, Henry, China SASAC Minister Meeting in Beijing China in 2004, Speech & Paper on China Energy Scenarios & Challenges, SASAC, Beijing, PRC, 2004.

Wang, Henry, UK Prime Minister Climate Change Adviser & DEFRA Director General Ministerial Meeting in London UK in 2004, Presentation & Paper on China Energy & Climate Change Outlooks, DEFRA, London, UK, 2004.

Wang, Henry, China Ministry of Foreign Affairs & Institute of International Cooperation Meeting in Beijing in 2004, Speech & Paper on China Energy Business Outlooks & International Co-operations, MOFCOM, Beijing, PRC, 2004.

Wang, Henry, USA & UK Counsel Generals Meetings in Shanghai China in 2004, Presentation & Paper on China Energy Outlooks, UK Embassy, Shanghai, PRC, 2004.

Wang, Henry, London School of Economics Lecture & Paper on China Outlooks & Opportunities, London School of Economics LSE, UK, 2004.

Wang, Henry, China Economics Round Table in Beijing Speech & Paper on China Clean Energy Sustainable Developments, China Economics Roundtable, Beijing, PRC, 2004.

Wang, Henry, China Ministry of Commerce & Foreign Trade MOFCOM Transnational Company Forum Speech on New Development Strategy of Transnational Companies in China, MOFCOM, Beijing, PRC, 2003.

Wang, Henry, China National Development Reform Commission NDRC Energy Research Institute ERI Report on China Medium & Long Term Energy & Carbon Scenarios Report in 2003 Jointly by China Energy Research Institute of the PRC Government National Development Reform Commission with USA Lawrence Berkley Lab of USA Government Department of Energy & Shell Group Planning, NDRC ERI, Beijing, PRC, 2003.

Wang, Henry, China Daily 2003 News Interview Report in Beijing on EU Work Group Energy Proposals to Government with Henry Wang, Chairman of EU Energy, Petrochemicals, Oil & Gas Committee, *China Daily*, Beijing, PRC, 2003.

Wang, Henry, Singapore Prime Minister Office High Level China Strategy Meeting Speech & Presentation on China Social, Economic and Industrial Developments & China Strategy Developments, Singapore, 2001.

Wang Henry, Imperial College of Science & Technology MSc DIC Thesis on Bubble Flow Biological Reactor Research & Developments, Imperial College London, UK, 1997.

Wang, Henry with Mobil USA & Raytheon USA Authors, Oil & Gas Journal OGJ Paper on UK Refinery Successful Demonstrations of New Ethyl Benzene Process, Oil & Gas Journal OGJ, USA, 1995.

Wang, Henry University of Leeds, Visiting Lecturer on the "Successful Chemical Plant Start-up & Commissioning" Course at the University of Leeds in UK from 1993 to 1996, Lectures on the "Major Ethyl Benzene Chemical Plant Start-up & Commissioning at Shell UK Stanlow Refinery", University of Leeds, UK, 1993.

Wang, Henry, Canada Patent CA2008347 "Removing Hydrogen Cyanide and Carbon Oxy-Sulphide from a Syngas Mixture", Shell Internationale, Canada, 1990.*Washington Post*, The United States Already Has a Carbon Tax, USA, 2019.

WECF Fact Sheet Dangerous Health Effects of Home Burning of Plastics and Waste, USA, 2005.

Wiseman, Ed, Everything You Need to Know about the New UK Emission Rules, UK, July 2017.

Wood Mckenzie Greentech Media GTM, GE and BlackRock Launch Distributed Solar and Storage Business, US, 2019.

Wood Mackenzie Greentech Media GTM, Shell New Energies Director on Investing in Clean Energy, USA, April 2019.

World Meteorological Organisation WMO, State of the Climate Report, Switzerland, 2019.

World Bank, Refugee by Country Data, USA, 2018.

World Bank, State and Trends of Carbon Pricing, USA, 2015.

World Bank, Developing East Asia Pacific Growth in 2015, USA, 13 April 2015.

World Bank, World Development Report 2010, USA, 2010.

World Bank Report, Groundswell: Preparing for Internal Climate Migration, USA, March 2018.

World City Summit, Innovative Cities of Opportunity, Singapore, 2016.

World Economic Forum (WEF), Fourth Industrial Revolution for the Earth Series, How Technology Is Leading Us to New Climate Change Solutions, Switzerland, 2018.

World Economic Forum, The Global Competitiveness Report 2010–2011, Switzerland, 2010.

World Ocean Review, Climate Change and Methane Hydrates, USA, 2010.

World Science, Industrial Map of China Energy, USA, 2013.

World Widelife Fund, WWF, Climate Change, Coral Reefs and the Coral Triangle, USA, 2019.

World Wind Energy Association (WWEA), Small Wind World Report, Bonn, Germany, 2017.

Xiaowen Tian, Managing International Businesses in China, Cambridge University Press, UK, 2007.

Xinhua, China to Create Xiongan New Area in Hebei, Beijing, PRC, 2017.

Xinhua China, PRC President Xi Jinping Joint Written Interview to the Media of Trinidad and Tobago, Costa Rica and Mexico on 31 May 2013, Xinhua News Agency, Beijing, PRC, 2013.

Xinhua News Agency, China to Reduce Coal Consumption for Better Air, Beijing, PRC, 2015.

Xinhua News Agency, Chinese Carbon Emissions to Peak in 2030, Beijing, PRC, 2014.Xinhua News Agency, China M&A 2012 Highlights, 22 May 2013, Beijing, PRC, 2013.

Yale Environment, China Waste to Energy Incineration, USA, 2017.

Yuen Linda, China Growth, Oxford University Press, UK, 2013.

Yuen Linda, Enterprising China, Oxford University Press, UK, 2011.

Zhang & He, MIT Joint Report Series, Carbon Emissions in China: How Far Can New Efforts Bend the Curve? MIT, USA, 2014.

Index

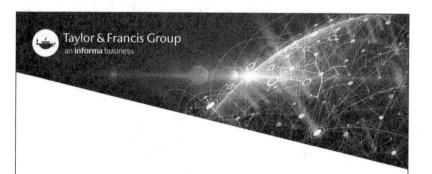